NATURE AND MAN

AND MAN

Paul Weiss

UNIVERSITY
PRESS OF
AMERICA

LANHAM • NEW YORK • LONDON

Copyright © 1983 by

University Press of America,™ Inc.

4720 Boston Way
Lanham, MD 20706

3 Henrietta Street
London WC2E 8LU England

Copyright 1947 by

Paul Weiss

The hardback edition was originally published in 1947
by Holt, Rinehart and Winston.

The paperback edition was originally published
in 1965 by Southern Illinois University Press.

Library of Congress Cataloging in Publication Data

Weiss, Paul, 1901-
    Nature and man.

    Reprint. Originally published: Carbondale: Southern
Illinois University Press, 1965, c1947.
    Includes index.
    1. Ethics.   2. Man.   I. Title.

BJ1012.W39   1983   171'.2   83-16823
ISBN 0-8191-3590-9 (pbk.: alk. paper)

To Victoria

DATE DUE

PREFACE

Can an ethics be grounded deep in the bedrock of nature and still do justice to the fact of duty, the nature of the good, the problem of guilt and related topics? This work was begun in an attempt to provide a systematic answer to that question.

It became evident quite soon that a correct answer implied that an ethical being must utilize powers analogous to those exhibited everywhere and by everything, and that he ought, therefore, to be dealt with as illustrating nonethical principles of universal application. The solution of the problems of ethics seems to depend in part on an antecedent mastery of the principles governing and exhibited in causation, action, being, life, consciousness, mind, will and self. The more thoroughly the special topics of ethics are probed, the more do they appear to presuppose a correct grasp of these principles. An attempt to answer the original question as to the possibility of a naturalistic ethics makes it necessary to engage in a prior systematic exploration of other questions. It is with this prior exploration that we are now concerned.

Nature and Man is a self-contained treatise dealing with fundamental features of nature, including those of ethics. There is a guiding thread running throughout which is revelatory of its motivation, and is indicative of the nature of the strictly ethical treatise to follow. That thread is the idea of freedom. The essence and vitality of natural beings involve the use of freedom. That freedom, universal but diversely exemplified, accounts for the fact that man and his problems are one with the rest of nature. Its acknowledgment makes it possible to show how nature provides a place for man, the being who is at once natural and responsible.

The specific problems of ethics are the topic of the next volume. Though grounded in and supplementing the present, that volume is an independent and complete unit, capable of being read separately by one concerned with ethics as a distinct discipline. The two volumes together constitute a single work, *The Foundations of Ethics*, and the introduction which immediately follows introduces that work as a whole. Together the two volumes—and particularly the second—aim to establish a basis for and to introduce a projected third volume on politics.

Dr. F. S. C. Northrop, Mrs. Max Roesler, and Dr. Erich Frank have been kind enough to give me the benefit of their opinions at several crucial points. Like my last work, the present book has had the benefit of my wife's painstaking, penetrating reading. The form and substance of the whole has been altered again and again in the effort to meet her searching criticisms. I am grateful that she at last grants me the privilege of dedicating the book to her.

P. W.

March, 1946.
Bryn Mawr, Pa.

CONTENTS

INTRODUCTION 1. The Danger of Thought—2. The Tradi-   ix
tions of Western Thought—3. Philosophic
Truth.

PART I · CAUSATION AND FREEDOM

CHAPTER ONE *Causation and Prediction*   3
1. Cause and Effect—2. The Rationale of
Causation—3. Prediction—4. Necessity and
Freedom.

TWO *Freedom and Process*   20
1. The Theory of Determinism—2. The
Paradox of Determinism—3. Half-way De-
terminisms—4. Activity—5. Freedom and
its Public Bonds.

THREE *The Nature of Beings*   39
1. The Inside and the Outside—2. Insistence
—3. Resistance—4. The Inside—5. Concern
—6. Summary.

FOUR *Action and Spontaneity*   58
1. The Motivation of Action—2. Self-adjustment—3. Expression—4. Compulsion—
5. Freedom of Action—6. Spontaneity—
7. From the Inanimate to the Animate—
8. Summary.

PART II · THE PSYCHE AND THE SELF

FIVE *The Wisdom of Living Things*   81
1. Metaphysical Biology—2. The "Extrinsic" and "Intrinsic" Ought—3. The Limitation of Natural Wisdom—4. The Check
on Folly—5. Grace—6. Evolution.

SIX *Consciousness*   103
1. The Expression of Sensitivity—2. Pain
and Pleasure—3. The Cartesian Hypothesis

—4. Environmental Sensitivity—5. Animal Perception and Intelligence—8. Transition to Man.

SEVEN *The Human Nature of Man* 121
1. Man's Late Origin—2. Darwin's Thesis —3. The Necessity for the Body—4. The Rational Soul—5. The Human Constant— 6. The Origin of Man.

EIGHT *Techniques and Habits* 145
1. The Unity of the Embryo—2. The Organs—3. Reflexes, Instincts and Habits— 4. The Organic Unity of Habits—5. Techniques.

NINE *Signs and Language* 166
1. The Objects of Signs—2. Expectation and Anticipation—3. Salutations and Occurrences—4. Words, Calls and Cries— 5. Exclamations—6. Names, Predicates and Metaphysicals—7. Conventional Discourse —8. The Nature of Language—9. Freedom and Language.

TEN *The Nature of Mind* 194
1. Man's Fourfold Bond—2. Man's Threefold Freedom—3. The Origin of Mind— 4. Levels of Mind—5. Inference—6. Mind and Freedom—7. The Mind-Body Problem.

ELEVEN *The Will* 224
1. Emotion and Desire—2. The Nature of the Will—3. Criticism and Objections— 4. Grades of Willed Objectives.

TWELVE *The Self* 241
1. The Self and the Body—2. Expressions of the Self—3. The Freudian View—4. The Concern of the Self—5. Natural Rights— 6. The Task of Man.

INDEX 269

INTRODUCTION

---

1. THE DANGER OF THOUGHT

IDEAS RELATE men to a world beyond. At the same time and even more surely, ideas hold men and the world apart. As a rule, they express more what things mean for men than what things are in fact.

To know reality as it truly is, we must use our minds creatively. We must transform our ideas—and incidentally our terms—from intellectual barriers into means and occasions for reaching to the heart of what exists.

Some intellectual barriers sum up the meaning of individual experiences; others report something of the temper of the day, the prejudices of a class, or the spirit of a civilization. All of them hide more than they reveal. Only by avoiding the habit of seeing things in purely conventional ways is it possible to get an intimate and direct grasp of the essence of things. Children, untaught as they are in the conventions to which the adult is inclined to conform so thoroughly and unawares, are more flexible and humble and therefore better able than the adult to see what tradition veils. But they are unable to understand and to communicate what it is they discern. Not blinded by convention, they are nevertheless unable to make use of it. Since it is only through the use of convention that it is possible to communicate and understand, children cannot say to themselves or to others what it is they clearly see. The more familiar they are with reality the less able are they to know and to report it.

Philosophy is insistent, creative, systematic thought, probing to the roots of things. Successful, it exposes in sophisticated prose truths open only to innocence. Since innocence is never entirely lost, a thinker's real concern is with what all know to some degree. To know the nature of things, we must make creative use of an established idiomatic thought and speech. We must grasp what the innocent do, but within and through the established means that the experienced use.

To achieve truth we must remold our daily categories to make them adequate to the facts they now obscure rather than disclose. "What," asked Blake, "it will be questioned, 'when the sun rises do you not see a round disk of fire somewhat like a guinea?' Oh, no! no! I see an innumerable company of heavenly host crying 'holy! holy! for the God Almighty.' I question not my corporeal eye any more than I would question a window concerning a sight. I look through it and not with it." Of course Blake, like everyone else, looked with his eyes. Otherwise he would not have known that it was the sun rather than the moon of which he was speaking. He did not see a disk, to be sure, for he did not use the spectacles of fashionable theory which hide the sun from men and make them see a roundish shape instead. But Blake did not see, as he wished, the sun known to innocence. Rather he saw the sun as it appears when one puts on the spectacles of a questionable theology. His report, as a consequence, was as inaccurate as those he opposed. The sun is an independent body with a characteristic power and promise. It is more than a disk and less than a heavenly host. To know it we must use spectacles of some kind, but must make allowance for the distortion they produce. We speak accurately of the sun when we use daily terms creatively, making them conform to what is there to know. Language, to communicate the nature of things, must stand between the tame discourse of daily life and the exultant shouts of a Blake.

Traditions of speech and thought often tell something about the nature of things as these have been understood by generations, but they also and more often nourish questionable beliefs and expectations. We must overcome the limitations of these traditions if we are to say what is so; in some places we must even break with large segments of those traditions in order to make effective use of the remainder. But, if we are not to produce new distortions in the effort to compensate for old, we must also avoid falling into the temptation to which Blake succumbed. Traditions must be treated critically, rejected where they obscure, and loosened where they bind.

A discipline comes to maturity by conquering the limitations which hem in unreflective thought and speech. But it begins almost at once to become traditional and soon or late itself presents an obstacle in the way of truth. This holds in philosophy no less than it does in science, art and history. Philosophy too has its shibboleths, follies and conceits which hosts of writers repeat. Every great thinker sees through them to some degree. But the more successful he is in thinking independently and in making his thoughts known, the more surely will he start a new tradition, provide a means for trapping men anew. The chains of today were forged by free men yesterday.

He who has a mind of his own masters the conventions endorsed by past philosophy and embodied in present thought and discourse. Those who follow him must penetrate further into the depths he failed to plumb and see that the truth he discerned does not keep others from the truth thereafter. No philosophy ever dies, but each must be resuscitated if its truths are to be truths for those who come later. And the best way to resuscitate a philosophy is to write it anew.

The conclusions of past systems are among the premises of present thought. We all uncritically use the results of thinkers of another age; they are pivots around which we constantly think and speak. If we break with past thought—and at most points break we must—we are bound, therefore, to reject some of the beliefs men today uncritically accept. Not all that is believed today, of course, is false, and we must hold on to the portion which is sound as firmly as we reject the portion which is not. And where we break away, in order to avoid rushing into the vacuum that is left behind with errors fresh and new, we must protect ourselves with a sound method by which we can distinguish truth from falsehood.

2. THE TRADITIONS OF WESTERN THOUGHT

To think truly is to think freely. We come close to the truth if we embrace much that our heritage asks us to keep at a distance. This means we must break through the barriers within which our thinkers have been content so long to remain.

Our Western thought has been in the tight grip of two powerful traditions. The first stems from Aristotle, the second from those who opposed him. In both there is truth streaked with error. For over a thousand years, the science, metaphysics, esthetics, ethics, economics, politics, logic and many lesser inquiries of Western man were almost completely Aristotelian in intent, method and result. There were rebels throughout the period, but their power was slight and their day was brief.

Not until "modern times"—this in fact is one of the basic meanings of the term—was the revolt against Aristotle carried through persistently and effectively in discipline after discipline under the brilliant leadership of Galileo, Descartes, Locke, Leibniz, Adam Smith and Darwin. Today almost all physicists are Galilean, philosophers Cartesian, political scientists Lockean, logicians Leibnizian, economists Smithean, and biologists Darwinian, rather than Aristotelian in principle and spirit. They have not, however, entirely freed us from Aristotle. He is still evident in our daily speech. When we talk of "matter and form," "potentiality," "actuality," "information," "sensation" and "truth" we make use of Aristotle's terms and remain quite faithful to his meaning. But on the whole we have broken away from him both as common sense men and as students of special disciplines.

We have lost and gained by this change. Much was rejected that might have been retained. Our range is wider than Aristotle's—but our ideas are thinner. Our disciplines do not let us affirm, as Aristotle's did, that there is a real, full-bodied world containing colored, substantial, self-determining men and things, that minds and bodies constantly interplay, that economics and politics presuppose the existence of ends they often ignore, that logic is a science of fact and not only of symbols, and that man is more than an animal. But gain there has been. We have discovered truths where Aristotelian error and darkness once held sway. We have naturalized the stars, seen the folly of slavery, achieved a universal physics and chemistry of great power, and know something of the bearing of economics on politics, of logic on mathematics, and of geology on biology.

In but one field—that of ethics—has opposition to Aristotle proved so far to be largely fruitless and futile. Though Christianity was, in its beginning, anti-Greek or at least non-Greek in spirit, it was not long before the great theologians had the one fitted neatly to the other. Even the apparently non-Aristotelian ethical systems of Hobbes, Spinoza, Kant, and Bentham exhibit the unmistakeable marks of a Greek-tainted view. And, in any case, they have had but a short life and few disciples. There is no vigorous, radically non-Aristotelian school of ethics today.

Yet the non-Aristotelian temper is strong and will not down. Having failed to replace Aristotle's ethics, we are nevertheless unwilling to accept it. As a result, the Aristotelian ethics occupies the singular position of a doctrine unrefuted but dismissed, rejected and yet opposed by nothing, and we today, as a consequence, do not know just what to say affirmatively or negatively about the meaning of virtue, the nature of the good, the purpose of the state, the aim of education, the duties of man and, above all, the essence of freedom.

The central thesis of Aristotle's ethics is that man is a being who never evolved, who has fixed, distinct and unalterable capacities, and who seeks and ought to seek his own good. It is a view which stands in the way of the truth that man had an animal origin, that his capacities have been modified in the course of history, that he ought to and does devote himself to the realization of impersonal ends, even at a cost to himself. It touches only on the freedom characteristic of man and fails to see that other beings are free and are possessed of rights as well. It slights the virtues of altruism, humility and self-sacrifice, and is indifferent to the values which subhuman beings embody. Aristotle's ethics is a static ethics and too, all too human.

An adequate ethics is non-Aristotelian in temper and result. To obtain such an ethics, it would, at first glance, seem desirable to build it on the foundations laid by the creators of our typically modern modes of thought. But if, in place of Aristotle's philosophic system, we try to put the scheme made possible by Galileo, Descartes, etc., we will not only be without an adequate ethics but will lose much of the world and knowledge that is in fact available to us every day. Though the Galileos and Descartes have taken us part of the way we should go, and at least far enough to enable us to see that the Aristotelian view is not entirely sound, they have denied to us in principle the right to say that we are part of a rich and multicolored world of substantial active beings, each with a nature and freedom of its own. Neither the philosophy of Aristotle nor that of his opponents does justice to both the human and the subhuman. Neither can be accepted therefore as offering a satisfactory account of the nature of the world and of the men who live in it.

Aristotle was mistaken in many of his views on nature; he did not take full account of the powers and flexibility of man. But unlike his opponents he did support the double truth that man is in nature and that he possesses powers and is therefore subject to duties not possible to other beings. The modern non-Aristotelians avoided many of the errors Aristotle made in his treatment of nature, and made good many of the omissions to be found in his account of man. But they did not do both together, because they rejected one or the other of the two truths Aristotle affirmed. Either they defined man as a complicated kind of subhuman being, getting him into nature by ignoring the traits he alone possesses, or they insisted on his characteristic powers but separated him off from the rest of the world. They thus either naturalized man but denied he was free, or gave freedom to man but denied he was natural. Though they rightly rejected Aristotle's account of nature and of man, they conceived of nature as being so rigid and mechanical that it could provide no place for a full-bodied man acting freely and responsibly.

What is needed today is a philosophy which is adequate to all aspects of existence and thus has room to assert that man is a being who is both natural and free. A satisfactory philosophy is one which recognizes that nature is quite different from what both Aristotle and the moderns take it to be, and that man, as part of nature, has powers and duties both Aristotle and the moderns had to ignore. Such a philosophy would be able to place its ethics within a cosmic frame, or—what is the same thing—see the freedom that concerns ethics as a special case of the freedom which is at the core of every being. The powers that man uses when ethical, though they enable him to do what others cannot, are as natural as those which he uses when he acts as a physical, a biological or a chemical being.

Man is a free being in nature. Otherwise he would be supernatural, in part at least, or would not be responsible for the things he does. The freedom that pertains to him is but a special illustration of a freedom embodied in every other natural being.

We must be on guard against the error of unwarranted subtraction, the denial that entities possess the characters they do. This error is occasionally evident in Aristotle, but it never was fully exploited until the modern age. The attempt to show that men are subject to the same laws that govern other beings, combined with the claim that the scope of natural science is universal and its mastery complete, has inclined modern thinkers to subtract from men their characteristic life, desires, hopes, feelings, values and minds. As a result they have viewed men as little more than inanimate physical things. Having sacrificed man at the altar of an arbitrary theory, such a view can hardly shed light on human needs, goals and concerns. A philosophy which speaks of the human as though it were dead or subhuman can but provide an excuse for ignoring the problems of men.

In escaping from this error, it is possible to fall into another, exploiting the opposite extreme. The error of unwarranted subtraction can be replaced by the error of unwarranted addition. This latter error is encouraged by the worthy effort to understand all entities as interactive with and as knowable by real men, and by the laudable desire to avoid the deep dualisms which have made mysteries of the union of mind and body and of the origin of life and thought. It attributes minds, feelings and life to atoms, rocks, oceans and stars. Instead, however, of explaining anything, this view obscures matters by loading down the rest of nature with human characters there is no reason to believe it possesses.

The present contention, that all things have a freedom similar to man's, appears to verge on the error of unwarranted addition, apparently attributing to nonhuman beings traits which belong to human beings alone. But this is an illusion furthered by the fact that we have so long been under the dominance of a view which has expertly deprived the rest of nature of its powers. We too often speak of freedom as though it were illusory or attributable to man alone. We react to the contention that there is freedom in the subhuman realm as though it expressed an unwarranted anthropomorphism. But we should say that there is freedom in the rest of nature, even if we had to deny that man was free. If we did not, we would be unable to do justice to the nature of causation, the origin of life and the character of laws. Men have freedom precisely because they are natural beings, for freedom is a part of whatever is a part of nature.

To commit the error of unwarranted subtraction is to deny a truth; to commit the error of unwarranted addition is to exaggerate one. Both errors have a common root. They are consequences of the supposition that if all beings are free they must exhibit that freedom in the same way and with the same results. But a common power can be expressed with different degrees of strength, in divergent ways and with diverse results. A mammal is still a mammal though it flies like a bat, walks like a cat or swims like a whale; a being can be free though it falls like a stone, feeds like a plant or thinks like a man. The rejection of the supposition, that free beings must exhibit their freedom in the same ways, makes it possible to avoid the errors of subtraction and addition, and affirm that man is part of nature, subject to the same categories which embrace the smallest and most insignificant piece of matter, but still different from all other beings in range, interest, promise and aim.

There are gaps between man and man, between men and the apes, between the snail and the stone. Sudden and novel beginnings, abrupt and surprising endings confront us on every side. Nature is more an affair of fits and starts, of breaks and bumps, than of smooth and easy passage, of continuity and harmony.

The existence of gaps does not mean that the distance between the different entities and acts had not once been bridged, or that what lies on one side of the gap is unconcerned with and is quickened by a different type of power from that which lies on the other. Some bodies rise, others float and still others drop straight down. To move up is other than to move down, to move to and fro is not the same as to move round and round. Yet we now know that all these different motions have a single explanation. A piece of paper and a piano fall at different rates. But there is not one law for paper that rides on the air and another for pianos that plummet to the ground; the same law of motion applies to both with equal force, the difference in result being due to the structures and composition of the paper and the piano and the way they interplay with air and wind. Just so, there is one power of freedom, exhibited by all beings in divergent ways in diverse circumstances and with diverse results. This freedom, unlike motion, accounts moreover for the origin of the living from the nonliving and the human from the animal. The nonliving and the animal are not only free to act; they are free to become different in nature.

In the present volume an attempt is made to make manifest that freedom is of the essence of all beings and that it explains why and how new existents arise. The account begins with a consideration of the nature of causation and inanimate beings so as to make evident how deep-rooted and unavoidable the fact of freedom is. From there it moves on to show how obstacles in the way of the exercise of freedom promote a new attempt to exercise freedom in ways which are characteristic of new and perhaps superior types of beings. It is freedom which makes it possible to understand and relate the human and the subhuman, and eventually to see the rights and duties of the former in their cosmic setting. It allows us to move step by step from lower beings and limited acts to man himself, the ethical yet natural being.

3. PHILOSOPHIC TRUTH

A philosophy is more than a report of opinions; it affirms what is true. It is more than a catalogue of what happens to be the case; it deals with what must be so. It speaks of the permanent and essential in undeniable ways, to provide a revelation of the nature of things, holding everywhere and always.

Like the truths of logic, the truths of philosophy cannot be denied without absurdity. But whereas the denial of a logical truth yields the absurdity of an assertion which contradicts itself, the denial of a philosophical truth yields the absurdity of an assertion which contradicts the existence of full-bodied beings, some of whom have minds, dwelling in a full-bodied spatio-temporal world.

A philosophy is more than a set of logical truths; its truths are existential, dealing with the inescapable substance of knowledge and being.

That "x is x" is a logical truth. Its denial is the self-contradiction, "x is not x." The logical truth tells us nothing about the nature of the world we confront every day except, of course, that nothing in the world violates it; it is too abstract and formal to serve a philosophic purpose. Philosophical truths are more concrete, discoursing about those aspects of being and knowledge which must be exemplified always. One such truth is "I cannot meet myself coming toward me." To deny this is to commit the absurdity of denying one's uniqueness, and ultimately therefore the fact that one utters the denial as an individual in an individual way. Another philosophic truth is "When I feel pain I am in pain," for the denial of this involves the absurdity that what exists only for consciousness can be characterized as having a nature other than that which consciousness reveals it to have. A third philosophical truth is "It is wrong wantonly to kill one's friend," for to deny this is to commit the absurdity of maintaining that it is either right or indifferent to reduce values unnecessarily. It is possible to deny these three truths and yet speak intelligibly; it is not possible to deny them without letting go some vital aspect of being or knowledge.

There are many philosophical truths. Some of them are obvious and their denials obviously absurd; others require some analysis to make evident how inescapable they are and how disastrous their rejection would be. In the course of the following work a number of them will be formulated; almost every one of them will serve to articulate the nature of freedom as resident in some basic aspect of existence. To deny them is to deny the fundamental fact of freedom in some way, and incidentally make impossible an understanding of causation, nature, value and obligation.

Such truths, and others not yet explored, are in one sense rather easy and in another sense very difficult to uncover. Once we have put our finger on the pulse of the universe to deny which is to deny one's sanity, it is a comparatively simple thing to express the nature of that which we have isolated. But we do not usually get to the heart of things without going through a number of preliminaries, for we cherish many assertions whose denials are thought absurd only because of traditional beliefs we have refused to criticize, and we usually have to struggle long and hard to get beneath these to truths more substantial and sound. We all know that there is nothing really amiss in the claim that a large, flying being is not necessarily a bird, but there was a time when such a claim would have been universally deemed absurd. If we are to avoid identifying such beliefs with indubitable truths, we must make a strenuous effort to suppose the beliefs are mistaken. In most cases we will find it almost impossible to do this, except with regard to details. It is easier to reject the belief that "flying beings with red wings are birds" than to reject the less specific "flying beings with wings of some kind may be birds."

The truths we daily accept ought to be generalized until they express a structural fact so basic and comprehensive that every item is bound to illustrate it. The denials of such generalized truths involve the rejection of those aspects of the universe presupposed in all action, existence or thought. Because every assertion and fact must provide an instance of such generalized truths, it is possible to start with any statement and any fact and, by a process of generalization achieved by imaginatively rejecting details, move inevitably to truths which cannot be denied without absurdity. Whether the original statements be true or false and the facts minor or crucial, they must illustrate a truth which covers all there is and can be.

All thought begins with some present belief, and it is this which must be generalized to get a beginning in philosophy. Now, to me it seems evident at this moment that "I have just written something." Still, it is possible that I may be in error, for I often mistake the extent of a lapse of past time. I feel confident but not certain that my assertion is true and its denial foolish. I am more sure, however, that the generalization: "I wrote something" cannot be denied without absurdity. My memory may play me false in its report that a lapse of time was short rather than long, but I am not willing, except in the face of a good deal of counterevidence, to agree that my memory is playing me false in testifying that I did write something sometime. Still, such evidence could conceivably be produced. It is possible that I am in error when I affirm that "I wrote something." I may not have written anything at all. The possibility is, for me, a very remote one, but I confess that it is a possibility after all. Caution requires me therefore to retreat to the more general formulation: "Something was written here." To deny this I would have to question the insistent testimony of my memory to the effect that the page was blank before, and the insistent testimony of my senses that there is writing there now. Still, it is conceivable that this, which I take to be writing, is nothing more than a series of natural marks and that I have somehow become deluded to the point of believing that it was put down by myself or another as a communication of some kind. Such a supposition I shall not take seriously; as a practical man who trusts his memory, senses, observations and inferences until forced to question them, I will not yield in my contention that "something was written here." But as more than a practical man, as a being in search of an absolutely solid ground on which to base a host of speculations, I must drive myself to question even that of which I am very confident, until I get to the point where it is not plausible to doubt at all. And I can obtain this result by generalizing further to "something occurred." Here is an indubitable truth; if it were not, ours would be a static world, a world in which nothing—not even my assertion—occurred.

If this cannot be a static world, it must be a dynamic one. But then it is not only necessarily true that something occurred, but necessarily true that everything in the world must have come to be, if only in the sense of reappearing at every moment of time. The assertion that "everything in this universe comes to be" is a philosophic truth achieved, as all of them can be, by generalizing a simple proposition of daily experience and extracting the truth which the absurdity of its denial lays bare. It is, of course, possible to construct a scheme in which some things do not come to be, where time is nothing, where there is no passage of any kind. Such a scheme might describe some actual state of affairs—a Nirvana, a Divine Mind, a logical system and so on. But it does not describe this world, the concern of our philosophy.

Our method has not been that of denying or doubting all things. It is a method which allows each belief to be indubitable in the particular context in which no evidence serves to bring it into question, but which requires us to abandon it in its specificity as the range of our interest increases in scope. It does not require us to affirm that the details abstracted from are not details in fact; it merely leaves these details behind in an attempt to reach the more generalized truth they specialize and adorn.

There are many philosophical truths to be obtained in this way, and it is part of our task to bring their implications into focus. We cannot escape the task by claiming to be modest. We are, to be sure, finite, bewildered and far from omniscient. But unless we try to live up to the ideal of having a sound, universal knowledge, we are bound to be entangled in a tissue of preconceptions and prejudices. We do not achieve modesty by refusing to ask after the real nature of things. That is but a device for riding on the crest of current beliefs and preparing our ideas for passage into the limbo of historic errors. True modesty demands a courageous attempt to express systematically, in intelligible language, truths that are at least faintly discernible to a child.

For our present purpose we can take our start with the truth that in our universe all things come to be. We can then proceed to make evident that they come to be because they are free. All beings embody a freedom which is responsible for the origin of the living and the human, and which comes to final and most complete expression in the ethical activities of man.

PART ONE

_____

CAUSATION AND FREEDOM

CAUSATION AND PREDICTION

1. CAUSE AND EFFECT

WHATEVER EXISTS in this world of ours has come to be. Whatever comes to be is an effect. And for each effect there is a cause.

Were there no causes, what happens would have had to produce itself and thus exist before it existed, or it would be unconnected with anything past, take place though there was nothing which enabled it to occur. The first supposition is self-contradictory; the second is intelligible but absurd. We can think of a world in which each episode is a miracle, unrelated to any other, but such a world we deny is ours every time we pull to open a door or drink to quench a thirst.

Every quality, every thing, every state of affairs has its cause. Love and fear, impulse and gait, weight, structure and height, you, the stone, the cloud and I, all these and more have their preceding causes.

This is a causal world. Hume suggested that there was no causation in fact, but that we have a habit of thinking and acting as if there were. His view cannot ultimately be sustained. Either the habit is uncaused and no reason can therefore be given for its presence, or the habit has a cause and the suggestion that there is no causation is withdrawn in being explained. We cannot follow Hume without prohibiting an explanation of why we think and act as though there were causes. To account for the belief is self-contradictorily to acknowledge a cause for it. On the other hand,

3

to say that the belief just happens to be is to say that it is an irreducible matter of fact which can be rejected only verbally. If we now, as a matter of brute inexplicable fact, happen to believe in causation, even though we may at some later time happen not to believe in it, causation is beyond the reach of an actual denial now. Only an uncaused belief in causation could possibly be mistaken, but such a belief could not possibly be put aside. If we believe in causation—as we do—we cannot think and ought not say "this is not a causal world."

A correct understanding of the nature of causation is a prerequisite to a correct understanding of man as an ethical yet natural being. If causation, as is sometimes thought, precludes the possibility of freedom, then either man is free but is so far not part of a causal world, or he is part of such a world but is so far not free. But if man is both natural and free, there must be causes for everything he does and yet he must possess a power of acting in ways those causes do not prescribe. In fact, as will be immediately evident, there is always a gap between cause and effect. In that gap freedom makes its presence felt.

A cause precedes its effect. There is a temporal distance between the two. Were there no such distance the cause would coexist with its effect, and the effect of that effect would coexist with it, and so on endlessly. Nothing would take place in such a case, for every consequence of a cause would then exist at the moment the cause appeared. The whole of history would be here before one could blink an eye. To be sure, we sometimes speak of a ball pressing on a cushion and simultaneously "causing" a depression there. But the cause of the depression in the cushion is the ball as not yet resting on the cushion; as resting on the cushion it is an analytic component of the effect, "ball resting on a depressed cushion." As such a component it is simultaneous with the depression; it is not a cause of the depression any more than clenched fingers are the cause of a fist or pages are the cause of a book.

A real cause has a real effect. The effect follows it in time. For a thing to be a real cause, therefore, it must await the occurrence of its effect. Until the effect appears, that which precedes the effect cannot have the status of a cause. One would be speaking carelessly if one were to call the conjunction of a lighted match and gasoline the cause of an explosion if no explosion occurred. It is only after the initial coming together of the two has given way to a process of interplay and then terminated in an explosion, that the union of match and gasoline could possibly achieve the role of a cause for the explosion.

What is present cannot, as present, be a cause. As present, it has no effects as yet; there is nothing then of which it could be the cause. Cause and effect are correlative terms, and it is only when the effect has come about that what preceded the effect can be a cause of it. Causes are dependent for their status as causes on the occurrences which succeed them. But as having actual effects, causes are already in the past, crowded out of present existence by the arrival of these effects. Presupposing as they do the existence of effects in order to achieve the status of causes, causes could not possibly produce effects.

When an effect occurs, and not before, there is a real cause for it. And as we shift our interest from one factor to another of the effect, we stress different subordinate effects and thereby different causes. We usually say that a lighted match is the cause of the burning of gasoline, but we can also say that the burning of gasoline is the cause of the match being blown to smithereens. The former and usual mode of speaking stresses a more signal subordinate effect, but the latter—despite its unimportance—refers to an effect which is equally a component of the total effect, the explosion, whose cause is the union of lighted match and gasoline.

An effect is made possible by the co-presence of antecedent things, its "cause"; it comes to be as the outcome of a dynamic *course* of "causation." The togetherness of lighted match and gasoline determine what *can* happen; their interplay determines what *does* happen. And what does happen is what can happen, made determinate, concrete and present. The interplay of match and gasoline is an event, an ongoing in which each participates and in which each is modified, a *course* by which a prospective effect, a possible kind of explosion, is made determinate, to become a present, actual, unique explosion which never was before and never will be again. As the means by which the possible is made actual, the indeterminate determinate, the abstract concrete, the process of becoming is necessarily free. Freedom, as the dynamic agency for turning the general into the particular, is always to be found filling in that temporal gap which separates an actual concrete antecedent "cause" and its actual concrete subsequent "effect."

If there were no determination of a *possible* state of affairs, anything could occur, no matter what the antecedents. If there were no production of an *actual* state of affairs, nothing in fact would ever happen. And if the course of causation were not a way of producing determinations allowed by the antecedents, it would be impossible to predict, as we do in science and practice, the kind of effects which actually take place in this world of ours. A prospective explosion makes no noise and hurts no one; only an actual explosion, produced in the course of time, has power. But if the latter were not a determination of the former we could not reasonably make plans to prevent its occurrence when we open a can of gasoline.

This is a world of canalized courses, having definite beginnings and endings. Each course is a localized *durée*, a concrete slab of time, a specific mode by which an effect comes to be, a limited, unique route originating in a limited definite past and terminating in a limited definite present. The nature of the course in its concreteness and detail is not determined and not determinable in advance. It cannot possibly be explained by or reduced to its origin, for it is related to its origin as a line to a point, the changing to the fixed, becoming to being, the present to the past. It never was before and never will be again, having its entire nature exhausted in the act of occurring. To know the course of the becoming of an effect one must go through it toward an as yet undetermined future, leaving the past behind.

Every effect is the outcome of specific antecedents and a limited process in time. To forget either component or to hold them apart is to abandon oneself to paradox and perplexity. Yet this is evidently what eminent representatives of three dominant schools of thought have done.

The rationalists, in the person of Spinoza, acknowledged only antecedent things and could, as a consequence, find no room for time. If only antecedent things are required for an effect to occur, the effect follows at once. There is no temporal distance between them. The romantics, in the person of Bergson, took the opposite tack. They acknowledged only a course of becoming, and as a consequence could find no room for science. If there is only a course, there are no boundaries, no limits given within which the course must be confined, and therefore nothing specific to know. The empiricists, in the person of Hume, acknowledged both the antecedents and the course but, because they did not bring them both together, could find no need for the effect to come about. If the two are kept apart, there can be no accounting for the result which their union alone provides.

Let us imagine these three philosophers watching two men in an argument ending in an agreement. The disputants are reasonable men, let us say, who are looking for a common truth. They are antecedents who make an agreement possible. Their argument is a course through which they remove their doubts and ambiguities, the outcome of which is the effect, a definite, actual agreement.

Spinoza is the only one of the three philosophers who is sure that the men will agree. He deduces that result from the antecedent natures of the men. But he ignores the course of events; he does not treat the dispute of the men as another factor, helping determine the outcome. As a consequence, he concludes that somehow men who have not yet conversed are men in agreement. Yet the men agreed only because they discussed. Bergson, who allows only for the course, concerns himself instead with the argument. He knows that the agreement is not itself the argument but its outcome, and supposes therefore that the dispute itself produces the agreement. Yet how can a dispute of itself yield an agreement? Hume alone takes into account the men and the fact that they are arguing, though he sometimes supposes that the dispute is an illusion. In neither the men nor the discussion does he find agreement. He therefore concludes that the agreement has nothing to do with the fact that there were two men and that they were disputing. But how else but by being two men and arguing did the men come to agree?

Most thinkers believe it is possible to say in advance that the men will agree. Like Spinoza, they confound the possible agreement, which can be anticipated, with the actual unanticipatable agreement which will be reached only if there happens to be a course of disputing. They are left with the problem of how there can be a temporal distance between cause and effect. If causes necessitate, there is no reason why there should be any delay in the appearance of the effect. Some thinkers, the Occasionalists, call on God to force a temporal gap between the cause and effect which their theory would otherwise require to be related without interval. But the most daring suggestion is that of the Hegelians who suppose that the men change into the dispute, and that this in turn becomes the agreement by holding on to and uniting with the men as not yet having disputed. These and other variations reveal how ingenious thinkers must and can become, once they deny that what all the rest daily know is true. Unreflectively and with surety, ordinary men rightly treat the agreement as the outcome of a specific argument conducted for a time by living men. Subtlety is misplaced when it serves only to make one distort such an obtrusive truth.

It is necessary to affirm with Hume that there is a temporal gap between the men before they began to dispute and those men as in agreement. The actual agreement the men reach must be recognized, with Bergson, to be the outcome of a course of disputing, a process unique and unanticipatable. And with Spinoza, one must hold that an accurate knowledge of the men would make it possible to know that the men could agree. But it is vital that the points which these three philosophers make should not be isolated, for an understanding of causation requires the acknowledgment of all of them together.

Neither antecedents nor courses are alone productive of effects. The antecedents provide one condition, the courses another, and only the two together determine what actually will be. If, for the purpose of analysis, a course is held apart from antecedents, it must in the end be brought together with it again, to make possible an understanding of how an effect could come to be.

2. THE RATIONALE OF CAUSATION

The syllogism tells us that Socrates can die. It relates him abstractly to an abstract conclusion. It does not tell us how Socrates' life will end. Only the actual course of living through which he goes, the way in which he eats and sleeps, teaches and thinks, yields the fact that he is a mortal who dies in prison, surrounded by his friends. Socrates died as he did, not because men are mortal, but because he lived in Athens in a un-Athenian way. The conclusion of his life was not the conclusion of a syllogism. But the concrete result, the actual fact of his dying as he did, is just as necessary as is the conclusion which a formal syllogism might provide. His death is logically deducible *after* it occurred, for then it is possible to add, to the fact that he is Socrates, an account of his career, as terminating in his death.

Antecedent causes and subsequent effects are not related as premises and inevitable conclusions. The nature of the consequent or effect is in part determined by the nature of the course by which it comes to be. It is the antecedents and the course together which make the effect what it is. The antecedents by themselves yield only a possible result, the course by itself yields nothing but itself. To get a concrete specific result, the two must be inter-related.

The process of the coming to be of an effect provides a condition which, together with the antecedents, suffices for the logical as well as for the actual derivation of the effect. Whatever occurs is rational, not in the sense that antecedent existents are premises for the inevitable presence of foregone conclusions, but in the sense that the effect follows inevitably from those antecedents as supplemented by the additional condition provided by the course of moving to the effect. The character of the effect must be learned from experience, not because it defies logic and reason, but because the course by which it comes to be is a concrete empirical event, unknowable before it takes place. The course of coming to be is an unanticipatable second condition which makes possible the actual and logical, the factual and necessary occurrence of an effect.

Once a course of becoming is completed, the effect is necessarily what it is, and when. There is no coming to be of something from nothing. The antecedent of the effect and the course as terminating in it (or, if an effect is an event, taking time to be, the course as embracing the entire career of the effect) together determine what that effect is. Before the effect occurs, it is not a determinate result, for the course by which it comes to be is not yet itself determinate. Given the antecedent conditions, one cannot get to the effect without going through the course, and thus without following a novel route which the effect terminates.

The effect is necessarily what it is. In terms of what has gone before, it is inevitable. Yet it need not have been. Taken in isolation from the course by which it actually comes to be, it is a posibility which did not have to occur. What necessarily is, need not have been. Once the die has been cast, it cannot be recalled, but it did not have to be thrown or to turn up as it did. The past allows for a subsequent, free course which helps determine the necessary effect that ensues.

This result has bearing in every domain—even in that chaste and abstract realm where men presumably engage in acts of pure, formal, logical reasoning. "Leibniz is a rationalist" is a contingent truth. It is conceivable that the fact might have been otherwise. Yet it is a necessary consequence of an inference which starts from the premises, "all members of the Cartesian School are rationalists, and Leibniz is a member of that school." These premises do not produce the conclusion; the conclusion does not issue out of them. For the conclusion to be, some one must conclude, infer to it from the premises. No premises pick out the conclusion—that is done by the thinker. When we say that "Leibniz is a rationalist" is a conclusion from such and such premises, we should mean therefore that we have already gone through the course of reaching that conclusion, starting from those premises. We ought not to suppose that the conclusion is wrapped up in the premises, awaiting only to be uncovered, or that it already exists apart from the premises, awaiting only to be discovered. A conclusion does not exist before it is concluded to.

The laws of logic to which one's inferences conform are general, universal. In reasoning one makes these general laws pertinent to the particular situation, exemplifies them in a limited context in the free act of moving from the premise to the conclusion. Until one actually goes through the course of inferring that conclusion, one does not have it as a conclusion.

3. PREDICTION

The future can occasionally be predicted in the large, as abstract, indeterminate, and general; it defies prediction in the little, as concrete, determinate, and particular. A study of a "cause" may reveal a range of possible effects, but to get to the one actual effect that occurs, in its concreteness and full detail, one must go beyond that "cause" to and through a free course of causation, up to the point where the effect fully is. The past limits the range of what might occur; the course of causation, a process in time, the becoming of the present, is the means for making what is now undetermined in that range, present and determinate.

Some beings act time after time with little variation, others charge their acts with considerable and variable degrees of novelty from moment to moment. The effects of neither are given in advance. A predictable outcome is a possible outcome, not something neat and complete awaiting merely the external passage of time in order to be able to appear on the scene, irrelevantly decorated with one date rather than another.

No matter how short the course, no matter how clear and well-defined the "cause," no matter how simple and familiar the effect, we do not and cannot know that effect in advance. The future cannot now be known, not because our knowledge is a limited knowledge, but because there is nothing concrete in the future that can now be known. We cannot take refuge in the idea that the future is intrinsically knowable, but that it is unknown or unknowable to men. A reasonable argument to the effect that the nature of the future is unknown or unknowable to us cannot be based on the grounds that we cannot master the countless details and intersecting lines of causation which lead to that future. There *are* countless details and multiple, intersecting lines of causation beyond the possible reach of *our* knowledge. But each detail and line must itself first come to be before it can be known. It is not the complexity of the process of causation which makes it impossible for us to know the future in its concreteness. The actual terminus of the simplest course is unknowable in advance for the simple reason that there is no such terminus yet to know.

It is necessary to come to be in the future in order to have a concrete future to know. That concrete future is nought but a new present replacing the present that now exists. It would be antecedently unknowable in its concreteness even if there were but a single line of causation and even if all things were perfectly simple; it is not concrete except as the outcome of a free, unique course of causation.

A concrete future has no being or meaning until it is fully present. Until then there is only the future as possibly concrete, as general, abstract, as that which can be made determinate, as that which lacks details. The details the future will contain are thus beyond the possible reach of *any* knowledge now.

What the future holds in store is beyond the power of a God to know, granted even that He be omniscient, for God cannot do the impossible. He cannot contradict Himself, do evil for the sake of evil, make Himself impotent, ignorant or debased. His omnipotence is the power to do all that *can* be done, and His omniscience is the power to know all that *can* be known. He has not the power to do what cannot be done, the power to know what cannot be known. He cannot now know the future in its concreteness, for such a future is not, and thus is not knowable. Even if He thoroughly grasped the nature of things that now exist, their habits and the kind of power they exert, He could not tell in advance just what in detail their effects would be, for there are no such details before they actually occur. One might conceive of effects to be, but these effects and every feature of them would be general, abstract. The details of actual effects cannot be known in advance, for there are no such details to be known. Not even God can know just what will be. It is foolish for a man to expect to achieve what is beyond the reach even of omniscience.

"It is true," it might be argued in reply, "no one can predict the concrete outcome of a causal process. But we must go further. No one can know such an outcome when it occurs, or after it has occurred. The concrete is beyond the reach of knowledge at any time. To know is to dismember, to analyze, to abstract from the concrete and thus to lose it as concrete. Even a God must fall short of knowing the world in its full being. The concrete is lived through, not known or knowable." Such an objection supposes that there is no intuitive knowledge, no way of reaching the being of another. Yet when we know that another is a person, that he is sympathetic, when we grieve or laugh with him, we know him intimately and immediately. Presumably an omniscient God would have an even more intimate contact with beings, and grasp what they are from within. The possibility of knowledge does not require that one destroy, discard or distort the concrete.

It is true, of course, that what is normally termed knowledge involves distinction, abstraction and analysis. To know something before me I must distinguish *that* it is from *what* it is, and bring the two together in a judgment. Though a book in its concreteness is a that and a what in one, undivided and undistinguished, to know the book I must distinguish them, and then bring them together in the judgment, "this is a book." The judgment, though one, contains distinct and separate elements which are not separate in the actual book. But this does not mean that to know something is to distort its nature as objective and concrete. This, perhaps an elementary dilemma may make clear.

We either do or do not know that the elements used in the judgment are not separate in the actual book. If we know that the elements are not separate in the book, we must obviously somehow grasp the book in its concreteness; our knowledge then, instead of requiring the loss of the concrete, demands its acknowledgment. On the other hand, if we do not know whether or not the elements used in judgment are separate in the book, we do not know that there is something which knowledge fails to reach. But then we cannot claim to have a knowledge of anything. To have knowledge is to refer abstracted and distinct elements to a concrete in which they are one and indistinguishable. Instead of requiring the view that the concrete is abandoned or dismembered when we know, the very nature of the act of judgment requires rather the admission that the concrete is acknowledged in its full concreteness.

There is knowledge only if one possesses content in terms of which one can know, and confronts a concrete object to which the possessed content can be referred. Knowledge involves the use of abstract content and a reference to a concrete subject matter which lies outside that abstract content. It is like vision; to be known a thing must be kept at and acknowledged from a distance. The act of knowing is the act of relating abstract content to the concrete being which lies outside it. Knowledge is always "knowledge of" what is outside the content of knowledge. Concrete occurrences are accordingly knowable, but *that* in terms of which we know them is distinct from them.

To know the determinate we must refer to it by means of what is not entirely determinate. And if we wish to know what is not entirely determinate we must have recourse to other indeterminate content, in terms of which we can articulate and thereby judge the single concrete fact. If it were impossible, then, to know the concrete, it would also be impossible to know the abstract, for the latter is, relative to our knowledge of it, as concrete as the former.

"We can bring the abstract into our minds. We can contemplate it, know it. Able to know the possible by contemplating it, we are therefore able in principle to know everything that occurs, for an actual occurrence differs from a possible one only in its mode of existence. The former is here and now, while the latter is merely future." But an actuality is more than a possibility in the present. It possesses determinations not contained in itself as possible. It is the possible transformed. The knowledge we have of the possible is, therefore, never entirely appropriate to the actual. A possibility is determinate only relative to the means by which we know it; it acquires actual determinations when it is referred to a transforming concrete which lies beyond it.

These conclusions can be used to illuminate the nature of predictions, i.e., articulate judgments about that which is not yet, but is expected to be present. Because they refer to the future, predictions, no matter how detailed and precise they may be, necessarily express the nature of something general, indeterminate and possible. They ought not to be confounded with judgments regarding present matters of fact, unless one's purpose is to reveal oneself to be a disciple of Dewey. To confirm a prediction, a judgment about a possibility must be referred to a present occurrence. But the present is particular, determinate; it is the possible enriched and transformed. It can constitute a confirmation of a prediction only if a confirmation is not the recovery of the possibility originally judged but is instead the acknowledgment of that possibility as altered and concrete.

Predictions are not identical with the possibilities which they articulate. They are human modes of expressing these. Nor are they formulations of the actual events that ensue. They articulate not those events, but their possibility. When we confirm a prediction, therefore, we must transform our knowledge of a judged possibility by referring our judgment to an actual concrete situation in which that possibility has been made determinate. The judgment, in being referred to the actual concrete case, is enriched, specified, provided with details it did not possess as a judgment of a possibility. It is then no longer the judgment it was.

A judgment about a possibility can be abstracted from, generalized out of a judgment about a concrete case in which that possibility has been made determinate. Similarly, we can recover the original predicted possibility in the present, if we are willing to generalize and thereby make indeterminate the particular case that occurs. But if we generalize what occurs we ought to generalize our judgment too. Our judgments must be generalized when and as our subject matter is.

If we are interested in recovering an original possibility, we must also try to recover our judgment about it, for only then will our judgment relate to the possibility as abstracted from the concrete. By referring to such a possibility we would not, of course, confirm a prediction. At most we would repeat it, but as that which had been rather than as that which was to be confirmed. An exact confirmation of a prediction is not possible. But we can recover the predicted as an abstract element derived from the concrete, unpredictable event that actually occurs.

In becoming actual, the possible is transformed. We cannot know, however, whether or not a transformation of a possibility will be great or small at the next moment. Nor is it very important, for the most part, for us to know this. Even the most exact and exacting of sciences do not require a perfect exhibition of rigid laws. They require only that possibilities in the future be subjected to transformations somewhat similar to those they suffered in the past. A successful science is one which the world happens to support for a time, by realizing its possibilities in an orderly, i.e., lawful way.

For the ancient Hebrews, Jehovah laid down inviolable moral laws, to defy which was to become morally extinct. For classical science, He laid down physical laws instead and punished violation by physical extermination—or what is even more distressing, by calling on physicists to deny that the recalcitrant thing was even capable of existing. Classical physics is Hebraic morality in a new dress. It supposes that laws are iron bonds holding things in an inflexible grip, that what is merely possible controls what is actual. The reverse is closer to the truth.

The laws of nature have a threefold status. They are the substance of what occurred, they are components in what occurs, and they are possibilities defining the nature of what can occur. None of them is imposed from on high. As the substance of what occurred, the laws of nature are perfectly exemplified; as components in what occurs they are unstable, changing in character as the things in the world change in activity; as possibilities they change in character in being exemplified.

The past is a tissue of perfectly fulfilled laws. The present is a domain in which changing laws are components of concrete occurrences. The future is a domain of possible laws. The march of time is the free conversion of possibilities first into the components and then into the substance of things.

Science has application to this world, not because the world is a tissue of possibilities, but because the distance between those possibilities and the concrete happens to vary but slightly from case to case, particularly when the cases considered include whole ranges of individual items whose separate variations are slight or balance one another. Precisely because the relation between the general predicted and the specific actual occurrence is fairly constant it can be constantly ignored, if it is possibilities rather than concrete facts with which one is concerned. Science is possible because the things in the world act in somewhat monotonous ways, yielding a fairly constant relation between the predicted and the actual occurrence.

4. NECESSITY AND FREEDOM

Every effect is necessitated. It must be what it is, because the process started with just those antecedents and ended with just that effect. But though necessitated the effect is freely produced, the outcome of a free course which works its way out here and now in ways impossible to know with surety in advance. Whatever necessities there are, result from the exercise of freedom. A thunderclap, the moving of a billiard ball, an impulsive act or an act of design are on a par because they are all the outcome of free occurrences by which indeterminate possibilities are made into determinate actualities.

Every effect is a cause. It is the beginning of a new course in which another effect will be freely brought about. The exercise of freedom ends with a necessity for a free course to occur. Whatever freedom there is, is the necessary outcome of what has gone before.

The course by which an effect comes about is a free occurrence whose outcome is necessary. It ends with the necessity that another free course take place. Freedom and necessity are thus inseparable. They presuppose one another. Because freedom has been exercised, an effect is necessarily produced; because an effect has been produced, it must be followed by a free course moving to and terminating in a new future occurrence.

If there could be necessity without freedom there would be no spread between present and future. Necessity without freedom allows no place for time and thus makes causation impossible. Causation is a temporal phenomenon, a concrete free course linking past "causes" with subsequent determinate effects.

If there could be freedom without necessity, the process of coming to be would have neither beginning nor end. It would start independently of what had occurred, and would end before the effect took place. Every process that occurs is forced to begin, and ends with what has to be. Freedom is a temporal power then and there turning the indeterminate into the determinate. It neither pushes from behind nor pulls from ahead; it constitutes from within.

A world of necessity without freedom is a world in which logicians dwell. It is a world in which there are logical connections between existents, but no real movement from one to the other. A world in which there is freedom without necessity is a world in which romantics live. There is movement and life in it, but nothing definite and fixed before or after. Our world is more complex. To be at home in it we must be both rational and practical, constrained yet free, humble and adventurous, beings who know that they have been determined to determine for themselves what they will be.

CHAPTER TWO

FREEDOM AND PROCESS

1. THE THEORY OF DETERMINISM

ACCORDING TO WHAT was once the most widely held theory of causation—the theory of the determinists—effects are not produced by causes. The determinists distorted their insight, however, by insisting that the impotence of causes is a consequence of the fact that whatever occurs is nought but the manifestation of a single, cosmic force, and that everything else is merely a passive place where the force could be manifested. To know the nature of an effect one need know, according to their theory, only how this unitary force was exhibited in the antecedent causes and the law of its nature according to which its subsequent manifestations necessarily take place.

For the determinist, antecedents serve only to point to a possible effect; it is the cosmic force which "actualizes" the effect by giving it a predictable date and position in this world. The actual effect is, on his theory, only the possible effect as embodying for the moment an expression of the cosmic force. The actual and possible effects are thus thought to differ only in date and position, and then only because the one does and the other does not serve as a locus for the predetermined expression of the force.

Spinoza's view can be deduced from the determinist's when the law supposed to control the exhibition of the force is attributed to the antecedents. Bergson's view can be derived from it by treating the force as an ultimate changing power, and denying reality to any specific localized course. And if we look at Spinoza's theory through the eyes of Bergson and Bergson's through the eyes of Spinoza, thereby depriving both the antecedents and the course of all bearing on the effect, we get the view of Hume. The theory of determinism is a matrix for a host of subsequent and less adequate views. None of them holds as closely as this theory does to what appears to be empirically known.

A stone appears to remain where it is, stolid and unmoved, so long as it is not disturbed. Not a leaf seems to rustle until the birds and the breeze begin to stir. Animals appear to remain quiescent, so long as all about them continues silent and undisturbed. And men, though more complicated than stones, leaves and animals, seem like them to be but places where an external force may be expressed.

The things in nature seem to be passive. We find them moving and changing only under the pressure of external compulsions. The things, to which these compulsions seem to be traceable, appear on examination also to be passive and inert—mere places where an external force once entered and later departed.

No theory, therefore, sounds so plausible and so right as one which asserts that whatever occurs is the result of a single force passively exhibited by specific things. It checks with what seems to be observed; it is simple, direct, clear-eyed. There is little difficulty in giving it a mathematical form or in shaping it so that it becomes a mainstay of a science intolerant of mysteries and vagueness, a science which tries to make successful predictions and to control nature.

Laplace stated the view in its simplest form. According to him, the cosmic force is a single physical power prescribing the position and velocity of whatever bodies might exist. He thought that if we knew where all the bodies in nature were and the velocities with which they moved, our knowledge of the laws of motion—laws perfectly fulfilled by the cosmic force—would make it possible to predict precisely what the future would be.

Laplace thought he knew the formulae according to which one could deduce subsequent expressions of the cosmic force from a knowledge of its antecedent expressions. But he did not claim that he or any man could ever know the position and velocity of every body. He supposed merely that such knowledge was possible and that it was of scientific interest. Determinism, for Laplace, described what was the case, and it was the business of science to make the fact manifest in its accounts.

The Laplacian view no longer finds the favor with scientists that it once did. Others of course still hold to the view—and in the name of science. There is a cultural lag between science and the texts and popular books through which it is spread, so that many a man today mumbles in the name of science views which scientists already reject. The words of God are whispered on Mount Sinai and are spread abroad on broken tablets.

Most physicists reject the Laplacian view and accept Heisenberg's instead. They use the term "indeterminacy" to express direct and conscious opposition to the Laplacian concept of "determinacy." They have no concern with the question of free will, chance or self-determination. Theirs and Heisenberg's thesis is simply that it is *intrinsically* impossible to ascertain precisely both the momentum and the position of the ultimate entities which supposedly constitute the physical universe. The exact specification of one of these quantities, they maintain, precludes the specification of the other. Laplace's theory, for them and Heisenberg, is an hypothesis about a state of affairs which it is beyond the province of physics to ascertain, and would be useless even if what it said were true.

When Heisenberg's theory was first stated, there was dancing in many philosophic streets. Quite a number of philosophers were jubilant over the fact that physicists found no scientific truth in the hypothesis of Laplace. But their jubilation was premature.

Firstly, there is no surety that the Heisenberg principle will always be accepted by scientists. It is merely the theory which *now* best accords with the facts which scientists know and consider. If one is willing to hang theories of free will, chance and self-determination or the like on the momentary and transitory theses which science finds it desirable to hold, one must be ready to believe in them one week and be ready to reject them the next. Whether or not men have a free will is a question whose answer does not depend on the nature of the transitory hypotheses a science may find it desirable to maintain in the course of its development.

Secondly, the Heisenberg principle does not deny that Laplace provided an accurate statement of the true nature of things. It is silent on that point. It denies only that Laplace made a significant statement for physics. It is possible for both to be right. Laplace may have accurately described an objective state of affairs, and Heisenberg may have accurately described the state of affairs which science can significantly acknowledge. No disciple of Heisenberg need give up the Laplacian view; but he ought to add, for clarity's sake, that he has no scientific warrant or scientific use for it. A Laplacian today is a philosopher, speculating about an aspect of the universe which present day science confesses it cannot possibly know.

Thirdly, and most important, is the fact that both views—Laplace's and Heisenberg's—have a very limited scope. They say nothing about the nature of ends, desires and values. Human actions, at least, are more than motions. They are drenched with values. Since one says nothing of these values when he adopts the Laplacian account, he says nothing about them when he rejects the account, either as a physicist or as a philosopher.

2. THE PARADOX OF DETERMINISM

To be a determinist having some regard for the facts, one must be somewhat bolder than Laplace. Instead of maintaining that bodies are determined with respect to their positions and velocities, one ought to say that they are determined to do whatever they in fact do, whether this be to move or to think, to change a state or a position, to move at a steady or at an irregular rate. One will then achieve what is at once the most unyielding and most flexible, the most thoroughgoing and yet the most accommodating version of determinism. One would still be affirming, tacitly or explicitly, that there was a cosmic force, momentarily felt and suffered by passive particulars, but would credit that force with the ability to do more than make bodies move. As a result, one would trench on the Hegelian and Marxist theory of an over-all spirit or historical process which made itself manifest in countless ways to yield the rich world we daily know. Laplacianism is a thin view; Hegelianism takes in many more of the facts, since for it the single force makes things not only move, but eat, think and form a state.

A comprehensive determinism allows for assertions and denials; the thin view of Laplace grants the possibility of motions only. Since determinism is a theory which men affirm, only the more comprehensive scheme is significant, for only it allows for the possible formulation of a *theory* of determinism. The thinner the determinism, the less provision does it make for the possibility of its own formulation. Yet the more comprehensive the determinism, the more obviously is it untenable. In adjusting itself to the facts, it becomes so accommodating, as we shall see immediately, that it allows equal status to a denial and to an affirmation of itself. The statement that this was a deterministic world and the statement that it was not would, for a comprehensive determinism, be on a level, equally true and equally false, and therefore—since truth and falsehood are mutually exclusive—really incapable of either truth or falsehood.

If this were a deterministic world, both the assertion and the denial that it was so would be predetermined, unavoidable effects. Both would be necessitated to occur as they do by an alien force which was inevitably expressed in different men in these opposing ways. A determinist might say that those who did not speak as he did were mistaken, confused, unenlightened or misinformed, but that would just happen to be the kind of expression which was forced from the determinist when he was confronted with one who said the opposite of what he did. It is consistent—in fact, it is required by the determinist's position—that it might happen that he replies to his opponent with nods and a cry of "true!" Such a reply would be no less a determined result than the preceding one. When a determinist says that the determinist's position is fruitful, desirable, confirmable and so on, he is, according to his own theory, expressing something he *had* to say and which others could not say unless they had been similarly compelled. The determinist's theory allows one to say that there is nothing wrong or right in holding to the theory and nothing wrong or right in opposing it. The formulation of the theory and the acceptance or rejection of it are, by that theory itself, predetermined, unavoidable expressions of an external force, and any supposed comment or evaluation of them, favorable or unfavorable, is also predetermined by the alien power. The determinist can claim nothing; he can only exhibit the fact that an external force compels him to say something.

If this were a deterministic world, the statement that it was so would be followed by one set of occurrences here and by another there. In such a world there would also be occurrences following on the opposite statement, "this is not a deterministic world." If each statement were followed by statements of agreement or disagreement, there would be a semblance of discourse. Yet none of the statements would be judged or argued, if by judgment or argument we mean that which is deliberately affirmed in the light of what is meant. There can be no deliberately asserted truth in a completely deterministic world.

If a determinist is willing to affirm that his theory is true, he must affirm that it is something which can be freely considered and responsibly adopted, and thus that those who know it are so far not determined by an alien power. No matter how comprehensive the determinism, no matter how accommodating its scheme, it always leaves out at least the fact that someone is making a responsible judgment of its merits. If a determinist, on the other hand, denies that he freely considers and responsibly adopts his position, he denies that he has a view which opposes others; his view is then acknowledged to be but one verbal fact among a multitude, no better or worse, no more or less important, than any other.

The more convinced a determinist is, that he has a theory, that it is true, and that it is something other men *ought* also to accept, the more surely must he grant that it is false, since only thus can he expect to have someone pass a responsible judgment on its value and meaning, or follow the trend and evaluate the arguments on its behalf. If determinism rules the day, we cannot know that it does. We must wait for the course of events to make us say that it is true, without being able to judge whether it is or no. A deterministic world is one in which the deterministic thesis could not be offered as true because such a world allows no place for beings who are responsible for asserting truths.

3. HALF-WAY DETERMINISMS

So long as there are determinists who mean what they say, so long must it be true that there is something more than blind forces making men affirm, willy-nilly, what they do. Nevertheless, the deterministic view is so intriguing that one is tempted to save it by marking off a portion of nature and maintaining that it applies there, while some other principle is in operation elsewhere. Thus one might contend that determinism holds of all of nature, but not of all of man. Such an answer, however, eventually ends by dividing man in two. It supposes that man has a body which necessarily moves under the pressure of forces exerted from without, and that in addition he has a soul or self which acts freely, and thus independently of that body. It supposes that man as a body is a delimited region within the whole of nature, while as a soul he stands above and outside nature, a being really free.

We cannot put a man's body into a determined world and keep his soul outside, without making him, as both Descartes and Kant were forced to do, into two distinct beings. To see man as one again, we must suppose that the soul has nothing to do or that it interplays with the body in such a way as to make man an exception in nature, affected as he is by the acts of a soul which is not caught within the controls that dominate other things. It is hard to decide which of these alternatives is worse. The former affirms that man has a soul, but has no reason for saying so; the latter says that he can act, but only because he has been defined as an exceptional kind of being, possessed of a mysterious and private power totally unlike that which any another being can have. A man may be said to have a soul which quickens and sustains his body, but that soul ought to be comparable to the "souls" within other things. If man needs a "soul" to provide his body with vitality and energy, other beings need "souls" as well for similar reasons. But then man will not be an exception in nature; the laws of his behavior will be comparable to the laws that govern the behavior of other beings.

Once grant that a man can judge or be persuaded, and it is granted that he can act and decide on his own responsibility and is so far not caught within a deterministic scheme, whether this be Laplacian or Hegelian in temper. And if man is a single natural being, the indeterminism which characterizes him must also characterize other beings. The only tenable theories of determinism, in a world where men are part of nature and can decide the question of determinism, are the theories that there will be an eventual determinism following upon the present indeterminism, or that there was a deterministism once which somehow gave way to the present indeterminism. Both affirm that with the elimination of men and a change in the rest of nature, a determinism would hold complete sway. The determinism would not, of course, be known or judged at the time that it existed, but if the determinism were possible, the inability to know it would also, of course, not prevent it from occurring.

The universe of the determinist is one in which time assumes the shape of a spatial line over which one can move forwards or backwards indifferently, but which itself has no passage in it and thus is not really time at all. Or his universe is one in which time has the status of an external reality which beats out intervals regardless of what goes on elsewhere. A determinism denies real becoming and therefore precludes the possibility of a time that is integral to the things and processes of the world.

If there could be a deterministic universe it could replace ours only if an external time could be made to change places with our characteristic ingredient time. Such an interchange could take place only in a third time, and that time alone could serve to connect those universes and our own. In terms of their own characteristic times those universes and ours would be independent of, and discontinuous with, one another.

A determinism is impossible in any world continuous with ours. Because there is no determinism now, our universe could never have been and can never become deterministic. Our universe can be arbitrarily said to be externally related, in a third unknown time, to an entirely independent deterministic world, but there is no way in which we can possibly know whether such an assertion makes sense or not.

Determinism is not internally discrepant. It conflicts only with the world as it is. It is impossible as a theory of our universe, not impossible in itself. There might have been a universe in which there was no ingredient time, or in which there were only passive particulars. Such a universe could conceivably be created and then annihilated to make room for ours, or ours could be destroyed to give place to it. But in neither case would the deterministic scheme be one that could be reached through any extension, backwards or forwards, of the time which is integral to our universe.

But though there never was a time when our universe was deterministic in nature, and though there never will be a time when this will be true, there is a sense in which a deterministic account of this world is always pertinent. After an effect has occurred, it is a determinate result, as are all its conditions and the course by which it came about. Determinism is relevant to what is past, never to the world as present or as future. Since it is historians, not scientists, who are concerned with the world as having passed away, it is therefore historians and not scientists who should take the theory of determinism seriously. Scientists, not historians, should be antideterministic in spirit, for it is scientists and not historians who are concerned with the present and future.

Historians and scientists usually reverse their proper roles. Historians are inclined to look at the past as though it were still future —as though it were a domain of unpredictable occurrences and probabilities. Scientists, on the other hand, tend to deal with the present and future as though it were already past—as though it were a field of certainties and foregone conclusions. Only historians can deduce actual effects; scientists must be content to surmise.

A historian does not have to abandon his freedom to deal with the past, any more than a scientist must abandon his habits to deal with the future. The one must conform to the determinations of fact; the other must conform to the determinations which will ensue in fact. As the historian traces the relation holding between one portion of the past and another, he moves as a free being who is now trying to make his freedom conform to the contours of the necessity with which he is concerned. The scientist is neither more nor less free, though there is no given necessity for him to which his freedom must conform, but only a necessity which is in the process of coming to be.

What men want to know and are prepared for is the concrete that is not yet but can be. But what can be is now indeterminate; it is general, possible, lacking concreteness, specificity, details. The desire to know what the future holds in store leads men to try to specify the nature of that future in advance of that concrete course of becoming by which alone the future is made specific and actual, present and concrete. They tend to *anticipate* the future; they endow it with specifications it does not yet and may never possess. Their assertions regarding the future, accordingly, involve an overdetermination of the nature of the general possibilities which constitute that future. Their tendency to overdetermine the content of the future is one of the primary sources of their victories in thought and act—and also of their failures.

All men are inclined to overdetermine their data. Those who follow the romantics and cherish the vague and amorphous, exhibit the same error of overdetermination that is characteristic of their opponents, the classicists. They recognize that the classicists overdetermine their data. They think, however, that this is an inevitable result of the use of a mind, the favored tool of the classicists. They therefore urge us not to use our minds, and to try instead to know the nature of things by some other device. Yet any other device we might employ can also serve to impose determinations in advance of a concrete course of becoming.

The mind the romantics criticize is itself an object which they themselves tend to overdetermine. The romantics know that the position of their opponents is the result of an overdetermination of data, but they themselves tend to overdetermine the operations of the mind in order to account for the preceding error. The classicists reciprocate; they recognize that romantics overdetermine data. They try to explain this as the inevitable outcome of the fact that the romantics give excessive weight to the emotions as a source of knowledge. Both sides make similar errors and similarly misunderstand why their opponents erred. Many of the controversies which beset philosophy seem to be characterizable in a similar way. Each side recognizes that the other overdetermines its data, but then it in turn tends to give an overdetermined account of the power by which the original error arose.

Most philosophers show great ability in ferretting out the errors of others, but their explanations of those errors are usually inadequate. Their explanations too often exhibit the very vice of overdetermination which they are so anxious to condemn. In noting this fact one need not of course commit a similar error. It is one thing to say that overdetermination is a tempting vice. It is another thing to say that all thinkers must overdetermine their data, or that the character and outcome of an overdetermination can be known in advance. The latter alone is an overdetermined account of the vice of overdetermination.

There is no need to overdetermine any particular content. The tendency to overdetermine need not eventuate in an error; it may in fact assume the form of a lucky hit. We cannot, therefore, know in advance what errors will be committed. But we can know in advance what errors men tend to commit once we know that they exaggerate some phase or power to the detriment of others. If the past is determinate as error, we can anticipate some of the errors that will thereafter ensue. But we have no guarantee they will occur. Nor can we know just what form they will take.

4. ACTIVITY

There are independent beings in nature as well as events, energy and fields of force. These beings act with freedom, i.e., with a strength, character, and direction not predetermined. Because they act in this way, there are multiple effects all of which, though rigorously deducible once they have occurred, are not intrinsically anticipatable in their concreteness and detail. It is often possible, however, to make a shrewd guess as to what will ensue. Freedom is exercised within determinable limits and is usually exhibited in a monotonous way, making possible predictions in the large and often satisfying expectations in the little. The world in which we live is loose-jointed; it leaves space for slip between cup and lip, it slows up and speeds on in novel ways. But on the whole it moves along a fairly even course, and those who know what has been done know in part something of what is likely to be. No one, however, knows and no one can possibly know just what will actually be. The nature of what will actually be is made determinate when and as it occurs.

Determinism erroneously treats what will be as though it were fully determinate before it occurs in fact. It is a possible view if one is willing to detach time from the universe and identify the possible and the actual. Determinism also supposes that all activity is the expression of an undivided force to be viewed as an ultimate matter of fact. It thereby misses one of the most obtrusive of phenomena,—the occurrence of multiple independent lines of causation each of which owes its being to the interplay of a limited number of active beings.

There are many courses of causation. Each is a function of a number of freely produced, independent *activities*. The breaking of a stone is a course embracing the action of a man with a hammer and the action of a resisting stone. The course is constituted by these activities and exists only while and because they do. It takes place independently of such concurrent processes as a cow's chewing of a cud and a bird's flight through the air.

A number of activities constitute a single course. The activities may be termed the "causes" of the course of causation which they constitute, if one is willing to use "cause" in somewhat the same way that Aristotle did at times—as an essential analytic component of what exists. But this would be to speak strangely. Activities are no more the "cause" of a course than the shape and size of a circle are the causes of a circle, or speaking and answering are the causes of a conversation. Activities are causes of a course only in the sense that they are essential to its being, existing when and where it does. They are its constituents, and the course is the whole which they constitute.

Activities, like courses, begin at one moment and end at another. Each one can be subdivided into smaller and smaller parts, until we reach an atomic activity which cannot, without destroying the unity of the act and the fact of time, be divided further.* In each unit activity there is a part that is before and another part that is after, but no part which is earlier or later than another. Each unit is freshly produced and, together with some collateral unit activity produced by another being, constitutes an indivisible unit of a course of causation.

Each activity can be said to mark the end of a course constituted by preceding activities. But if we treat it in this way we neglect the fact that an activity, like anything else having a temporal stretch, is determinate only after the stretch has been covered. As determinate, an activity is not an effect of what has gone before, unless in "gone before" we include the whole activity itself. What has "gone before" in any other sense is merely that which makes it *possible* for an activity to take place.

An activity is a free occurrence which, over and above what the past determines, is self-determined; or, more accurately (since an activity presupposes an agent), an activity is determined and thus produced freely when and as it occurs. The agent is compelled to act by what has gone before, but the action is his own, then and there made to be what it is.

Each activity bears the marks of habits and experiences its agent acquired in the past, the resistance of the agent's body and the opposition offered by neighbors and the world beyond. Together with those barriers, the activities—direct, free expressions of their agents—constitute a public course. Each course is thus the resultant of a free activity interplaying with activities and resistances outside it.

Because it is constituted by activities, a course is not explicable by what has gone before. Because a course is unpredictable, the effect which follows it cannot be known until the course is finished. If account is taken of a course, however, an effect can be

* See *Reality*, chapters 6 and 7.

known not only as a free but as a factual and rationally necessary outcome of what preceded it.

5. FREEDOM AND ITS PUBLIC BONDS

Every course is free and every one is constrained. Each is foreshadowed by the possibility of its occurrence. That possibility is constituted by the possibilities of the constituents of a previous course, and limits the shape which a present course can assume. Thus, like all processes, the present inclement weather has subordinate constituents, and these together constitute the possibility which is the essence of future weather. That future weather includes, as part of its being and meaning, a possible course of raining, hailing, or snowing. If it does rain, the broad possibility of weather as allowing for rain, hail, etc., is realized in one of many alternative determinate ways. Actual rain is possible weather transformed in a special and unpredictable manner.

Radical individualists doubt that a course is anything more than a passive resultant of the interplay of its constituents. They think that a history of a nation is synonymous with the biography of individual heroes or of a multitude of independent but interacting creative figures. Their position depends on the neglect of the fact that the different possibilities correlative to the different constituents constitute a single possibility which is correlative to a course of becoming, embracing those constituents. Were they persistent, they would have to say that all causal chains, physical or nonphysical, human and subhuman, were nothing more than summary statements of the activities of separate self-determining beings. But it is just as sound to deny that a nation has a nature and a possibility of its own, which constrains that nation and incidentally its members, as it is to deny that it is water and not oxygen or hydrogen that is wet, or that the possible career of the water limits the possible careers of its constituents. Men sometimes start wars deliberately and always sustain them through their activities, but wars have a nature of their own with characteristic futures. Men may die, be frustrated, conquered or disarmed, but a war can only stop or continue, being incapable of death or conquest. Beings create bigger than they know. The whole they make possible may be good or may be bad. In either case a future is defined which limits what the beings and the whole they constitute can do.

At the other extreme are those who speak of group minds, the Constitution, a nation, or an institution as creative forces having an internal wisdom and a private objective. They think of these as substantial realities, ruthlessly using men and things as instruments. Since these supposed realities stand with respect to an all-embracing Absolute as they stand to individual beings, rigor would require these thinkers to treat the world as the expression of a single cosmic power. The position is a variant of determinism with its passive or unreal particulars, even when, as in the case of Hegel, the Absolute is endowed with infinite flexibility and is described as being free. It is, however, just as sound to say that a conversation is a reality using men as instruments as it is to say that a process, cosmic or local, alone has internal vitality, and that concrete things and their acts are nought but instruments for this process. There are no wars when men stop shooting at their enemies. A war is bigger than men, but every step of it depends on how men act. Having finished shooting at the enemy, an army can turn into a riotous mob in which soldiers shoot at their countrymen. No spirit from on high turns the soldiers in this way; individual discontent and suspicion, fear and anger multiplied a thousandfold define the riot as a new possibility which some random act may help make real. It is never the institution that is alone to blame; men always have the power to alter the direction in which it goes.

Neither the extreme of individualism nor of groupism is satisfactory. Nor is the situation saved by balancing one with the other. We cannot say that there is a separate life to groups and another to individual things without dividing the world into two parts, the one made up of individuals who are outside all states, institutions and organizations, the other existing as an indifferent unity which hovers over them all but goes its own way. Institutions are not things; they are courses made possible by individuals. The individuals act on their own, but the results of their actions are limited by the future characteristic of the course which the actions of those beings constitute. Each course has a future of its own, which is a function of the futures its constituents define. The course has no power to become. But as it becomes through the agency of constituent activities, it transforms the meaning of the future which lay before it, and faces a different future which is then and there freshly constituted.

There is no law to which a course blindly conforms, no end towards which it strives. Laws are general, a course is concrete; and striving is something only things can do. We can speak significantly of the decline and fall of nations, of the dialectic of history, or of the spirit of the time. But we then must, at least tacitly, acknowledge that what will be may be quite different from what had been before, and that a possibility is general, allowing for endless divergent determinations which always add content and sometimes radically change the meaning of that possibility.

Each course is a concrete occurrence which realizes a possibility that was foreshadowed. In realizing the possibility, the course changes the status and meaning of the possibility. It is, therefore, just as correct to say that a possibility is fulfilled as it is to say that it is reconstituted, for fulfillment is reconstitution, reconstitution a fulfillment. If it were true that every nation had a characteristic rhythm, that it contracted only to expand, rose only to decline, conquered only to be conquered, the stage which it had not yet gone through would be a constraint which it vitalized in its own way to make into a more or less significant aspect of itself. The prospective decline which it faced it could forestall to any degree, and for an endless time, by virtue of the way in which it actually came to be. Each course constantly reassesses the meaning which a prospect has for it.

A course is also constrained by its constituents. It is because beings have their own capacities which they fulfill independently and freely that a course develops as it does. Because men interest themselves in other things, institutions lag and disintegrate. Each course, conversely, infects its constituents with its own nature, changing them into participants of it. A nation changes the acts of men into the acts of citizens, endowing them with meanings they otherwise would not have.

Each course is also constrained by its neighbors. The futures of the course and its neighbors constitute a wider and more inclusive future, and what one course does to isolate and utilize its characteristic future, limits what the others can do. Each constrains and is in turn constrained by the others; each vitalizes and transforms the others as surely as they vitalize and transform it. There are independent but no perfectly isolated systems in the world; there are no courses which go on entirely undisturbed by what happens elsewhere. The way one family develops affects the way other families can and do.

Each course that is less than the whole universe as becoming, is a part of more inclusive courses and ultimately of the whole universe as becoming. Each stands with respect to more inclusive courses somewhat as its own contituents stand with respect to it. Each course converges on a future which is the future of the world as a whole and which is what it is because of what the courses and existing things are. Each course and thing accordingly is, in the last analysis, constrained by a single cosmic future. Each vitalizes this future in its own way, separating out of it a limited and pertinent component in the act of coming to be.

The determinist is one for whom there are only unvitalized constraints, imposed from above. He subscribes to an Absolute, more real and powerful than any subordinate course or thing. But the only Absolute there is, is the cosmic future, the future as common to whatever is present. That future is almost amorphous; it cannot exert a force. It is made determinate and realized through the actions of actual present beings which diversely specify it as limited relevant possibilities and attempt to make these concrete.

The single cosmic future is divided and thereby transformed and enriched by being specified in the form of limited possibilities. Those possibilities in turn are realized and thereby enriched by being made the termini of actual specific courses of coming to be. Behind both acts of enrichment are individuals, concrete, independent, interacting, and free. It is they to whom all activities and ultimately all courses must be referred for substance, for origin, for explanation and for termination. They are the beings between which all becoming occurs.

CHAPTER THREE

THE NATURE OF BEINGS

1. THE INSIDE AND THE OUTSIDE

EACH BEING is concrete, independent, substantial, individual. Each is something on the inside. Otherwise it would be but an adjective, dependent for its nature and existence on something else, itself but an adjective of something further, and so on.

Each individual has an inside. It is, in addition, something from the inside. It is a being with a characteristic perspective. Otherwise it would not express itself in an individual way. Each has an individual approach to what concerns it.

Each individual is something on the outside. It is a bounded reality, restraining the influence of other beings. Otherwise, it would be completely permeated by others and could not appear as a public distinct being.

Each individual has an outside. It is, in addition, something from the outside. Otherwise account could not be taken of it until it was close by; nothing like vision or gravitation, stimulation or environment would therefore be possible. Each being is dealt with at a distance.

Each being is something *on* the inside and *from* the inside, something *on* the outside and *from* the outside. It is an independent, individual reality, countering and taking account of others. And it is all these at once. To suppose that any one, any pair or any triad of these aspects exhausts the nature of a being is to divide the indivisible. What is distinct in thought is not always clearly the fact. Distinction is determination; it may be excessive.

Leibniz thought that beings had only insides. His monads, with their tightly closed windows, were isolated universes. To make them constitute a single universe where each was pertinent to the others, he had to invoke a God in terms of which they could be related. The Hegelians went to the other extreme. They took account only of the outside of beings. According to them, the Absolute alone was real, all other beings having been denied substantiality and individuality. For them the objects of the world are mere surfaces, decorating nothing, insubstantial termini or facets of a single reality. Leibniz had only a Many, Hegel only a One.

The romantics and the empiricists, in contrast with Leibniz and Hegel, isolated and reified what beings were from the inside and from the outside. Schopenhauer, for example, tried to deal with beings from the vantage of their insides, with the result that he was unable to acknowledge them as provocative objects. On his theory, they had no substantial insides of their own, no boundaries where they resisted others, and no outside limits from which an approach to them could be made. Hume, on the other hand, viewed other beings only from the outside. For him, each was knowable only so far as it could make its presence felt. The beings in his experienced world had no substance, restrained nothing and never looked beyond their boundaries. Schopenhauer had only subjects but nothing to subject; Hume had only objects but nothing to object.

Whitehead recognizes that all beings are something from the outside and on the outside, on the inside and from the inside. He is a Humean Hegelian who nevertheless insists that there is truth in the Leibnizian and Schopenhauerian views. But instead of affirming that all four aspects are conjointly exemplified, he supposes that beings first assume the state of having insides and approaching others from those insides, and that they then move on to the state where they have only outsides and are approached from the outside. For him, the problem of how beings can be both private subjects and public objects is, as it were, solved in time. And when the problem is solved—this apparently being the essential task of every entity—an entity has, he thinks, no further need to be, and therefore gives way at once to a new being which begins to solve the problem over again, and so on, endlessly. But it is when and while a being is something on and from the inside that it is something on and from the outside. Its career does not consist in solving the problems of the one and the many, of subject and object; it is because the problems are already solved that it is able to have a career at all.

If, in Leibnizian fashion, one cuts off a being from the rest of the universe in the effort to keep it private and self-enclosed, one achieves the paradoxical result that, in order to be one private being among others, it must have relation to them. If, in Hegelian fashion, one denies independent reality to beings in the effort to make them all members of a single universe, one achieves the paradoxical result that they do not have sufficient substance to exist anywhere or for anything. Each being is at once public and private, with an outside and an inside. The windows of Leibniz' monads are open, but despite Hegel, the walls still hold.

If, with Schopenhauer, one tries to hold that beings have characteristic perspectives but no individual natures, one achieves the paradoxical result that there is nothing for or on which to take a perspective. If, with Hume, one insists that beings can be dealt with only from the vantage of their outsides, one achieves the paradoxical result that there are no beings to approach. Each being is at once subject and object, approaching others from its own inside and being approached by them from its outside. Humean objects are also subjects, and despite Schopenhauer have something individual to express.

2. INSISTENCE

Though all four aspects of a being are in fact inseparable, they can be partly separated in thought and examined one after the other. It makes little difference in what order they are dealt with, so long as all of them are understood as being inseparately together. We are all accustomed, however, to approach things first from the outside. That aspect, then, might as well be dealt with first.

Other beings make their presence felt here where we now are. They insist on themselves and thereby give us relative positions and characters with respect to them. Their *insistence* is a means by which they delimit us, holding us in place.

An insistence elicits a counteracting *resistance*. If it did not, other beings would be blank tablets on which the insistent being wrote its signature without blur; they would be unbiased, passive, unable to provide places at which an insistence could be felt. If by experience, then, one intends to refer to insistence alone, it must be confessed that no one can learn from experience, since no insistence is ever met outside the context of an opposing resistance, reflecting something of the nature of the individual intruded upon.

The shape, the color, the taste, the texture of a being are sometimes spoken of as though they were pure manifestations of it, or as though they had a different nature in different contexts, existing by virtue of the power of an intruding eye, tongue or finger. Public colors and shapes vary from context to context, but they vary in this way because there are private, constant, resistant colors and shapes which are being manifested in these different contexts. Each being resists the intrusion of others in a characteristic way; each has its own color but exhibits it only in the course of a resistence to an external insistence. The public color of a being is not its actual private color; it is that private color in the context of an alien insistence.

A public trait is a resisted insistence viewed as the possession of an intruded being. The resisted insistence belongs also to the insistent being. As such, it constitutes the public outside limit of that insistent being. Public traits and public outside limits are thus two sides of the same fact. The public traits are the result of a qualification of a resistance by an alien insistence; the outside limits are the result of the qualification of the insistence by the alien resistant. Every being has public traits as a consequence of its resistance to an intruding insistence; everyone has a public limit at the boundaries of other beings, for there its characteristic insistence is countered by an effective resistance.

Each being has public traits and outside limits. Each not only resists the intrusion of others but itself insists and is resisted by those others. As mutually resisting one another, existents have the status of localized, detached individuals; as reciprocally insisting on themselves they dwell in a common space.

Each being spreads beyond the borders where we normally locate it; it is a static, extensive continuum of decreasing insistency. Its spread is overlapped by the insistent spread of others. The result is space. Space is thus a product, presupposing mutual extensive insistencies. That space is flat and homogeneous when the insistencies which constitute it have a minimum of common content. Curved space is the result of an increase in the degree of such minimum, concordant, reciprocal insistencies. The space between distant inanimate beings is flat, for these beings impose themselves on one another with a minimum intensity. In all other cases, space is "curved." Curved space is the space of inanimate beings in close proximity; it is the space also in which the living always dwell.

All beings exist in different types of space—or better, all live in a physical space intensified and contorted in different degrees and ways. It is well known that the members of a mob affect one another considerably. The fly on the pavement is nothing to them; they are closer to one another than they are to the fly, and this though they are at opposite ends of the courtyard. Their contortion of space is as basic a fact as is the contortion produced by two physical bodies which, by approaching closer, reciprocally insist more effectively than they did before. The astronomical world is a variant of worlds long familiar to painters and psychologists.

The most contorted space is that which intervenes between highly interested beings close together. It is physical space, intensified and contorted, not a new space or an illusion of space some-how hovering over and partly obscuring a real space beneath. There is no warrant for believing that space is an independent ulti-mate entity, or that it exists only to relate or frame physical bodies. Such beliefs preclude the possibility of space being contorted in proportion to the degree that concordant beings are more insistent, and they ask us to deny arbitrarily that the space in which we daily live is real.

Living beings dwell in a contorted space. So far as they are interested in one another, they contort their space still further. Each insists on itself in the face of opposing insistencies. Each takes account of the others, insistently approaching them from their outside limits. Each insistently looks backwards, as it were, along the insistence through which others manifested themselves at the point where it is.

Beings exist in an environment. They insistently take account of other beings. Were this not true, bodies would not gravitate towards one another, electrons would not jump orbits, it would be impossible to perceive. These all presuppose reciprocal abilities on the part of beings to insist on themselves and thereby contort the space that would otherwise intervene between them.

New elements, without apparent limit, are producible by bind-ing together spatially limited wholes to form single, more con-torted spatial unities. Elements can be made to disintegrate, on the other hand, when they are forced to form distinct, subordinate, less contorted spatial unities. If the alteration is sudden the result is an explosion.

It would be a mistake to follow Hume and try to build a theory of nature solely on the basis of what can be discovered by attend-ing to the outside limits of beings. Hume leads one to treat en-countered insistencies as though they were unqualified by a re-sistance. He asks us to abstract from the substantial nature of things; he wants us to ignore the fact that all beings dwell in an environment which they help constitute. Hume saw that by restricting himself to what is known from the outside, he could go no further than to acknowledge a world of distinct atomic surfaces, present to the knower but not presented to him, owned by nothing, indifferent to the existence of anything else. The tragedy of Hume was that he thought that this was a sound philosophical result, rather than an opportunity for getting rid of inherited, incorrect assumptions.

3. RESISTANCE

All beings show defiance at attempts to intrude upon them. The softest, most unstable and fluid being is as opposed to intrusion as the hardest, most stable and rigid, differing from the latter only in the degree to which it can retain its public shape, traits and place in the face of an alien insistence. A rock is no more opposed to an attempted intrusion than butter. But the latter we can mould and push about with comparative ease, the former with difficulty. Both resist with equal power and effect an attempt to disturb their privacy, but the one is forced to undergo a change in public properties, while the other continues to have more or less the public traits it had before. Air opposes us as surely as iron. But air so readily assumes the shape of our bodies, so readily bears and is decorated with colors, sounds and odors, that we almost forget it exists, as reluctant as iron to submit to the intrusion of another.

Each being has the power to resist the onslaught of all the world. If it could not, it would lose its status as an individual independent being and become the creature of another. The space between them would become a space inside the intruder, intervening between its substantial self and the creature it possessed. The intruded being would thereby be deprived of all power to insist as well as to resist and could neither take account of the intruder nor be in a public world with it. The intruder would therefore no longer have outside limits at the intruded being. But then the intruded would no longer be anything possessed; it would be reduced to the status of a component of the being which intruded on it.

Resistance is the counterpart of an independence cherished and capable of being threatened. I impose myself on the book before me when I pick it up. The book resists me to the degree to which I press against it. When I let it go it resists me still to some extent as an independent being, a part of the same contemporary spatial world with me. But the degree of resistance which it then exhibits is less than it was before. Since the book is able to increase its resistance when I pick it up again, it must have resistance in reserve. The harder I press on it the more surely it reveals that it is persistently opposed to all possible intrusion.

All beings are resistant. To annihilate any one would take as much power as would be necesary to create it. The distance from something to nothing is as great as is the distance from nothing to something. Only a God, therefore, could conceivably overcome the resistance of the most feeble thing in existence. Whatever exists has sufficient resistance in reserve to withstand the insistence of any and every finite being, severally and together. Each is adamantine, expressing that fact in an actual resistance to attempted intrusions and a readiness to resist still further. Others can alter its shape and change its traits, but none can annihilate it in the sense of turning its being into nothing. It may pass away, but that will be due in part to its own action, provoked, constrained, and directed though it may be by others.

The public traits of a being, the boundaries of it as a localized entity, are a function of the resistance it expresses and the insistence it suffers. The being's outside is the resistance it *can* express; it is the power to acquire public traits when an insistence is encountered.

Knowledge of an outside is achieved by negating the insistence a being encounters and reducing the remaining resistance to potentiality. This can be done in one of two ways: either by inferring what the being would be like were it infinitely distant from everything else, or by pointing to it as something to which reference is being made. The first method requires one to know how its actual resistance progressively diminishes as it recedes from others, and extrapolating to the limit; the second method requires that it be viewed as standing in a one-to-one relation to the observer. By the first method we get the result that its individual outside is a quantity of potential energy which it actualizes as it comes into finite relation with other beings; by the second method we get the result that its outside is a bare "this" or "it," the object of a pure denotation. The two methods converge. To treat a being as a mere "it" is to treat it as though it were infinitely distant. And conversely, to view a being as infinitely distant is to credit it with no other actual nature than that of being denotable. The object of a denotation is an abstraction, however; nothing is infinitely distant from everything else. Each being has some public traits and thus is actually as well as potentially resistant.

An act of indication terminates in a bare "it," in an object as though it were infinitely distant. The "it" at which it terminates is a contentless point. If knowledge of the object is to be possible, that point must be united with the traits which the object has in relation to others. The judgment, "It is a cat" thus brings together the infinitely distant outside, the being as a bare "it," with its related outside, with the traits the being possesses due to the insistence of others. The "it" gives us little information, but it does refer to what the outside is by itself; the "cat" tells us much, but what it tells is in part a testimony of the relation the being bears to things beyond.

"It" refers to a being as it stands apart; "cat" refers to it as it stands in actual relation. Neither refers to the cat as it is on the inside. As Hegel saw, both the "it" and the "cat" are universals. But his theory, that the Absolute alone was real, required a denial that there were any things individual and concrete beyond the universals. As a consequence, "it" for him became a universal on a level with "cat," which was itself treated as nothing more than an "it" multiplied and congealed. Hegel tried to get to things as they were on their outsides, but since those outsides were for him nowhere and were the outsides of nothing, they could be, as he readily admitted, naught but terms in discourse or in the mind.

Hegel knew that an "it" is a mediated result, something derivative, not an object in its concreteness. But he drew the false conclusion that it was therefore not the immediate outside of the object denoted. What was denoted, instead of being acknowledged as possessed immediately by an individual being, became for Hegel an entity existing and known only through mediation. He viewed it as an outside which the Absolute mind, through a process of self-expression, knew and made at the same time. Because he treated outsides as though they were the outside limits of an Absolute rather than as the outsides of individual beings, Hegel was compelled to tear the outsides away from the beings to which they belonged and thus had to deny that they were real outsides at all.

The supposition that beings are only outsides drives one to deny that they possess those outsides. The outsides will then have to be attributed to an Absolute as that which alone can possess anything. Since an Absolute is immediately what it is, and since a known outside is mediated, to acknowledge any outside for the Absolute is to affirm that those outsides are self-mediated, that they are the borders of the Absolute viewed from and produced from the inside of that Absolute.

The Hegelian, by acknowledging only the outsides of beings, is driven to deny that there are beings for which they could be outsides. It is one of the ironies of history that contemporary positivistic and pragmatic thought, while claiming to be anti-Hegelian in temper, nevertheless accepts this Hegelian conclusion. For it, too, there are only outsides. Instead of those outsides being produced by an Hegelian Absolute substance however, they are produced, according to contemporaries, by an Absolute language or science. It is difficult to believe that this represents an advance over Hegel.

The immediate can be known only through mediation. To deal

with beings as having outsides by themselves, we must approach them from their outsides. Our knowledge of an "it" is mediated knowledge, requiring an act of abstraction. To deal with a being as it is immediately on its outside, we must transcend its actual resistance. The Hegelian, by identifying mediated knowledge and mediated existence, inevitably identifies the known outsides of beings with the self-imposed limits of an Absolute. If, in contrast with the Hegelians, we are to acknowledge a being as having an outside, it is necessary to acknowledge it as also having outside limits restrained by others, and as having an inside to which its outside can be the correlate.

4. THE INSIDE

Each being spreads endlessly outwards, insisting on itself with decreasing intensity. Its inside is the focus of all its diversely exhibited insistencies; it is there that it is infinitely insistent, ready to impose its nature on anything which could reach it. Could another being ever get to its inside, that other would be swallowed without remainder.

The inside of a being is inviolable. This is the truth which Leibniz so clearly saw, and which led him to affirm that each being was completely sundered from every other. But, though a being as private is ineluctably private, that does not mean that it makes no contact with anything beyond. It is not merely private; its privacy is but one of its aspects. And though no one can force himself into it, it still can be known. The resistance which one offers it can be abstracted from, and the insistence remaining considered as maximized, either by inferring what the being would be like were it infinitely close, or by submitting our judgments for judgment to the being that is judged. The first method requires a knowledge of how a being's insistence increases as it is approached, and an extrapolation to the limit; the second method requires us to submit passively to the being as the arbiter of what is true and false. By the first method we get the result that on its inside the being is infinitely insistent, the unitary focus of its diverse insistencies; by the second, that its inside is the substantial correlate of what we articulately know of it. The two methods converge, for to treat a being as the substantial correlate of articulate knowledge is to treat it as infinitely insistent on being itself.

If by "knowledge" we mean "what is articulated," if we mean by it what results from the welding in judgment of an abstracted subject or subjects with a predicate or relation, then the inside of a being is not an object of knowledge. It is an unknown thing-in-itself. The inside of a being never comes into a judgment. But in a broader sense we can know the inside of a being. We can adumbrate it. In fact, we acknowledge it every moment as the correlate of our knowledge, and report it whenever we employ a copula to unite a subject and a predicate, or whenever we use a relation to link denoted subjects together.

The adumbrated is the real as outside articulate knowledge, a unity of subject and predicate freed from extraneous additions and acknowledged as more substantial than their judged togetherness. It can be reached by submitting the content of the mind to the thing known. We act to know, but that whole activity is framed against a background of a passivity which allows the being about which we know to shape our minds according to its nature. We submit our minds to the thing while standing apart from the thing. If we merely submitted, we would lose what is submitted, just as, if we held ourselves entirely apart, we would lose the being about which we know.

Knowledge is always of what is other than itself; otherwise it would be neither true nor false. It is less concrete than the object known; otherwise what we knew would exhaust the being of what we know. All knowledge has a subject matter with which we are in contact, making evident that there is still more to be articulately known. We come in contact with the insides of beings directly, by submitting what we have in mind to those insides. We exhaust the activity of the mind, as it were, before we exhaust the mind's potentialities. We allow the remaining potentialities of the mind to be determined by what lies beyond, the result of our previous activity limiting the extent to which our minds can be moulded by what lies outside them. We adumbrate at the same time that we articulate and thereby grasp others as having an infinite insistence supporting their acknowledged resistance. As a consequence, we assert "This is a cat" of an actual concrete being, recognizing the being when and as we assert something of it.

As infinitely resistant, a being is entirely potential. When it becomes active, it acquires public traits. Its public traits are not specifications of the being as an "it": the predicates of the being are not contained in it as a subject. If we supposed they were, we would, with Leibniz, confound subject matter with subject. Public traits are specifications of the subject matter not of the subject. To confound a subject with a subject matter, to make a subject into an object of knowledge, is to turn an infinite resistance into an infinite insistence and thereby give up the possibility of denoting altogether. Though "cat" is a result of expressing the resistance of an "it," it tells us something which the "it" does not—what the being is in a public setting. Each being is an "it," but only some, in this setting, can assume the shape of a public cat. To refer to these as "cats" is not to predicate anything of the beings as denoted or as private; it is to find a public trait, the correlate of an "it," in terms of which the infinitely insistent inside can be judged.

There are schools of thought which deny that beings have insides, or that the insides can be adumbrated. There is nothing, then, which they can claim their knowledge is about. In opposition to them are those who deny that beings are more than self-contained insides. There is no knowledge, then, which they can claim to have about those beings. The one cut themselves away from the world, the other cut the world away from themselves. Neither can distinguish fact from fancy, supposition from truth, knowledge from being, for such distinctions require that one be faced simultaneously with content judged and with that of which the judgment is made.

We can get to the inside of beings as surely as we can to their outsides. If we can know a being as an infinitely resistant "it," we can know it as an infinitely insistent inside as well. To know either facet we must extrapolate to the limit, or transcend an expressed resistance. Those who deny that a being can be grasped in either of these ways can acknowledge only public traits belonging to nothing, without power or substance. But whereas when we say that a being is an "it," we fully represent a real facet of it, we cannot completely express what it is on its inside. An inside is undivided and concrete; our representations of it are divided and abstract. Because as an "it" a being is naked, without determinate characters, we can exhaust all that can be said of it by using a merely denotative term; we cannot, however, exhaust what it is on the inside, for there it is infinitely rich.

We can get to an inside most readily by submissively presenting a being with the result of our judgment of it. But it takes a creative artist to obtain a fairly accurate judgment, and it takes the humility of a saint to yield the result wholly to the substance judged. We probe deeper and deeper to the inside the more we attempt to express it and the more readily we allow our judgment to be supported and perhaps therefore altered by the object we seek to know. Privacy is open to humility and never to force. It is the adumbrated background of an outside as integrated with an expressed resistance. For some it is very obscure, for others quite clear, depending on how submissively they present to the inside what they abstractly know. But whether clearly or obscurely noted, the inside is always discerned. All beings get something of the outside of others and submit the result to the insides of those others for support.

Nothing is easier, Hegel observed, than to get in contact with a thing-in-itself. Though he intended by this to refer only to the Absolute, what he said applies to every individual being. The inside of each is always available. Whatever we know is known as an abstraction from a real being beyond, directly discerned.

What is strange is not that the inside can be discerned, despite the being's irresistible antagonism to intrusion and its insistence on itself, but that men have been at such pains to deny that it exists or can be encountered in any sense. Once we refuse to exaggerate a distinction into a division, to force an arbitrary, unbridgeable chasm between the discursive and the intuitive, the surface and the substance, judgment and that which is judged, knowledge and being, syntax and semantics, the public and the private, subject and subject matter, the articulated and the adumbrated, there is however no longer anything in the way of an admission of the truth of Hegel's insight. As beings we all have at least a trace of humility; only in theory do we attain the height of arrogance which cuts us off from the vital substance of other beings.

5. CONCERN

Each being has a *concern*, a way of reaching from the concrete present into the abstract future. Its concern enables it to lay hold of the future in an individual way. It is the agency by which the future, as common to all beings, is focused on in the shape of a limited, pertinent possibility. Since the common future is a single harmonious totality of all that can be, it is neither more nor less than the good as possible and all-embracing. Any specification of that good is necessarily a specific limited good. The specific good with which a being is concerned is a single, cosmic, absolute good, congealed and individualized in one of many possible ways.

From the inside, to be is to be concerned with a pertinent good. If that good is not to be discrepant with the goods which concern other beings, it must be made to determine what goods are to be available to those others. So far as a being fails to limit the goods that might concern others, its good is either not in accord with or is not independent of the goods of those others. The highest good possible to an individual is independent of but in harmony with the goods that concern other beings.

Each being, through the agency of its concern, tries to focus on the highest relevant good which is in harmony with the goods that are possible to others. This requires the concern not only to carve out a good of its own but to *prescribe* what goods are to be available to the rest, to condition their concerns, to make contact with them as they are from their insides and thereby limit what they can become on the inside. All beings, however, are finite. None is the complete master of others. The good of each both defies and yields to the prescriptions of the rest.

The good of each being is a good whose nature is to some degree prescribed by others. As a consequence, the good with which a being is actually concerned fails to some degree to be as good as it would be were the being alone or all-powerful, and at the same time fails to some degree to accord with the goods which are the concern of others.

In the very act of concentrating on its good, a being loses part of the total good. By submitting to or rejecting the prescriptions imposed by others it qualifies what it concentrates on. And since its efforts are restrained and opposed by others, it can only partially realize this qualified good. What is realized is, accordingly, three removes from perfection, the total good as cosmic and common. Hope for a being and hope for the world lies in the ability of each to focus on a good which is richer than that which it now embodies and expresses, and in its ability to realize this new good at least as fully as it had realized a lesser good before.

What is possible for the acorn depends in part on what is possible to the soil, and what is possible to the soil depends in part on what is possible to the acorn. There is no firm and perfect oak quickening the acorn now, or awaiting the acorn in the firmament. A change in the nature of the actual soil makes a different soil possible in the future and this limits the kind of oaks that can exist in that soil. And those oaks, as merely possible, are partly indeterminate, awaiting full determination by the action of the acorn. A radical enough change in the constitution of the soil would so alter the future possible to the acorn that the oak it could become would be quite different from the oaks we know. Aristotelian final causes are possibilities which change in the course of time. And it takes the conjoint efforts of different concerns to make them into pertinent goods.

Knowledge of the good which concerns others is embodied in our expectations; knowledge of our own good is embodied in our hopes. We always know something of our own good and something of the good of others; expectation and hope are ingredient in all knowledge. Because we expectantly know other things, we know them not merely as they are from the outside and on the inside, but also as they are from the inside as pointing, like us, towards limited, pertinent possibilities. If we did not know that an apple could not write or speak but could grow and be eaten, we would not know the apple as a substantial being with a definite predilection towards the limited possibility of being ripe, nourishing and fruitful. To know anything is to know it as having a special, limited kind of future.

The attempt to deal with a being as though it were nothing from the inside is an attempt to deal with it as though nothing or everything were possible to it. Yet the most elementary acquaintance with an apple involves a reference to what it is concerned with realizing. An apple impervious to an expectation would be known as wholly in the present. It would not be acknowledged as a being whose behavior was relevant to what it was in the present and was going to be in the future.

The converse attempt to deal with a being as though it could be grasped only from the inside is an attempt to deal with it as though it were nothing but a unique mode of striving. If we take that Schopenhauerian approach, we overlook the fact that there is a being which strives, that there is something against which it strives and something for which it strives. A being strives from its inside, resisting interference from contemporaries while taking account of their presence and the character of their goods. Treated as nought but a striving, its inside becomes indistinguishable from what it is from the inside. The fact that it has an outside then becomes an illusion. Yet, paradoxically, that illusion could not appear to anyone, since there is nothing, by hypothesis, but other strivings.

6. SUMMARY

Whatever is, is both resistant and insistent, concerned with some limited good. It dwells in an environment, in space and in the future, taking account of others as contemporaries and as beings which specify the future conjointly with it. No one of them can be located wholly in some limited region of space, for its outside limits are at the outsides of all the others. No one of them can be properly treated as without an appropriate outside, for each is denotable and resistant. No one of them is all on the surface; each has a private nature which irresistibly insists on itself. And no one of them is merely in the present; each stretches out towards the future to concern itself with a limited individual objective. All four facets are essential, together exhausting the nature of beings.

Each being has a public career, a public nature, an inside, and a concern of its own. Each of these facets can itself be analyzed to yield a similar set of four. No matter to what aspect we turn, we find that it both contains and refers to the other aspects. The one basic category governing and embodied in every being and every part is the structure of noncontradiction, "x is not non-x." * If the x is taken to refer to one facet, e.g., the good as an object of concern, and the non-x is taken to refer to another facet, e.g., the public nature, the x and non-x together will refer to the third facet, e.g., the inside, which is partly expressed as the fourth facet, an insistence interplaying with other beings.

*See *Reality*, p. 154.

Whatever exists is a limited individual, resistant, insistent and concerned. As resistant, it offers an outside limit to the insistence of others. As privately insistent, it is a barrier to which others can only submit; as publicly insistent it is what others resist. And as having a concern it is ready to act with respect to others in the light of its elected good.

Each being is both actually insistent and resistant in different degrees. Each forms different degrees of union with all the others. As independent of but intimately united with those others, each is a component in a "cause." Because each is also absolutely insistent and resistant, each is more than such a component. It is an active, ultimate, substantial reality. It acts to realize its good as something concrete, determinate and present.

CHAPTER FOUR

ACTION AND SPONTANEITY

1. THE MOTIVATION OF ACTION

ACTION HAS a reason. It is begun and carried through because the acting being seeks to close the gap separating what exists from the good which is the object of concern.

A being may act in one of three ways. It may try to realize the object of concern in itself, by an act of *self-adjustment*. It may try to infect its outside with the object of its concern, by an act of *expression*. Or it may try, by an act of *compulsion*, to sustain or alter the traits of others to make them conform to the prescriptions its good imposes on their goods.

A being which failed to make an adequate self-adjustment would fail to embody the good with which it was concerned. If it failed in the expression of its good, its outside would be discrepant with its inward nature. If it failed to exert the proper kind and degree of compulsion, other beings would be in conflict with it. The perfect act realizes, inside and out, the object of a concern as it is in itself and in relation to other goods.

No act is absolutely perfect. Each is countered by the acts of others and its aim is spoiled. There are distortions at the end of an act as surely as there are at the beginning, and the being must once again focus on a relevant good and act to make it real. But one act may be more perfect than another and may attain a result which could not have been attained at a previous time.

The best of acts can completely fulfill only ideals already left behind. The heavens of the past are now within grasp, but beyond them are further heavens now beyond all reach. After the masters come the disciples who rid him of his flaws. But these we rightly ignore for the new masters who imperfectly realize a higher good beyond. Today a schoolboy can deduce a proposition in Euclid, but in Euclid's time it took genius to state it even in an inadequate way. A thoroughgoing logician today knows more logic and knows it better than did Aristotle, but anyone who might scale the new heights beyond would produce a work as full of flaws as his. It is now easy to see the errors committed by genius in the past; it is still hard to do great things in the present. More difficult than the former and less difficult than the latter is the perfect fulfillment of the promise that past masters only partly fulfilled.

It is possible for unrealizable ideals of the past to become realizable today, but the ideals of today are as difficult to fulfill today as were yesterday's ideals yesterday. We progress by conquering what was once beyond conquest; we retrogress when we try to repeat the past with all its flaws, and we stand on a par with the great of the past to the degree that we storm heavens as far away from us as theirs were in their day.

2. SELF-ADJUSTMENT

The object of concern is a great or minor good which may or may not be in harmony with other goods. It may be realized privately by an act of self-adjustment, it may be realized publicly by an act of expression, or it may be compulsively realized in others.

Those who hold themselves aloof from all the world but seek an inner peace, act primarily to adjust themselves to their ideals. They entertain and try to embody a good which clashes with those goods others might also embody. Theirs is the goal of the reflective, discouraged men of all ages, trying to live a life apart so as to realize a good for themselves which does not cohere with the goods sought by others. It can and sometimes does happen that this good, when realized, is concordant with the goods others happen to realize. The men will then live in harmony with others but only because those others or they themselves failed to realize all the goods available to them. If they are in accord with the others because those others failed to realize what they should, they are in the position of tolerated iconoclasts. Too readily do they delude themselves that the world in which they live is as it should be. If they are in accord because they did not do full justice to their own ideals, they are practical idealists, men who think high and live low. Tolerance is a great enemy of those who burn with heresy; zeal for the ideal is fed by a failure to fit in the world as it is.

Thoughtful, political men attempt to adjust themselves to a high or low ideal in harmony with the lower or higher ideals available to others. They adjust themselves to a good which they believe coheres with different types possible to other beings. If the good is a high one they are leaders, if a low one they are followers, in spirit. Epicurus set an arrogant ideal before his wise men and Plato set a servile one before his lower classes. The Epicurean wise man was not supposed to express his virtues; the Platonic citizen was not supposed to compel others. Both were supposed to be peaceful men who adjusted themselves to their own goods, while others acted concordantly. The peace characteristic of the arrogant and servile in spirit is one which is achieved by a process of self-adjustment to values which form a harmonious totality with whatever values are available to the rest. It is a peace which is possible in a world where government is at a minimum, in an aristocracy where harmony is bought by having some men achieve greater values than are allowed to the others.

It is possible, however, for a man to embody ideal values while others fail to embody their proper goods. He, though his values are concordant with what others might realize, will then nevertheless be out of harmony with them. The Epicurean wise man might achieve wisdom in a world of folly and the Platonic tradesman might acquire temperance while the rulers went astray. It is sometimes desirable for men to be in conflict, providing the conflict is a precondition for their trying to realize a future in which high values are harmonized, for they then would make a state where they might soon realize great goods concordantly.

To realize great goods concordantly, to be, as W. H. Auden says, "Within the peace where all desires/ Find each in each what each requires," it is necessary for each being to adjust itself to an individual good in harmony with the rich goods of others. Though each then ignores the need to express and refuses to compel, something precious is obtained. High-minded men, men who are concerned only with concordant private goods, have this as their ideal. Their aspiration is to belong to a democracy in which all beings privately and harmoniously attain their highest possible goods. Unfortunately, achievement lags behind aspiration. Others fail to elect and realize the goods available to them and as a consequence the high-minded man, though concerned with a social good, stands out in history as a lonely soul, because he realizes that good only in himself.

An act of self-adjustment is performed by a being in the attempt to realize in itself the goods with which it is concerned. Only beings capable of growth, however, have the ability to concentrate their energies so as to transform their inward natures in a radical enough way to make adequate room for the possibilities they confront, and only men seem able to incorporate a great good which is in harmony with great goods open to others. Not everyone, however, succeeds in adjusting himself to the good with which he is concerned. Many love truth whose lives are lies. They live too much in the world, do not concentrate their energies enough to enable them to bring the miracle about by which they become in fact what they are in aspiration. It is necessary at times to retreat from the world so as to make easier the realization of the good that is the object of one's concern. The retreat is dangerous if one does not have sufficient strength of character to prevent one's loneliness from feeding an incipient madness. To become inwardly what one is in aspiration it is necessary to retreat from the world but with power enough to withstand the temptations that haunt those who are alone.

The peace that passes understanding requires that the understanding remain intact. It is the product of a resolute retreat from the world with a compensatory concentration on a good superior to that can be realized by meeting and mastering external barriers. It comes, as a rule, only after a valiant struggle to bring some good into the world has revealed that greater goods ought to have been realized. We usually learn what it is to which we ought to adjust ourselves only after we have tried to express and impose some inferior good.

3. EXPRESSION

The full realization of a good requires that a being adjust itself to that good and express that good externally. Each being, in the attempt to realize its good, engages therefore in an act which is both an act of self-adjustment and an act of expression.

Whenever a being engages in an act of self-adjustment, it also expresses itself, altering the mode in which it is manifest outwardly. It is possible, however, for a being to stress the mode of expression at the expense of self-adjustment, to exaggerate the free act by which the meaning of the good is carried into the open. The object with which the being is concerned is then not embodied in it to the same degree that it is made manifest externally. Though the being does that which its concern requires, it fails to be as it ought. The converse is also true. A being may adjust itself to its ideal and yet fail to express this fact adequately, stressing self-adjustment at the expense of expression. The exuberant and extroverted are inclined to adjust themselves inadequately, just as those who seek an inward peace are inclined to express themselves less than they ought.

A great or minor good may be out of harmony with goods available to the rest. He who expresses such a good, will act well in the light of his own good but not so well in the light of the goods of others. Conflict and chaos is the inevitable outcome of the successful expression on the part of many to be the leaders of the rest; where servants multiply, service degenerates. Sometimes, however, a man of action succeeds in expressing himself in a way which is concordant, not with the goods others ought to, but with the goods they actually embody or express. Though the upshot is harmony, either they or he fail to express goods to the degree they should be expressed. It is not high ideals which mark the statesman, but the ability to bring into the open goods that cohere with those which others enjoy or defend. The harmony he achieves is of the kind that is bought by compromise.

Men ought to live together in harmony. The harmony should, however, be that which results when all most fully realize the objects of their concerns. Such harmony may of course be achieved by some beings concerning themselves only with minor goods. In an ideal caste society, different groups successfully realize different but concordant grades of good. It is not often, however, that all those whose ideals are in harmony succeed in realizing them to the same extent. Though all might express the concordant ideals that are available to them, their modes and degrees of expression might still bring them into conflict. The most rigid caste system is a whirlpool of antagonisms, the outcome of conflicting expressions of concordant ideals.

The conflict which results from a failure to realize compatible aims is more desirable than a harmony that results because of a failure to realize incompatible aims. Though conflict is not ultimately desirable it is better to have it as a consequence of one's fulfillment of a good in the face of a failure on the part of others to realize fully the goods that were available to them, than it would be to have a harmony as a consequence of a common failure to do justice to any good whatsoever.

The ideals which men ought to set before themselves are the richest possible goods that are in harmony with one another. If they could succeed in expressing such ideals, they would succeed in bringing about a public realization of a harmonious set of great values. But the most that can be expected is that a few men only will publicly realize such goods and that they will therefore inevitably come in conflict with the rest.

Great practical men and truly creative artists are highly sensitive to the values that could be made available to others. But their histories are largely tragedies; the goods they express, though compatible with the equally rich goods available to others, do not cohere with what those others actually express or embody. Men are unusually successful if they express the values they have reserved for themselves; they are singularly fortunate if such expressions cohere with the values embodied elsewhere. As a rule, what they express falls short of what they want and conflicts with what others achieve.

Expression is an art, requiring a concentration of energy in the shape of acts which embody the meaning of the good with which one is concerned. It is quite different from exposure, the overflow of energy in unconventional channels. To express is to create and control in the light of the good; to expose is to reveal oneself as apart from the good, and then as one who is not in sufficient control of himself. Inanimate beings seem capable of only a minimum degree of expression; their public manifestations are primarily modes of exposure. They are what they do. Subhuman living beings seem capable of expressing minor goods in partial harmony with the goods available to others. They can be more than they have been. Men alone seem able to express rich goods which harmonize with the rich goods available to others. They can and should make manifest goods that allow room for growth on the part of others, and thereby make themselves into beings who express great goods in a world of great goods. Men ought to be more than they are.

The object of a concern is rarely both embodied and expressed with equal success. Men are in a perpetual dilemma of deciding whether they are primarily to be but not to express the good, or primarily to express but not to be good. They should aim at both equally. Forced to make a choice, they ought to lean towards being good, for not only will a successful act of self-adjustment make possible better acts of expression and with respect to higher ideals, but a good man is more valuable than a good work. A Socrates contemplating in solitude has a value greater than a painting of Rembrandt's. Both are irreplaceable, but no matter how perfect the latter and no matter how excellent an expression of cherished beauty, it is less valuable than the result of a self-adjustment. One must in fact go even further. A man who failed to adjust himself to his good, precisely because he was still capable of self-adjustment, would be more valuable than any expression of the good he made possible. It is a crime to destroy even a bad man in order to preserve a masterpiece. Here is one point where the ethical and legal meaning of "crime" coincide.

4. COMPULSION

Under the influence of the mechanistic creed, it has become common to treat action as though it were a brute, ultimate fact requiring no explanation. Under the influence of the deterministic creed, it has become common to treat it as though it occurred independently of the needs or aims of the beings from which it issued. As a consequence, we have become accustomed to think of action as a momentary, arbitrary use of energy serving only to sustain or alter the traits of other beings. But all action is adjustive and expressive as well as compulsive. A means for altering others, it is at the same time a means for realizing and expressing a possible good.

As compulsive, action is the agency for making the outside of others conform to the ideals one wants them to embody. It is the means for realizing in other beings the goods one has prescribed for them. To the degree it is inadequate, a being will have put before others objectives that it itself either defies or ignores.

A benevolent despot tends towards the realization of great goods for himself and attempts to mold others in conformity with the lesser prescribed goods that remain. A public servant tends to cherish minor goods for himself and attempts to mold others in conformity with the greater prescribed goods that remain. In both cases the goods prescribed are goods which others may cherish. However, since no action is absolutely perfect, neither the despot nor the servant can reach his objective. Both mold the outside of others in ways which are discrepant with what those others in fact internally want, are, or can be. Both compulsively act in such a way as to defy what they themselves prescribed.

An act ought to make a being outwardly what it can and ought to be inwardly. A being rarely, however, realizes inwardly the goods it ought. Even if one acted in conformity with one's own prescriptions, other beings would not necessarily be inwardly what one was outwardly making them be.

To act on others so as to make their outsides conform to the goods they ought to realize inwardly, is often to make them externally what they are not internally. Of this the law-maker is often acutely aware. He puts aside the question as to what men make of themselves internally, contenting himself with the attempt to make their outsides conform to the goods he prescribes for them. He would like them to be internally courageous, honest, intelligent, thoughtful, etc., but is satisfied if he can so act on them that they will become these outwardly, whether or not they attain these states inwardly as well. He sees no way of distinguishing between the law-abiding and the enslaved, between those who are and those who are not inwardly what they are outwardly compelled to be. Freedom, to him, means a right to do something without fear of punishment—a permission not a power. He is inclined to ignore questions of mercy, sympathy, love, right intention and good character and to interest himself instead in the problems of liberty, justice, the influence of the environment, security, etc. As a consequence he tends to adopt the attitude and to follow the practices of those who believe that others have no souls. To avoid seeing men as empty husks the lawmaker ought to view them as beings who always have the freedom to become inwardly good no matter what they are outwardly made to be, while legally insisting that they ought outwardly to be what they ought to be inwardly.

An inanimate being seems capable only of compulsive acts which mold the outside of others in conformity with prescribed goods. A subhuman living being seems capable at best of producing compulsive acts which mold the outside of a few beings (their offspring, as a rule) in conformity with their appropriate goods. It is only man who seems capable of molding the outside of all other beings in consonance with their appropriate goods. No one of these types, however, engages in acts which are exclusively compulsive. All of them adjust and express themselves. The problem for all is to see that their acts perform all three functions equally well. Inanimate beings, however, seem to overstress compulsion, animals expression, and men adjustment. In different ways each fails to do all it ought.

5. FREEDOM OF ACTION

Action takes its character from the nature of the actor, the nature of the good with which he is concerned, and the obstacles it encounters. Conditioned in all these ways, action is nevertheless free. It converts an undetermined future good into a determinate present content in an intrinsically unpredictable way. The occasions prompting it and the ends towards which it is directed can be specified; its nature and effects can often be successfully predicted. But whatever actual character it has, action achieves only when and as it occurs. We know in advance that we will be prompted to engage in it in the effort to realize a good, but the actual form it will assume and the specific effects it will produce cannot be antecedently determined.

That action is free is most evident when it takes the form of a mode of self-adjustment. As such, it is freshly initiated in response to a good with which one is concerned. Almost at once, however, the action is constrained by the inherited past which imposes limits on the action's possible range.

The self-adjusting being behaves as he does because of the objective he has before him, under the limitations which his past imposes. There are forms of adjustment in which he will not now engage and there are results which are now beyond his power to achieve. But within these limits his act is free, a novel determinate mode of producing determinations in an undetermined good.

The attempt to express the good with which one is concerned is limited by the past. It is limited, too, by the nature and the bias of the body through which it must pass. He who is dexterous will act in one way, he who is awkward in another, he who is tired in a third. Yet all might have somewhat the same experiences and objectives. There are acts which the body does not allow, but within the limits it assigns, the nature of an expressive act is free. Every attempt at expression is restrained by the body and the counter-acts of those beyond. Free as and when it occurs, it is conditioned before, behind and alongside, so that it inevitably falls short of its goal.

Action in the mode of compulsion is also free. It too is restrained by the body and the counter-acts of those beyond. But in addition it is opposed by others which, in consonance with their independent attempts to realize the objects of their concerns, alter their own public natures in the face of attempts to compel them to have a different form.

An act is at once a form of adjustment, expression and compulsion. It is hemmed in by barriers which make the actor fall short of its objective. If the actor is to realize the object of its concern it must, to bring its result in closer conformity to what is intended, redouble its efforts in the course of its act. Even when (as in the case of beings with will and intellect) acts are forged in the light of the resistance they are expected to encounter, some correction must be introduced into the act to overcome the unpredictable concrete opposition which the act inevitably encounters. This correction of the act, this change in its nature which is introduced to compensate for the distortions the act inevitably suffers, is a product of *spontaneity*. It serves to help realize the object of concern. The greater the spontaneity, the more the attained result will be what the realization of one's good demands.

6. SPONTANEITY

Before an act is completed, an effort is made to alter it so that it conforms more closely to the demands of the concern. The act is thereby charged with spontaneity, a supplemental dose of freedom serving to change the direction and upshot of the act.

There is a modicum of spontaneity in every act. Even the supposedly routine and monotonous exhibit variations throughout. For the most part, and particularly with inanimate beings, the degree of effective spontaneity is slight. The spontaneous alteration brings about only minute changes in the act and makes no real difference to the result. But occasionally even inanimate beings will spontaneously express their concerns with such force as to make a radical difference both to the character of the act and to its upshot. Again and again, they will exhibit the intent of their concerns in ways which redress the qualifications to which their acts are being subjected. The remainder of the time they also act freely and with some degree of spontaneity, but in such a way that the general character of previous acts and their outcomes are more or less preserved.

Action is freedom manifest in the face of obstacles; spontaneity is freedom overcoming obstacles. Since every being meets opposition from others, there can be no result achieved by spontaneity alone. Every result is in part determined by what other beings are and do. Spontaneity enables a being to realize the object of its concern more effectively than a routine action would; it does not enable it to realize its good perfectly. Action at its best, action charged in midflight with new energy and given new direction, is always restrained by others.

Few beings act with the degree of spontaneity possible to them. The incipient failure to realize the objects of their concerns does not often provoke in them a strong attempt to alter the act which they have begun. For spontaneity to be manifest at its highest, a greater concentration on the good than is usual is necessary.

When the inanimate acts with spontaneity, it is for the moment keeping the object of its concern in focus, and is blindly but freely responding to the discrepancy between that object and the act which has been produced. Higher types of being can fairly steadily, though only dimly, discern the objects of their concerns, and as a consequence can act with spontaneity more effectively than lower beings can. But man can know the good. He, therefore, alone can radically alter the character of his actions by charging them with appropriate doses of spontaneity.

The most spontaneously vitalized of acts may at times not enable a being to realize the object of its concern to any significant degree. Faced with the fact that it cannot, no matter how spontaneously it acts, realize the good with which it is concerned, the being will then try to employ its freedom to change the nature of its concern and thereby have a new objective which it can realize more successfully. There are multiple ways in which it can be frustrated and thereby provoked to try to alter its concern and thus aim at a new objective. The most obvious and most effective is provided by the body. Soon or late the body of almost every being successfully resists every attempt to realize the object of concern, no matter how fresh, creative, subtle and spontaneous the attempt might be. The being must then change its concern and objective, for it cannot exist as permanently frustrated by its own body without being divided against itself and thus somehow existing as two beings instead of as one.

7. FROM THE INANIMATE TO THE ANIMATE

Each individual has a single individual concern. Each allocates to its body the task of satisfying a part of that concern. The body is an instrument for the being, an instrument which functions in part without supervision, and which may bring about results that go counter to those the concern requires. Having allocated part of its total concern to its body, each being is driven to bring the un-allocated portion into play in the form of a spontaneity, so as to make the resultant expression one which conforms to the intent of the entire concern. At every moment each tries to modify spontaneously the course of its acts in the light of the divergency which exists between what its body is about to do and what the adequate satisfaction of its concern demands.

Sometimes a body is recalcitrant to an expression even when that expression is charged with spontaneity. At such times the being spontaneously attempts to retreat from the obstacle which the body provides. It tries to focus on a new good so as to be able to engage in new acts which can successfully exhibit that good in and through the body. It is this power of retreat and refocusing which makes possible the coming to be of higher types of beings from lower ones, the human from the animal, the animal from the plant, and the animate from the inanimate.

An animate being differs in radical ways from an inanimate one. It is a different type of entity. But through death it changes in type, becoming inanimate where before it was animate. It is a moot question whether the process could ever be reversed, whether the living could ever come from the nonliving. The question is evaded if, with the panpsychist, one supposes that everything, no matter how apparently dead and inert, is nevertheless alive. That supposition not only forces one to deny that when a living being dies it is dead, but it still leaves one with the problem as to just how the things that appear to be dead are different from those that appear to be alive—which is the original question over again in a slightly different form.

It is possible to answer the question and yet avoid meeting it. When one says that life owes its origin to God's inscrutable wisdom and miraculous acts, one avoids supposing that the dead are really alive. But then no provision is made for understanding how the living and nonliving can be part of a single natural world; how it is possible to produce organic compounds, such as urea, in the laboratory, or why or how evolution can occur. An adequate account of the origin of life should not and need not transcend this world of ours.

Nonliving beings can be changed into living ones, just as surely, though not as readily, as living beings can be changed into nonliving ones. This contention one might expect to find denied only by those who hold that the living and the nonliving are cut on entirely different patterns, forever distinguished from one another as fixed and unalterable kinds. Yet it is one of the striking paradoxes in the history of thought that Aristotle, who held that there was a definite and fixed division between the living and the nonliving, believed that occasionally a living being could originate out of nonliving matter, while many biologists, despite their belief in the possibility of reducing biology to chemistry and chemistry to physics, despite their ability to produce organic compounds, and despite their knowledge of the way in which the animate adjusts itself to a world largely inanimate, are inclined to follow Pasteur and deny that what was once nonliving could possibly become alive. What Pasteur showed was that living beings could not be obtained in the way that Aristotle thought they might be. It is of the essence of modern science to insist that it was Aristotle and not Pasteur who was right in principle regarding the origin of life, though Aristotle's contention was made in the face of his own philosophic view. Pasteur made Aristotle's philosophy more consistent. Aristotle made a point which our philosophy must, but his could not, digest. The living can arise from the nonliving.

It is possible that there never was a time when life was not. Geology can provide evidence of the late arrival of living beings with structured bodies, but it cannot tell anything about the existence of those whose bodies cannot be or were not fossilized. In asserting that the living can arise from the nonliving, nothing more need be maintained therefore than that living beings *could* have followed nonliving ones in the course of history, and that they *can* be made to arise from them, even though there was and always had been life somewhere.

The problem of the origin of life is to understand how a change in circumstance will enable a nonliving being to become a living one. The answer lies in the fact that the body of an inanimate being can become so recalcitrant to its concern that the only way of having an effective concern is for the being to change the nature of that concern. The living arise from the nonliving when the latter modify their concerns so as to overcome the recalcitrance which their bodies offer to expression of those concerns.

Inanimate beings with excessively recalcitrant bodies do not usually become animate; as a rule they change into other kinds of inanimate beings. Take a thing, for example, like iron. It can accrete to itself other items, such as oxygen, and thereby achieve a new bulk, structure and way of acting. To the extent that iron is oxydized, it no longer accretes oxygen. It ceases to interplay with it as it had before. Rusted iron is a thing with a body distinct from that of nonrusted iron. That new body prevents the expression of the concern characteristic of nonrusted iron. When its body rusts, the iron must therefore alter its concern to avoid permanent frustration —to escape being divided against itself with an impotent concern on the one hand, and a body which it cannot control, on the other. When iron is outwardly rusted, it changes inwardly to become the new thing, rusted iron—with a new concern, a new objective and a new way of acting.

Both iron and rusted iron are things. Neither is alive. Each places a minimum of prescription on the objects which concern others; each engages in a minimum degree of self-adjustment and expression, spending most of its energy in compulsive acts. Let it be supposed now that, when iron is rusted, it not only has a new object of concern but that it increases the degree of prescription to which it subjects the objectives which are the concern of others. It would then have the kind of concern characteristic of a living being. Unlike rusted iron, the new being would, despite its rusted body, be able to interplay with oxygen; unlike rusted iron, it would interplay with oxygen without thereby getting in the way of the continued expression of its own good. Its compulsive acts would have regard for what other beings could become. Its acts would be infected with expectations and would be designed to bring about results which cohere with what some of the others ought to achieve. It would be a living being, exerting compulsions in terms of prescribed goods, at the same time that it expressed the nature of its own good in the light of which those prescriptions were imposed.

The living arises from the nonliving when the latter freely alters its concern, both to express itself and to act compulsively through an otherwise recalcitrant body. The state of being alive is thus the reward of a successful strategy, a consequence of the fact that a being, in retreat from its body, was able to find an objective which could realize in and through that body.

A living being is one whose activities are sustained by a concern, not only for its own good but also for the good of other beings. It loses abilities it once had and acquires other abilities in the course of time, but throughout its career it is able to persist in such activities as digesting, breathing, giving off carbon dioxide and so on. The tempo and pattern of these may vary. They do entail significant changes in the body of the being that engages in them. But the being is alive so long as it has a concern which enables it, through the medium of its changing body, to engage in these acts, and through them to satisfy its concern to some degree and thereby help realize the goods its own good prescribes.

For life to arise, a being must so change its concern that it is thereafter able to act on the same kind of material it did before. Such a being must be provided with the material and must, after it has changed, be given the opportunity to encounter similar material again. Only thus will it be able to continue to act, under the influence of its new concern, on the same kind of things it had acted on before. Whether or not such material is available and whether or not its use will result in life are open questions. Their answers depend on the circumstances, and on the way in which the thing freely changes its concern when the expression of the concern is frustrated by the body.

It is not to be expected, of course, that all things of the same kind will become alive in the same circumstances. Not all of them will exercise their freedom to change the character of their concerns. Not all will be able to satisfy a new concern through the existing body. Not all will be able to act on others so as to help realize the goods prescribed for them. Life is the result of the exercise of freedom, and exists only so far as a being conquers the opposition which its body puts in the way of a continual exhibition of a concern for goods pertinent to itself and other beings.

When life first arose (granted there was a time when life was not) it undoubtedly appeared in a host of places in multiple forms. It seems likely in fact that living beings come from nonliving ones in myriads every day. The majority of newly generated living beings, however, die off almost at the instant of birth. They have no opportunity to make prolonged use of their newly achieved concerns. Circumstances are too much for them. Either the material they require is not available, or their bodies harden too soon and thereby prevent the production of acts exhibiting the intent of the new concerns. Beings die not because they have been deprived of a divine spark or mysterious breath; they die either because there is nothing on which they can act or because their bodies act too well, insistently behaving as a cancer does, without regard to what the total concern requires.

So long as an inanimate being can spontaneously infect its acts with the meaning of its concern, it has no need to change that concern. But when its body proves to be too recalcitrant to the spontaneous expression of that concern, the thing is compelled to change its nature. Spontaneity is the highest type of freedom it can exhibit; that failing, it must change in nature. If it changes its concern so as to become a living being, it is thereafter able to produce acts under the external prompting of stimuli rather than of pressures, and to respond rather than to interact with what it encounters.

8. SUMMARY

Acts have their source in the individual as concerned with a good which it endeavors to realize through the use of freedom. Each action is countered by other actions and meets barriers which make it fall short of its objective. The being, as a consequence, is prompted to act spontaneously in order better to realize its good. When such an introduction of spontaneity is necessarily ineffective, the being is forced to change in nature. It is driven to employ its freedom so as to alter its concern and the kind of good it will act to realize. Should it so alter its concern as to be able to act on others in terms of the goods it prescribes for them, it becomes a living being. Those beings are alive which have and express a concern for goods pertinent at least to offspring or kind.

We can help make the living arise, but it is acts of the being itself which alone can make it alive. Strictly speaking therefore, living beings can never be produced in the laboratory. All that can be done is to restrain the nonliving in such a way as to compel it to use its freedom to focus on a new good which it may be able to realize to some extent through the agency of the body we have altered.

The power to become alive is analogous to the power by which lower-grade living beings become high-grade ones, and nonethical infants become ethical men. If, to this fact, we add a knowledge of the nature of life and the nature of man, we should be able to explain how and why higher beings and ethical men come to be and what their function is.

PART TWO

THE PSYCHE AND THE SELF

CHAPTER FIVE

THE WISDOM OF LIVING THINGS

1. METAPHYSICAL BIOLOGY

SOME OF THE preceding remarks (particularly those referring to living beings), some that will follow, and some contained in the present chapter are far from familiar turns of thought. They have a strange sound, particularly when compared with the conclusions of contemporary biologists and psychologists. Part of the reason undoubtedly is the fact that familiar terms have here been used in novel ways. But there is a further reason. What is here stated is bound to sound strange and even fantastic to many today in part because the philosophers, who should set the tone and pace for thought, failed to do all they ought and could. Modern philosophers, perhaps even more than other men, have been intimidated by the experimental successes of the biological and psychological sciences. They have abandoned, to the injury of themselves and others, a quest which they by definition ought to have pursued.

Before modern biology and psychology matured, philosophers did try to understand the nature of the living as well as the nature of nonliving beings. Some of them were overdogmatic and were trapped in errors which experiment revealed. But there was much that was sound in what they said; their views have been constantly confirmed by those who study animals and men as living individuals rather than as mere instances of general laws. Today we have reached the stage where we can see that a transplanted tissue is altered in nature by virtue of its place in the total organism, and we are therefore a little more ready to admit that living beings are single beings, and not mere collections of independent parts. And since we have now succeeded in making mice go mad, we are somewhat more inclined to admit with the ancients that even a mouse has a psyche. But we are still hesitant to think what we almost believe, and are disinclined to interpret even the most obtrusive data. We lack some of the courage of the ancients. We avoid their follies by avoiding their questions. What they tried to do we must try to do again, or arbitrarily define a large and in one sense familiar part of the universe as beyond our interest or ken.

Fields which philosophers once ploughed have been abandoned in the face of the advance of specialized scientific disciplines. From this a wrong moral has been drawn to the effect that philosophy is anticipatory science, and that it occupies a field only until science is ready to work it in its own way. But it is questionable whether there have ever been any advances in science which have touched the soil philosophers can and ought to till. There is a metaphysics of physics, mathematics, biology and psychology awaiting study today just as there was in Thales', Plato's, Descartes', and Hegel's time. The neglect of it has deprived us of an understanding of the nature of time, space, number, body, force, gravitation, life and mind, except as instruments or counters in the expression of hypotheses and conclusions which fit in with current interests and are capable of being dealt with by means of those techniques that have been mastered by contemporary experimenters.

Philosophers who allow scientists to do their thinking for them are unfair to themselves and to the scientists. A good biologist knows that he fails to touch on many questions which a geologist can answer; a good scientist knows that there are many questions which are answerable only by philosophers. The Galileos, Newtons, Einsteins and Darwins are never positivists, men who believe that science tells all and nothing but the truth. Positivists, philosophers who refuse to philosophize, are as unjust to the world and to their subject as a geologist would be who claimed that all truth was to be found in biology.

Because so many contemporary "philosophers" have refused to speculate, scientists with a philosophic bent have been forced, overnight, to think philosophically. The result has been unfortunate. Our scientific philosophers have produced, in place of the needed results of genuine, disciplined, speculative thought, a crop of apparently scientific hypotheses which have only a metaphysical sense, and a crop of philosophic theories which philosophers long ago abandoned because so obviously untenable. Supposedly scientific terms such as "entelechy," "evolution," "the organism," "adjustment," "complex," "instinct," "will," and "gestalt" have been allowed to blur the truths that observation and experiment reveal, and to hide a meaning which lies behind all that living beings publicly do. On the other hand, scientists have put forward philosophical theories which cannot stand the light of a critical reason. There are excellent scientific men who call themselves solipsists; Dingle is one. There are others who, like Soddy, are afraid of such a number as the square root of minus one. Others call themselves followers of Aristotle but deny the fixity of species, followers of Berkeley but still abandon the world of common sense, or followers of Hume and yet hold that the future is predetermined.

The philosophy of a scientist is usually an overnight philosophy. It is rarely pursued by the scientist with the same care and devotion that he gives to his science. He is strongly tempted to take some central scientific term and swell it up to cosmic proportions without regard for what is pushed away, confounding thereby the scientific and the philosophical meanings of terms, and a respectable theory with one which ultimately denies what it wanted to say. In such an atmosphere a deliberate philosophical discussion of bodies, living beings and minds must take on a strange hue.

A second and more serious reason why a speculative account of the nature of living beings sounds strange today is that we have too long taken our knowledge of lower beings to provide an adequate guide to the nature of higher ones, despite the fact that none of us has really exploited the art of penetrating to the inward substance of what is lower, or knows how to go from them to the higher. We have been too long content to speak of lower beings as though they had only outsides and have tried too long to understand all others in terms of what we learned from this inadequate standpoint.

There is at least a theoretical continuity connecting the lowest and the highest of beings. But if, with so many contemporaries, we take as our basic data only what we have experimentally learnt about the subhuman, and then try to apply the principle of continuity, we shall be unable to describe man except in terms of a few sadly inadequate concepts, extended and magnified. If we refuse to take what we know of man as a clue to the nature of other types of being, we will have to content ourselves with the thin and external knowledge which our experiments and observations provide and imply. A reverse procedure would have been better. We learn more if we begin with what we know of man and then apply the principle of continuity, for then we do not lose sight of the fact that there is a richness and promise in every being which it never fully manifests at any moment.

Better still would be an attempt to take each living being as it is and show how it is possible to go from one type to the others. After all, we know very little of ourselves and if ourselves are to be our guide, we will fail to see what other beings are. Some things about the inanimate are better known than are corresponding things about the animate—the probable behavior. Some things are better known about men—their concerns. Neither the human nor the subhuman provides a sufficient guide to all the others. Each must be examined on its own merits.

2. THE "EXTRINSIC" AND "INTRINSIC" OUGHT

Subhuman living beings occasionally act in ways which are not calculated to make them prosper. On this truth a number of theories precariously rest. The simplest is that of the experimental animal psychologist who is opposed to all speculation. He contents himself with noting the kinds of behavior which animals actually exhibit and does not suppose that some other type of behavior should have been—or in the circumstances, could have been—exhibited instead. His mood finds justification the further one goes down the scale of life. As one approaches the amoeba, it becomes more and more difficut to say that it would be better for it to do anything other than what it does. What justification is there for judging a living being in terms of a standard of "right" behavior which may never be exhibited? Such an approach leads one unwarrantedly to hold that there is something other than what goes on here and now; it tempts one to suppose, in violation of much good scientific practice, that there are tendencies in a being which cannot then be observed and may never be manifest. Why not instead view all living beings as complicated machines which always respond as they ought, since they respond as they must, given their causes and natures and the situation in which they are?

These questions contain their own answers in part. It is a supposition going far beyond the obtrusive facts to say that a living being always acts as it ought; yet this is what is said when it is maintained that what it ought to do is nothing other than what it does or must do. One inevitably, though perhaps only tacitly, is making use of a standard of "right" behavior in affirming that whatever occurs is right by that very fact. It is to adopt the daring metaphysical assumption that this is a well-oiled world, where whatever happens happens for the best.

To avoid making such a supposition it is necessary to free ourselves from all considerations of what ought to be, from the idea of the good, the bad and the indifferent, contenting ourselves with merely describing what happens to take place. This requires us to refrain from calling some living beings stupid and others bright, and forces us to look at the actions of a healthy being as different in pattern but not in value from that of one sick or distraught. We would have to content ourselves with describing and comparing the ways in which different animals behave in different moments —and that is all.

An easy method for seeing how much our perspectives have altered since the Middle Ages is to note how palatable this last suggestion is to the modern mind. The medievals were so impressed with the idea of the good and the ought that they could learn nothing from the diseased and the unfortunate except that they fell short of an ideal. They called them monsters, mistakes of nature, worthy of no man's attention. Men today are not so cavalier. They are interested in all nature's variegated forms and find as much to learn from those that ruin themselves as from those that do not. We have profited much from the decision to note what is to be seen and to avoid disparaging some things in nature because they fail to conform to some arbitrary norm.

The fact remains, however, that at least some men judge that the actions of themselves and others are wise or foolish, good or bad. To say that they are mistaken in doing this is but to repeat the "mistake" once more, for to describe them as mistaken is to evaluate their decisions and to point to another which is more respected, because more in consonance with the nature of things or the promise of inquiry.

No man can advocate the assumption of an attitude of indifference or impartiality without thereby making at least an implicit criticism of those who take another attitude; but then he at least implicitly repeats the very "mistake" he is criticizing. Even Adam, who originally knew neither good nor evil and thus was ideally suited to be an animal psychologist, must have made some errors or at least seen the possibility of making them, and knew that they stood in the way of his going where he wished, or of his doing what he would like to do. His subsequent knowledge of good and evil, which was one with his knowledge that Eve was human, was a grasp of the fact that she too made errors which it would have been better not to have made. Adam knew there was a distance between what he and Eve did, and what they ought to have done. He evaluated some of his and her acts and decisions as right and wrong. Even when we try to escape making similar evaluations we reveal ourselves to be true sons of Adam, for we judge others adversely for taking a different stand.

Man is a living being, the fruit of a long line of evolution. If it be legitimate to draw a distinction for him between what he does and what he should do, it ought to be legitimate to do the same for other things. To fail to make such a distinction is to run the risk of dividing man off from the rest of nature. To be a living being is to be finite and unwise, doing some things one ought not do.

For the moment this point need not be pressed. Grant that animals are mere machines; it would still be true that from man's standpoint a distinction between what they do and what they should do, can and should be made. From man's standpoint there are useful and useless animals, those that are dangerous and those that are harmless. In saying this, we impose a standard on them which orients them towards our world and does not measure them in their own terms. But we thereupon formulate a theory, the theory of the moralist, which is alternative to that which the animal psychologist desires to hold.

In terms of this moralistic theory, one can distinguish between what an animal does and what it ought to do. The distinction, to be sure, rests on evaluations which express the nature of human preferences. Since it limits the concept of the ought to but part of nature, more emphatically even than the other theory it has difficulty in bringing man into the scheme of nature and understanding him as a product of natural evolution. It leaves open too the question as to whether the preferences which a man expresses in holding the theory are the preferences he ought to express. Like that of the animal psychologist, this theory uncritically assumes that there is an "ought" for man, and only for man. The animal psychologist supposes that human detachment, the moralist that human interests alone provide proper perspectives in terms of which the behavior of other living beings is to be judged. Both presuppose anthropomorphic theories of value, subscribing to an arbitrary good whose realization is supposed to make nature translucent. But the investigator is just as surely in nature as his animals, and both he and his animals have tasks which they ought to fulfill.

A third theory, that of the individualist, combines the objectivity of the first with the distinctions made by the second. This third theory affirms that every being, whether it is aware of it or not, looks out at the universe from its own standpoint, and that it tries to do what is best for it to do. It assumes that each being has its own appropriate good, though the actual performance of the being may not conform to that standard. It affirms that each being has, from its standpoint, as much right to be and to continue to be as any other. It need not affirm that each tries to preserve itself— a supposition defied by the career of the male spider and the gluttony of the pig. It need affirm only that each would attempt to preserve itself were it only wise enough to act in accordance with what its true nature requires.

This third view, however, does not take into account that living beings are not only individuals but also members of species, that they ought and sometimes do abandon themselves for the sake of others. If we add this fact to our account and generalize it, we achieve a fourth view to the effect that living beings are to be judged in terms of what they do and ought to do to promote both their individual good and that of other beings. The other views depend on this for their sanction.

The animal psychologist demands that we deal with animals without referring to any goods. He insists that they be judged in terms of the natures they really have and what is relevant to those natures. He cannot then avoid holding the first part of the fourth view, that beings are to be judged in terms of the goods appropriate to them, since the good for an animal is what sustains and enriches its being. And since the nature of animals is one which, as a rule, requires that they benefit others and perhaps us to some extent, the animal psychologist is forced to hold the second part of the fourth view to some degree even when most insistent on denying it.

The moralist cannot avoid holding to the second part of the fourth view, for he affirms that the acts of animals ought to be evaluated in the light of the good they do to at least one other kind of being, man. But many animals succeed in benefiting men usually only so far as they themselves prosper. The moralist is thus forced to admit that there is a good for the animal which it is good for us that it obtain.

The individualist affirms that animals are to be judged in terms of what is good for them individually, but this is also at times what is good for others and ourselves. Like the other two, his view is a limited and reserved way of affirming the fourth. The three have difficulty in making the transition from animals to men, both because they view them as characterized by radically different drives and because they suppose that men and animals are governed by entirely different principles. But like the fourth view each of these three views really allows some room for a distinction between what a living being does and what it should do. It makes no difference to the fact but only to the import of the distinction that what they underscore as the good an animal ought to do is something useful to man or the animal itself, rather than what is needed both by itself and others.

What a living being ought to do is an *intrinsic* or *extrinsic* fact about it. It is intrinsic if the being has a characteristic concern for a possible good. It is extrinsic if the good it "ought" to realize is what other beings prefer it to realize. In that case if a living being fails to do what it ought, it fails to conform to a possibly irrelevant condition of excellence imposed from without.

To deal with living beings in terms of an extrinsic ought is to assume an anthropomorphic position. It is to impose on them an ought of our own. It is to evaluate them in terms not germane to their being. It is to look at them solely in the light of their conformity to human requirements, desires and obligations. Justice to the nature of living beings requires us to recognize that there is a good they ought to realize, though its realization may conflict with the realization of our own good. Long ago man gave up the Ptolemaic astronomy for the Copernican, but in the field of values there are but few who do not adhere to the anti-Copernican sentiment that values pertain to man alone. A cat has value as surely as it has shape; the one is no more bestowed on it by us than the other.

We ought not to read ourselves into animals; we ought not to evaluate them in the light of our demands, our possible prosperity, or the needs of our disciplines. To look at them in terms of human needs is to overhumanize them, even when we insist that they are below the level of human beings. We avoid reading ourselves into the beings we study only if we hold steadfast to the truth that there are goods which they ought to realize if they are to increase in value. The terms which we employ in speaking of them are bound to be our own, but we can use them with the qualification that they are to express the nature of what is not human.

To the degree a being is unable to realize its characteristic good, it is defective, no matter how serviceable it may be. If it is able to realize that good, it is so far intrinsically excellent, though it may at the same time be extrinsically useless or dangerous. Those animals we domesticate are usually or usually become defective. Those animals that endanger our lives or crops are extrinsically vicious, though they are often intrinsically excellent, realizing a good for themselves and their kind.

3. THE LIMITATION OF NATURAL WISDOM

Living beings have characteristic concerns for goods pertinent to them. Those goods they ought to realize. And they all have a kind of native wisdom which leads them to do much of what they ought. That wisdom is rooted deep within them, quite below consciousness, untaught by either parents or experience. They exhibit it in almost every act. Living beings show predilections for what benefits them; they reject what is harmful and ignore what is irrelevant. Without having been taught the benefits of corn or the danger of foxes, the new-born chick pecks at the one and runs from the other. A dog needs no brain in order to make evident that it prefers not to burn. Without a brain it withdraws its leg in the presence of heat as surely and as rapidly as it did before its brain was excised.

Living beings have a native wisdom driving them outside situations which have no pertinence to their welfare, towards those which would benefit them, and away from those which would harm them. For the most part, each selects what will nourish it, rejects that which endangers it and ignores that which is irrelevant to the growth and continuance of itself and its kind. The cow is tempted by grass and repelled by meat; it pays no attention to the sunset. The weed isolates oxygen and minerals and ignores almost everything else but the sun.

There are some who place the source of this wisdom in the juices and the tendons, defining it as a kind of chemical or mechanical reaction to what is beneficial or injurious to the organism. Since the juices and tendons have limited effects, whereas the wisdom of the organism seems to concern the welfare of the whole, this view eventually gives way to another which acknowledges that, in addition to these partial bits of wisdom, there is a wisdom of the organism which relates all the parts and makes them function for the benefit of the whole. The facts demand that one affirm that the organism is a single being with a wisdom of its own. Such an affirmation takes one beyond the doctrine that the source of the wisdom is in the parts of the body, to the doctrine that the organism has a set of native and unlearned drives appropriate to the welfare of itself and its kind.

Neither the theory that there is wisdom in the juices nor the theory there is wisdom in the organism can be satisfactory if it supposes that the wisdom is complete, or that it is ingrained from the start. Unfortunately no living being is wise enough for its own good, and fortunately it can grow in wisdom as it matures. There are times when even the most neatly organized animal will ignore what it needs and times when it will delight in what is bad for it; there are times when it will exhibit a desire for what is irrelevant or injurious and times when it will fly from that which it ought to have or which is without danger for it. Whatever bodily wisdom a being might have is tinged with folly; it does not always serve to make the body prosper. The dog is a high-grade animal but it would be a mistake to let it eat what, when and as much as it wants. Animals occasionally turn away from food which they desperately need, allowing themselves to waste away in the midst of plenty. They do not always attend to what is dangerous, paying in suffering, injury and death for their neglect. There are times, too, when they play or engage in random movements; there are times when they deliberately move towards the only place where danger looms, exhibiting a preference for what is indifferent or dangerous rather than for what is good for them. Curiosity kills more cats than cancer does. And there are other times when living beings spend their energies flying before harmless sounds and sometimes even from the food and drink they ought to have. Trigger-like timidity prevents many an animal from growing old.

There is some wisdom in the body. Otherwise living beings would perish sooner than they usually do. The world is highly complex and the body is in constant need of special things which it must have quickly, if health, strength, life and kind are not to be lost. A living thing is able, from the start, to focus on many of the things which make for its weal or woe, and to act accordingly. But the fact that an animal sometimes takes in poison as well as water, that it often eats the debilitating with as much avidity as the nourishing, and that it embraces but part of what it should and thus often lives on an unbalanced diet in the midst of plenty, indicates that animal wisdom is not perfect. The hope of the animal is that its wisdom will increase with experience.

4. THE CHECK ON FOLLY

Living beings are rarely as wise as they might be. Part of what they intrinsically ought to do is to attempt to prosper as individuals and as members of species. But quickly and too soon they act in ways which endanger their health and continuance. Their folly, fortunately, is subject to a fivefold check: (a) lack of opportunity, (b) teachability, (c) responsiveness, (d) sensitivity, and (e) purposiveness keep them from violating their own intent more than they otherwise would.

(a) Living beings have a limited opportunity to be as foolish as they might be. They are saved from much of their folly, not because they are so artfully contrived that they are inclined to do only what is best for them, but because they have too few occasions to show how unwise they can be. It is their constant need to struggle against oppressive forces which keeps their tendency to act in foolish ways at bay. If they did not have to struggle so much, they would have many more occasions to show how quickly and thoroughly they could injure themselves. Domesticated animals, those in circuses and zoos, do not have to struggle as much as those that run wild, and as a consequence usually have shorter spans and less healthy lives. It is good for an animal to struggle, not because struggle is a good thing, but because it prevents dominant bodily tendencies and well-intrenched habits from being exercised to the full, to the detriment of the body and in violation of what the animal ought to do. Wild animals do not overeat as a rule, largely because there is not enough for them to eat. The difficulties of existence, within limits, keep them in trim, enabling them to act with skill and grace, with a consequent benefit to themselves and others.

(b) The body of a living being is selective, attuned to some things and not to others. Depleted, needing water and food, it stretches or moves towards what it needs. With time it acquires habits enabling it to turn toward and utilize more quickly what it requires and to avoid many things that endanger its continuance. Living beings learn in the course of experience. There is a great difference in the caution exercised by a kitten and a cat; the old oak has habits the acorn is too young to have acquired.

Unfortunately, such bodily wisdom is never entirely adequate to all the situations which a living being confronts. Almost every moment has its novelty, and for this a bodily wisdom, acquired early or late, is not prepared. No matter how well trained a being is, there is always something more than training which it requires in order to act properly as an individual, as one of a species and as part of an environment. The structure and habits of its body never make a living being as wise as it need be, individually, for the species and environmentally.

(c) The body has various needs. As they come into dominance they favor the performance of certain acts rather than others. Whatever encourages the completion of one of those acts is a stimulus defining the act as a response to it. Living beings are accordingly responsive, expressing their bodily needs by acts directed towards stimulating objects.

Living beings act to satisfy their bodies through the agency of the objects which provoke and support the expression of their bodily needs. The satisfaction of their bodies may, however, prove detrimental to those bodies, and to the beings as more than bodies. Thirst may drive an animal to drink though the health of its body may require it to wait. It may lead it to take in fluid which will work havoc on its bodily economy. And even when it drinks the right fluids and to the right extent, drinking may not be what the animal ought to do. It might have been wiser to have waited a while until the enemy was at a distance, or to have spent the time working with others for the realization of some common good. Responses are rarely sufficiently selective or sufficiently under the control of a concern to help the body or the being to the degree its good requires.

(d) Each being has an object of concern. Others attempt to delimit that object while focusing on their own goods, and it attempts to delimit theirs while focusing on its own. As a consequence each being is subject to a double conflict. On one side there is a conflict between the good others demand that the being realize and the good it is concerned with realizing; on the other side, there is a conflict between the good it demands that others realize and the goods they are concerned with realizing. This double conflict is felt by a living being as a double tension standing in the way of possible action. At one and the same time it is ready to act to satisfy and to reject the prescriptions imposed by others, and to act in terms of the goods it prescribes for others and the goods with which those others are independently concerned. To allow action to occur, a living being must not only either reject or submit to the demands of others but must also approach those others as beings concerned with either prescribed or unprescribed goods. It is *sensitive* so far as it is keyed to act in terms of its decisions.

A living being is prepared to act as a social, domineering, dominated, or antagonistic being in relation to a few others. So far as it is sensitive that its prescriptions have been accepted and that it has accepted the prescriptions of others, it approaches those others as in accord with itself. So far as it is sensitive that its prescriptions have been accepted while it has rejected the prescriptions of others, it takes a domineering attitude. So far as it is sensitive that its prescriptions have been rejected while it accepts theirs, it takes a subservient attitude. And so far as it is sensitive that its prescriptions have been rejected and that it rejects theirs, it is in an attitude of antagonism towards them.

The lower down in the scale of life, the more is a being a part of a neighborhood than an inhabitant of a cosmos. The lower its grade the more restricted the environment with which it sensitively deals.

The fact that there is a restriction in the extent of a living being's sensitively apprehended environment has its compensations. Since a living being's possible actions are limited in number and range, were it more sensitive, keyed to more of the decisions it makes with respect to other beings, it could become greatly distressed. To be sensitive but impotent is often a prelude to despair. Each being decisively evaluates all the others, but because it is usually sensitive to the results of only those decisions which relate to beings in its environment, it can effectively act on what it sensitively discerns.

No being, to be sure, is so neatly organized that it is sensitive only to the degree that it can and will act with success. There would be gain in an increase of sensitivity which reached beyond a being's present capacities to act successfully, for it could then prepare to deal with things far off but eventually near by. But on the whole, its sensitivity is and ought to be limited to neighboring beings, and particularly to those which are of most importance for its continuance and prosperity, as an individual and as a member of a species.

The elm is sensitive to soil, air and sun, to wind, bee and bug, and as living confines itself to them, ignoring axes, stars and men. When the elm dies as a result of the blow of an axe, it is in part because it is not sensitive to the axe and is not therefore prepared for what the axe might do. Otherwise it could have attempted to avoid the axe. If an elm could have been sensitive to the result of its rejection of the prescriptions which an axe imposes, it could have assumed an attitude of antagonism towards the axe and readied itself to fend off the axe's blow. But an elm must blindly suffer the blow of an axe, though as a result it may undergo such a radical change in its body that it is unable thereafter to utilize that body adequately. Its insensitivity to the axe leaves it no alternative but to remain passive even though death threatens.

Because living beings are sensitive to some degree, they can attend to some of the beings which have bearing on their welfare. Were they more sensitive, they would take account of more beings and in more ways. Every one has less sensitivity than it could profitably use; but each is saved from much folly because it is somewhat sensitive to some of the beings which can affect it radically.

(e) The sparrow is sensitive to her young. When they cry from hunger she does not listen and grieve, flutter about, console them. Instead she feeds them. She might responsively feed them because the tendency to feed happens to be in ascendancy. But there are times when the sparrow is tired and keyed to act in other ways and yet continues to attend to her young. She does not merely respond to the young and hungry sparrows, but acts to realize values that never were and which she may never know—those sparrows older and satisfied. She assumes a social attitude towards them, submitting to their prescriptions while they submit to hers, and acts to satisfy the good she sensitively discerns.

The deer does not merely run away; it tries to run to safety. It rejects the prescriptions of its enemy and they reject its prescriptions. It is sensitive to the threat they embody, and acts in accord with what it sensitively discerns, but for an end it does not know.

Some male spiders sacrifice their lives in mating; the males are subservient to the females. The mating would be foolish did it not also serve to promote the good of the species.

A colt and a calf, fed in the same way, develop differently. The one becomes a horse and the other a cow because they are sensitive to different foods and utilize them in different ways. They assume different attitudes of dominance towards their bodies and their food. There is no need, with Aristotle, to invoke a grown horse or cow to lure them on and thereby make them grow. Each in its own way acts in terms of what it sensitively discerns so as to grow towards some other state whose nature it does not know.

The wisdom of a living being is most completely embodied in its *purposiveness*, which is a tendency to act in the light of what it sensitively discerns, so as to realize an unknown good. If the living being is below the level of a man it acts purposively but without a purpose. It feeds its young, but how and for what end it does not know. It grows without any desire to grow. It is blindly purposive, purposive without a purpose, and therefore does not act with the nicety which the fulfillment of its ends requires. The sparrow feeds its young though they are past recovery. The male spider sacrifices his life even though the mating may be unfruitful. The deer runs to its destruction. The calf cares for its tubercular body in somewhat the same way it would a healthy one. Purposiveness guides beings to do much they ought not do.

5. GRACE

In the ideal case, response—the reply to a stimulus—and purposiveness—the blind movement to an end—support one another. When responsiveness gets out of hand, the being acts aberrantly, living from moment to moment without order. When purposiveness gets out of hand, the being lives a life undirected and unbounded. The lioness eats her cubs and thereby makes nonsense of her act of reproduction. Her purposiveness should have controlled her responses. The acorn insists on reaching towards the sun though it burn for its folly. Its responsiveness to heat should have been controlled by its purposive need to grow.

The happy union of responsiveness and purposiveness is grace. A graceful being is one which, while acting appropriately to the situation in which it is, makes provision for the better future of itself or its kind. Gracefulness is a product of art, an art mastered in the course of living. Graceful beings are those which have had a world to combat and at maturity possess a stable mode of activity which they charge with a quiet purposiveness driving them towards a more perfect state.

Pampered beings become adults too effortlessly and are not therefore prompted to express much of their concern in the well-organized body that habit and training provide. Stultified beings have had too much with which to contend and have too little energy left by which to make manifest their interest in something beyond. The former are hardly individuals, being almost instances of a kind instead, bodies without life. The latter are hardly kinds of things. They are more like individuals turned inside out, having allowed too much of their vitality to be spent in mastering the bodies they have. Their lives are lost in their bodies. The pampered allow too much of their most characteristic power to sleep, the stultified bring too much of it within present confines. A properly matured being is neither the one nor the other. It has the structure and retains the freshness of the well-tended, and makes the effort and attains the stability of the stunted. It is not only a vigorous illustration of its kind, but an individual freely and energetically expressing itself, in novel ways, within a present bodily and public setting.

Only those beings which have matured with difficulty and still reveal, in their texture and organization, their rhythm and adjustments, a freshness and unpredictable movement to an unknown end, are truly graceful. An immature being might be said to be charming. It is not graceful because not enough of its power has been expressed in a stabilized mold. An aged being might be said to be interesting. It is not graceful because it no longer has enough strength to express its purposiveness effectively. Its established patterns of activity offer too much resistance to permit its concern to be adequately manifest. The immature are too unrestrained, living too much for the future, though immersed in the present; the aged are overconditioned, living too much in the present or past, though directed towards the future. Only a mature being can be at once young and steady, old but vigorous, purposive and responsive, free yet restrained, a private individual manifest in a public stable frame. Such a being is as wise as an animal of its type can be, for it alone is properly habituated in the ways of the world and acts purposively on what it confronts. It alone reaches the stage where it can became alive to what it intrinsically demands.

6. EVOLUTION

There is no place where a clear line can be drawn between the lower and the higher subhuman living beings. Yet there is a great difference between a tree and a horse. The fact that we cannot tell where a cloud begins and where it ends does not mean that we cannot tell when we are well under the cloud and when we are well above it. Just so, the fact that we cannot tell where to draw the line between the lower and the higher living beings does not means that we cannot distinguish the more obviously higher from the more obviously lower—horses from trees, owls from pansies, and pigs from oysters.

Animals are distinct from and superior to plants. But they are not necessarily superior in bodily ability, responsiveness or purposiveness. Some plants can move and some animals cannot. Some plants are carnivorous and some animals are not. Some species of plants have a longer history than some species of animal.

Plants, though they may be superior to animals in other respects, are nevertheless necessarily inferior to them because their sensitivity is less acute, because they cannot perceive, and because they are not conscious. An oyster and a pansy have little sensitivity, feed perpetually, have no consciousness, and perceive nothing. An owl and a pig are more acutely sensitive and to a wider range of things; they can see and hear, and can feel pain and pleasure.

Higher living beings arise from lower ones for the same reason that the living arise from the nonliving—the bodies of the lower beings effectively resist the expression of their concerns. Recalcitrant bodies provide an occasion for the free alteration of concerns, enabling the higher living beings to have intents which can be expressed in and through the bodies that before were so recalcitrant.

To give hands to a pig is to injure, not to benefit it; to give the mole eyes is to bewilder it. The ape is not a man, not because its thumb is less flexible than a man's, but because it lacks that human concern which alone promotes the use of the thumb in human ways. Radical changes in the organism remain useless or dangerous unless accompanied by a change within, enabling the being to express itself effectively in and through the altered body.

The usual theory, which bases evolution on the preservation of random variations useful to its owner or its kind, is unable, as Bergson and others have remarked, to account for the development of such a complex organ as the eye or the wing. These presuppose the occurrence and preservation of many useless and sometimes dangerous variations. Not all useful mutations are preserved and not all those that are preserved are good for the being or its kind. In fact, it is precisely because mutations are useless or jeopardize the existence of the mutating being that evolution is possible. The mutations prevent the being from expressing itself properly, and it is forced to alter internally in order to act effectively. The higher beings issue from the lower by a free act in which the concerns and objectives of the lower are so altered that the beings are thereafter able to use their mutated bodies.

A useful mutation presages a more effective existence and thus makes it unnecessary for a being to change its nature. A useless or dangerous mutation, on the other hand, challenges the being to change its nature. It is thus not the useful but the useless or dangerous mutations which mark the points at which new types of beings first emerge.

An evolutionary change comes after some mutation has occurred. There will, therefore, always be a "missing link" in the usual story of evolution, for the transition to man, just like the transition from any lower to any higher being, occurs while and because mutated bodies remain unchanged.

An evolutionary change may not produce a superior being; it may not even produce one which is well-adapted to the world as it is. The change which produced man, however, represents a genuine advance. It does involve a progress. Man arose because his inferior predecessors freely and successfully acted in and through uselessly mutated, recalcitrant bodies.

Evolution does not apply merely to parts of beings or to their bodies. It embraces the living being as a whole—its sensitivity, its concern and its end. It is a product of freedom. Freedom is the power behind evolution, responsible for whatever mutations occur and for the fact that higher beings have nonbodily powers such as sensitivity and purposiveness.

Freedom is responsible for evolution; it is responsible, too, for the fact that some individuals are conscious. Consciousness arises when sensitive beings freely keep their concerns steady despite changing bodies. Not essential, the presence of consciousness is nevertheless indicative of the fact that the being possessing it is superior to a plant.

CHAPTER SIX

CONSCIOUSNESS

1. THE EXPRESSION OF SENSITIVITY

LIVING BEINGS act on and through their bodies. They also act on their environments. Instead of dwelling quietly within bodily limits, accepting the position and status they happen to have, they reach outward to that which lies beyond. Beyond is where both sustenance and danger are to be found, and a being has the greatest hope of continuance if it can, from a distance, accurately discriminate the satisfying from the injurious, and act in the light of what has been discerned. This its *sensitivity* enables it to do.

The behavior of a living being is dictated by the demands of its *sensitive concern*, i.e., by its sensitivity for an objective as related to the objectives of other concerns. Its body is a *sensitized* body, a body infected by sensitivity.

There is a minimum degree of expression of sensitivity required to make the body alive; beyond that minimum, the expression of sensitivity is but a way of being *sensible*. A sensible being thus is one which expresses its sensitive concern through a sensitized body, thereby preparing itself to act appropriately. So far as it merely has a sensitized body, it is a being whose sensitive concern is only partly expressed in and through the body; it is able to be sensible to the degree that it is able to bring a reserve of sensitivity into play spontaneously, thereby modifying the direction and the result of the bodily activity.

Sensitivity is expressed in varying degrees throughout the day, making the body shrink and expand, close and open the avenues through which the external world is approached. A being is accordingly sensible in different degrees, and at different times, for it varies in the degree to which it supplements that minimum expression of sensitivity which is required for life.

So long as a body is alive it is sensitized, but the individual is not necessarily sensible. Thus, a man's body is sensitized when he is in a stupor, though he is not then sensible. The sensitive concern of a stupefied being is expressed in and through its body to a minimum degree only, leaving that body to behave largely as structure and habit dictate. But when something is about to destroy the body, the being infuses that body with more of the sensitive concern and thereby forces itself into wakefulness. The being is then sensible of some particular in its environment and is ready to act so as to bring about the result which the sensitive concern requires.

Each living being has a constant minimum hold on its body, making that body a sensitized one. When awake, it increases its hold on the body, becoming sensible. It is because the body is sensitized that the being can have sensibility; because it has sensibility, it can act appropriately. The body is a sensitized agency for sensibility, an avenue through which a sensitive concern is enabled to realize its objective more effectively than otherwise.

2. PAIN AND PLEASURE

The living being has a body which it sensitizes, and through whose medium it can become sensible of particular things. It is never the perfect master of its body, however. That is why it has moods, and why it can become conscious of its pains and pleasures.

An unconscious living being partly expresses its concern in its body, thereby sensitizing it. That sensitized body is constantly changing, thus creating a demand that the concern alter its expressions. But the concern refuses to contract with the contraction of the body, and insists on encompassing whatever the body accretes. Should there be a loss in the body, an increasing *tension* will then be produced between the concern that ought to be expressed and the body as now incapable of accommodating that concern; should there be a gain in the body there will be a decrease in the tension to the degree that the concern masters that gain.

If the body lets go of something, its owner suffers an increase in tension so far as it continues to hold on, by means of its sensitive concern, to what has been bodily lost; if its body accretes something, the being undergoes a decrease in whatever tension it may suffer, so far as it succeeds in sensitizing what has been bodily gained. Such change in the bodily reach of a sensitive concern, the fact that a being controls a smaller or larger bodily field than it did before, is recorded as a changing *mood*.

A mood fills out the gap between a changing body and a concern. Under the constant irritation of an ailing tooth, without an awareness of pain or any feeling of discomfort, a being turns morose. The irritation of its tooth ruffles its placidity. Thus the irritant creates a tension between the concern and the body. Or, well-nourished, without an awareness of health or a feeling of comfort, the being becomes relaxed and expansive. Having quietly increased the scope of the expression of its concern by mastering satisfying content, it decreases whatever tension existed between its concern and its body.

In all beings the relation between the concern and the body, in which that concern is partially expressed, varies from moment to moment; but it is only the living who record the change in the shape of a changing mood. The life of an unconscious being is one of increasing and decreasing irritations, of varying tensions between a concern and an altering body. But since the nonliving being is not sensitive to the decisions it makes with respect to the objects with which it and others are concerned, it does not undergo changes in mood as its body contracts or expands.

A living being is *conscious* if it feels, in the form of pain and pleasure, an increase or decrease in the opposition between the demands of its sensitive concern and the state of its body. Pains and pleasures are felt changes in mood. Not every change in mood, however, can be recorded as pain or pleasure. Changes in mood occur in beings which have only sensitized bodies; pain and pleasure presuppose that they have a bodily expressed sensibility as well. To be conscious it is necessary first to be sensible.

Consciousness, and thus pain and pleasure, occur only in those beings which constantly vary their approaches to the world; they are possible only to sensible beings which try to alter the province of their concerns to keep abreast of the states of their sensitized bodies. Consciousness is the feeling of a change in the distance between a present sensible expression of a sensitive concern and one that ought to be expressed.

Consciousness is one of life's by-products, possible only to some beings. Dried, put away for years, plants continue to have sensitized bodies. Growing, they are in addition sensible of foreign bodies, expanding and contracting as the circumstances change. Yet they are without consciousness. An animal or a man asleep is also without consciousness, though sensitive and perhaps even sensible. They become conscious when, as sensible, they insist on expressing their concerns in a constant way despite an altering body.

Pain and pleasure are felt changes in mood, existing when and as felt. There can be no illusions about them. To have a pain or pleasure is to be conscious; to be conscious of either is to have it. One might find nothing wrong with the body of one who complains of a pain, or see no reason why the being should suddenly be suffused with pleasure. But the fact that it is conscious of the pain or the pleasure should be enough for us. It certainly is enough for it. To deny that something is pained or pleased because *we* have no evidence that it is, is to carry the demand for evidence a little too far.

A bodily pain is a felt record of the tragic truth that something is in the process of passing from bodily control. It is evidence that the being is endeavoring to hold, through a bodily expressed sensibility, to that which it is about to lose in fact. Pain marks the truth that the being no longer controls the destiny of that which it had made an intimate part of itself, that its concern cannot be expressed where it had been expressed before. It informs the being that something is losing the value acquired by being encompassed by that being. The flesh, in being rent, is deprived of its status as a vital part of oneself; the process of losing such a part, while sensibly holding on to it, is felt as pain.

A being is pained because parts of it suffer the loss of a value which the concern once provided them. Pain is the expression of a natural conceit, even though it is primarily concerned with the disasters which beset other things. It is a kind of sympathy for other things about to lose the boon of being enhanced by oneself, a sign of the fact that one's regrets are rooted in an egotistic acceptance of one's own dignity and value.

Pain is a feudal passion. It arises because something which is being lost is still cherished. We are pained because something is being freed from its enslavement to us. The more a man has identified himself with his possessions, the more pain therefore does he feel on their loss. The life of a pantheistic God is a life of anguish, a perpetual suffering in the face of his impotence to stop the passage of time and the loss of values that had been in existence a moment before.

Pleasure is a consequence of a successful affirmation. It is a sign that one's concern is being expressed in one's body more adequately than it had been before, and thus that what is not alien from the standpoint of that body is not alien from the standpoint of the expressed concern. Pleasure blurs the distinction between the natures of other things and oneself; it is testimony that the being is sensitizing what its body is mastering.

Pleasure is predatory. It deprives others of an independent nature; it involves a neglect of what they want and need. Private pleasure has its taint of the diabolic, just as publicly suffered pain has its element of indecency. It is possible only to the satanic in its purity; only such a being could ignore completely the fate and fortune of others. We are forced to seek the company of others to enjoy ourselves to the full, for only by allowing them to use us as we use them can we achieve an equilibrium, feel ourselves one among many, and thus retain our sanity.

It is the tooth we say that pains, but the pleasure of relief we attribute to ourselves. We are pleased by the entrance of other things within the sphere of our influence, more for our sake than for theirs. It is in pain that we become aware that others have interests and values of their own; pleasure leads instead to a use of them for our own ends.

Pains and pleasures are rarely if ever had in isolation. Only one who is suddenly deprived of something perfectly mastered, or who has no difficulty in mastering something new could have pure pains or pleasures. But even in these cases the other follows almost at once, for a being both quickly adjusts itself to some degree to losses and always encounters some opposition and resistance. Because pains and pleasures usually occur together we are not altogether appreciative or unappreciative of the value and natures of other things.

Pain is the result of an increase in tension between a need for a bodily withdrawal and an effort to retain a hold on that which is disturbing. What a being bodily abandons, it yet sensibly holds on to; that is its pain. Pleasure is the result of a decrease in tension between the sensibility of a being and an alien world brought under the aegis of the body. What a being bodily conquers, its sensitivity adopts; that is its pleasure. Pleasure and pain are thus the result of a free expression of a sensitive concern endeavoring to maintain a steady position with respect to an expanding body and despite a contracting one.

Pleasure and pain can be deliberately produced and avoided. A being can subject itself to greater pleasure and pain by increasing the degree of expressed sensitivity in its body; it can decrease the degree of pain and pleasure by withdrawing its sensitivity. Both these movements are late achievements. Initially, naturally, automatically, and freely, every living thing tries to avoid contracting the reach of its concern, and tries to extend its control as and when the body expands.

3. THE CARTESIAN HYPOTHESIS

Both pleasure and pain are felt while, when, and where a changing tension occurs. Neither is projected from the brain or mind into a part of the body. They are conscious phenomena and exist only so far as they are objects of consciousness.

Yet, following Descartes, physiologists and philosophers rightly remark that since a man who has lost a leg will sometimes complain of a pain in his foot, what is felt cannot be where it is *said* to be felt. They then, however, treat the pain as an excitation in the brain which is attributed, for practical reasons, to other parts of the body. Who makes the attribution and how it is done, they neglect to say. They are content to affirm that one can be conscious of pains and pleasures whether or not the body is affected in any region outside the brain, and presumably whether or not the rest of the body is there at all.

Descartes thought that the body was a complicated machine for conveying impulses to a pineal gland in the brain—impulses which might be considerably modified in the course of their transmission and which, as felt, had no necessary pertinence to what was occurring at the point of stimulation. According to him, all that was necessary in order that pain or pleasure be felt was that the pineal gland in the brain be disturbed.

"The mind," Descartes remarks in his 6th *Meditation*, "does not receive impressions from all parts of the body immediately, but only from the brain, or perhaps even from one of its smallest parts ... which, whenever it is disposed in the same particular way, conveys the same thing in the mind, although *meanwhile* the other portions of the body may be differently disposed. . . . The nature of the body is such that none of its parts can be moved by another a little way off which cannot be also moved in the same way by each of the parts which are between the two, although this more remote part does not act at all. . . . When I feel a pain in my foot, my knowledge of physics teaches me that this sensation is communicated by means of nerves dispersed through the foot, which, being extended like cords from there to the brain, when they are contracted in the foot *at the same time* contract the inmost portions of the brain which is their extremity and place of origin. . . . It may happen that although the extremities which are in the foot are not affected . . . this action will excite the same movement in the brain that might have been excited by a hurt received in the foot, in consequence of which the mind will necessarily feel in the foot the same pain as if it had received a hurt."

Descartes seems undecided—as is evident from the words which I have italicized in the above quotation—as to whether the conveyance of an impulse from foot to brain takes time or not. Later thinkers are more definite on this point. For them all transmissions take time. If, then, there were a being who was thousands of miles high, one would, according to them, have to affirm that any pain that the being might feel as occurring in its foot occurred only in the brain and at an appreciable time after the foot had been disturbed. Imagine, then, a dextrous surgeon following the path of an impulse and cutting off each nerve immediately after the impulse had passed through it. By the time the impulse reached the brain, the entire body of the imaginary giant would be cut away, and though he then had neither foot, leg, heart nor head, he would, according to this doctrine, be conscious of a pain in the foot just as if his body were still there.

Some men, like Spinoza and Kant, will rightly have nothing to do with the Cartesian physiological explanation of the occurrence of a pain or pleasure. But if, with Spinoza and Kant, they separate the foot and its changes from the consciousness of pain and pleasure, they will, willy-nilly, still remain within the Cartesian corral, unable to understand how it is that a living body can painfully adjust itself to a pain in a part of it.

It seems quite evident, too, that it takes time for a disturbance to have its effect on an organism. Both the hypothesis of the transmission of a disturbance through the nerves and the supposition that it takes time for a being to respond to an irritation, have considerable experimental support. They ought to be sufficient, if anything is sufficient, to make the Cartesian point that pains and pleasures are directly felt only in the brain and then are referred to places where at most only a physical change could be occurring. But the point cannot be made. A pain exists where and as it is consciously suffered; a pleasure exists where and as it is consciously enjoyed. Pains and pleasure are no more in the brain than they are in any other part of the body; in fact, it is easier to feel disturbances which occur at points of the body other than the brain than it is to feel those that occur in the brain. Nor are they in the mind. They are in the body, though it is necessary to be conscious of them if they are to exist.

Neither sensitivity nor consciousness depend on the conveyance of a disturbance from nerve to nerve, from periphery to brain. Disturbances must be conveyed so that organized responses can take place. Such conveyance takes time; a provocation therefore may have already passed away before the organism is able to respond to it. At each point of the transmission the being is disturbed; from the standpoint of consciousness the function of the transmission is not to present an irritation to the brain, but to enable the being to feel it many times in a definite order.

A disturbance does not run its course through the body unaffected by anything else occurring at the same time. During the time it takes for it to be transmitted through the body, other disturbances occur which are immediately felt by the individual. Were a foot tickled and then instantly cut off, the cutting would be felt immediately. It would swell and modify the nature of that feeling which the transmission of the tickle makes possible. The being would thus feel the cutting in the context of a felt tickle.

Each disturbance, transmitted or not, if consciously is immediately apprehended. Beings do not, however, respond to each disturbance in turn, as the Cartesian hypothesis would prompt one to suppose. They do not first begin to respond to a disturbance which has been conveyed to the brain, and then inhibit that response in order to reply to the next disturbance and so on, until they come to something overwhelming or of major importance. When a foot is tickled and then cut, one does not first enjoy the tickle only to abandon that pleasure to concern oneself with the cut. The cut is directly felt *after* the tickle is *directly* felt, but *while* and *before* some *transmitted* versions of that tickle are felt. Both the tickle and the cut may be *located* where they are directly sensed or elsewhere.

An *experience* consists of at least two feelings, both referring to changes in the bodily status of an expressed concern. One of the feelings refers *directly* to one change. The other feeling refers to a *transmitted* version of the other change. Thus, a felt cut is part of an experience which also embraces a transmitted pleasurable tickle. The being experiences not a tickle now and a cut later, but a tickling in which there is an overwhelming accent on a cut. The cut and the tickle are directly sensed as painful and pleasurable, where and when they occur. The tickle alone, however, in this case is also transmitted.

A soldier whose leg has been shot away, if stimulated at the stump, feels a disturbance there and elsewhere at different moments. In the attempt to cut that experience short, he tries to focus on a limited region of his body. Without affecting the fact that he is then undergoing a painful experience, his attempt may be wrongly directed. If one cuts off the intervening places between the soldier's stump and his brain, the soldier dies. If one could cut off those intervening places quickly enough, he would die before he was able to respond to the disturbance in the stump. But he would nevertheless be conscious of the disturbance, at the instant it occurred, as an accent in any experience he might then be having.

There is no mystery in the fact that a stimulus is gone before a pain is felt; a stimulus is a stimulus for a response. Physiologists can tell how long it usually takes for a response to become manifest; they can tell nothing about the feeling that the disturbing stimulus immediately provokes, and thus nothing about consciousness, or pain and pleasure, or why we do not always respond effectively.

We have no sure knowledge of how to respond effectively. We attribute pains to places where they did not originate and where no disturbance can be found. Thus, we sometimes claim to have a pain in a healthy tooth—a pain, moreover, which can be provoked by irritating a decayed tooth in some other part of the jaw. We might sometimes attribute pains to places which are not part of us. Wounded, we may feel as though we had a twinge in a limb which is no longer there. It is fairly well authenticated that soldiers often do not feel any pain until hours after they have lost a limb.

Because a being does not know just where its pains originate it makes mistakes in response. It has to learn how to use its body. Its bodily acts are initially tentative, random; it does not know just what to do, and waits for success to dictate what paths it is thereafter to pursue. Its public movements are governed by an effort to eliminate the source of, and thereby decrease, the tension it suffers. Its actions are somewhat random at first, because it does not know just what will free it from pain. Those of its actions which happen to result in a decrease of tension are naturally associated with that decrease. When a similar tension is subsequently felt, those actions are repeated. The being is then on the way to achieving the habit of acting so as to increase its pleasure and decrease its pain effectively and promptly.

A conscious being tries to act so as to decrease the tension that it suffers. For some tensions it quickly finds a remedy, for others no remedy has as yet been discovered. As time goes on, the acts which were selected, because effective, are utilized as means for conquering new tensions. After tentative acts, comes association with effective bodily movement, and after such association comes the association of the selected movement with new tensions, and the perhaps mistaken identification of the source of the tension with the terminus of that movement.

Confronted with a new kind of tension, a being acts in habitual ways, and this the more surely the more mature and experienced it is. It is inevitable, then, that when a man feels a pain in the stump of his leg he will act as though he had a pain in his foot, and will suppose that he is feeling the pain at the place where he is accustomed to rid himself of it. He feels the pain in the stump, not in the non-existent foot or in the brain. He does not feel the same pain he would have felt if the foot had been disturbed, for the disturbance in the foot provokes a different tension from that which a disturbance of the stump does.

Descartes is wrong in claiming that a knowledge of physics teaches that sensation is communicated by means of nerves dispersed through the foot and reaching to the brain. Physics teaches nothing about sensations. And there is no evidence whatsoever that a sensation can be communicated by means of a nerve.

4. ENVIRONMENTAL SENSITIVITY

Men are sensitive—as most animals and plants also seem to be—not only to things inside or at, but also to things outside the borders of their bodies. Sensitivity extends far beyond the regions where most of us are inclined to look for it, but no further than the point where a living being can be sensitive to what occurs. And then a being is able to become morose because its environment is unpleasant, or to be filled with joy because the world is delightful, even though it acts and rests in the same way it did before.

Since a being can be irritated by and can experience things at a distance, it can be conscious of things beyond its body, as well as of things and irritations within that body or on its surface. One can sometimes feel an intruder in the room when deep in sleep; animals sometimes exhibit an uncanny awareness of the fact that there are changes going on at a distance quite beyond the reach of their eyes and ears. On good authority we learn that fish cannot hear, but every fisherman knows that it is better to be quiet if fish are to be caught.

There is no sharp line between what is felt inside or at the body, and what is felt at a distance. No being can be sure of just where its body ends and the rest of the world begins. We have difficulty in determining whether the heat we feel is in our bodies or in the world about, in knowing whether the apple is really sweet or merely that we think it is because we enjoy the pleasure of having it in contact with our tongues. Pains and pleasures, heat and cold stand out from the very beginning because they are vivid and intimate. Yet they are but the surface of a darker and richer content which fades off into the distance and of which we are constantly but dimly aware. They can be so acute as to make one almost forget that there is a world beyond; they can be so faint that we are aware only of that which is happening about us. But so long as we are conscious, we cannot avoid having both the clear and the dim, the near and the far.

Because living beings insist on expressing their concerns in a constant way on their environments, they feel pain and pleasure with respect to things at a distance from their bodies. A being is pained when its environment becomes impoverished, and it remains pained until it is able to adopt towards the new environment the attitude it had towards the old; it is pleased by the entrance of inviting things in its environment, until it succeeds in reducing them to the status of the old. Changes in the environment make for dimly felt pains and pleasures.

5. ANIMAL PERCEPTION AND INTELLIGENCE

Living beings, because their natures are changed with difficulty, allow bodily changes to continue far beyond the stage that inanimate things would tolerate. As a consequence, living beings are subject to a changing tension between the demands of their sensitive concerns and their changing bodies. If they can feel the changes in tension, they are conscious beings which successfully hold on to the opposed tendencies of sensitivity and body.

A sensitive concern is unsatisfied so long as the body and the environment are not mastered. But so far as a being insists on sensitively mastering its body and environment, it is bound to suffer a tension of increasing or decreasing magnitude which it feels as pain or pleasure. It must therefore charge its actions, as productive of pain and pleasure, with spontaneity, if it is to satisfy its sensitivity. To the degree it succeeds in bringing its sensitive concern to bear spontaneously on its body and the situation in which it is, to that degree it succeeds in freely responding and, when fortunate, in freely responding to the beings which are felt with or help cause pain or pleasure.

Consciousness, though it arises because the body resists the sensitivity, prompts a spontaneous reintroduction of that sensitivity into the body. It is a means by which an ineffective sensitivity becomes bodily effective once again, leading the being to act, not in the way which provoked the pain or pleasure in the first place, but in a new way which turns the being away from the pain towards another possible pleasure.

Pains and pleasures are most acute, and assume the forms of anguish and ecstasy when a being insists on remaining as it is despite a radical change in its body. Anguish and ecstasy are harbingers of death, marks of the fact that the contrast between sensitivity and the body is at its maximum, and that the being must act or change radically if it is to remain a single being. When pains or pleasures are at their height, the freedom of response and desire which consciousness entails is too late in coming, and the being is usually unable to recover its equilibrium. But should it succeed in warding off death and debilitation, the heightening of its pains and pleasures will be the prelude to activities and desires never possible before. Great tragedies and great joys start a being on a new career. It is one of the functions of religion and art to provoke anguish and ecstasy. If they are not to ruin, their effects must be controlled by ritual and the demands of their media. Free thinkers and the practical are inclined to see only the ill effects, the religious and the esthetes only the good in religion and art. But both types of effect can and do occur.

The pains which result from a lack of concordance between sensitivity and a bodily mastery of objects at a distance are almost all minor in nature. With respect to their occasions, no significant action is possible. To rid oneself of what is felt at a distance through the agency of sense organs, it is necessary to close the eyes and cover up the ears. Such acts must not only be learned, but have the disadvantage of shutting one up within oneself, preventing an adequate adjustment to the world about. A being may move, run away or towards an irritant; but this not only takes time, it brings it in contact with still other disturbances. Irritations provoked by distant objects cannot be avoided except by risking a loss of consciousness of things that might prove profitable or dangerous.

If a being could impress its concern on what it senses, it could remain in contact with what irritates, and nevertheless satisfy that concern. This it does when it *perceives*, for it then freely qualifies the sensed by an *interest*, which is a response to a distant object through the agency of a sense organ. Interest converts the sensed into the perceived by localizing, in the sensed, possibilities that had been sensitively discerned. It makes possible a fresh and new way of being sensible, utilizing the sense organs rather than the body as a whole as an avenue through which a sensitive concern is to be manifest. A living being has enlivened senses; if it is also interested, it uses its senses to perceive.

Perception occurs when a being reaches through its sense organs to distant objects and qualifies those objects by an interest expressive of the intent of its concern. Perception is thus sensitivity functioning through the sense organs and terminating in an object evaluated as being of interest, positive or negative.

Perceiving beings insist on viewing things in terms of established interests. This enables them to act persistently; but for that very reason they tend to rigidify the perceptual world and to treat it as promising what it does not promise any longer. The habitual approaches of daily life are attuned to what was once discerned but which all too often no longer exists.

Perceptions should be vitalized by new interests. This is a truth with which artists have long been familiar. They are constantly trying to look at things from the vantage of fresh interests appropriate to what they sensitively discern. Every artist, of course, is habituated and his works soon take on a definite pattern reflecting his habits and experiences. He can view things in terms of fresh interests only occasionally; but he is constantly aware (as other men are not) that so far as his is an habituated approach he is not doing full justice to the phenomena he encounters.

Habituated interests stand in the way of the realization of possibilities now sensitively discerned; they lead a being to attend to a familiar but perhaps painful and illusory world. To avoid such habituation, the sensitively discerned possibilities must, without the mediation of the body or its organs, be brought into relation with what is sensed. The perceived, as in the present, must be related to a sensitively discerned possibility dwelling in the future, if it is to be *meaningful*.

The act of bringing a sensitively discerned possibility into relation with what is perceived turns the perceived into a possible sign of what is sensitively discerned. As a consequence, the perceiver is converted into a being with *intelligence*. An intelligent being is an expectant one whose future is related to the future of the perceived; it is one who makes use of the perceived as a sign of a possibility which that being had sensitively discerned.

An animal can perceive, acknowledge meanings, and intelligently expect what is to come. Beyond this point it does not seem able to go. Its intelligence does not enable it to do more than to expect and to anticipate. It has no power of *knowing*, of grasping principles in terms of which the perceived can be related, explained and criticized. It treats other beings from the vantage of what it sensitively discerns; it does not deal with them in terms of the goods they are actually trying to realize. This only man is able to do.

6. TRANSITION TO MAN

Animals live; most are conscious, many perceive, some are intelligent. Those that are conscious have *psyches*. These are unified feelings, correlates of pleasurable and painful objects. They have these psyches only while they are conscious, just as the objects of which they are conscious exist as pleasurable or painful only so far as they are objects of consciousness.

Animals often act on that with respect to which they are not sensitive. They make their presence felt on a host of things about. If they run across an obstacle they can not master, they retreat from it in order to deal with some other obstacle within their powers. Similarly, a tree first tries to get through a rock and then probes around it, varying its activities in order to approach the state where, despite the rock, it can realize its good.

Living beings retreat from obstacles they find beyond their power to master. The retreat is preliminary to an attempt to impress their intent on some other phase of the body, neighbors or the world. Should the beings be unable to do this, they have no other recourse but to change in nature or prepare to die.

Unable to master its barriers, a living being may be fortunate enough to change in nature. It may freely concern itself with a new object so as to act on what it could not before. It is because some of the lower living beings successfully take this road that higher living beings have come to be; because some of the higher living beings have successfully changed their concerns in the face of otherwise insuperable obstacles, men came into the world.

Were man an animal, if he did not have a concern quite different from that characteristic of other living beings, the problem of his origin would raise no greater difficulties than would the problem of the origin of birds from reptiles. One can doubt whether the change from reptile to bird is a change to a higher grade or only a change to a type more fitted to the environment that happens to prevail. But if man be recognized to have powers and virtues, values and capacities which are, apart from their serviceability, of a higher grade than that characteristic of any animal, actual or possible, the question of his origin is not one of the origin of a being better adapted to its environment than its ancestors, but of the origin of a being who is superior to them and who may perhaps therefore be in a position to adapt itself better to the environment or the world at large. Man is not the best-adapted being; he is merely able to adapt himself more and more. Why then did he arise? To answer that question, it is necessary to know and keep in mind the peculiar nature that is his.

CHAPTER SEVEN

THE HUMAN NATURE OF MAN

1. MAN'S LATE ORIGIN

MAN IS A comparatively late arrival on the cosmic scene. On this point most thinkers are today agreed.

The view is not new. It was clearly stated by Empedocles over twenty-four hundred years ago. It is also to be found in the first chapter of Genesis.

The opening chapter of Genesis is frequently interpreted as unequivocally stating that God created the whole universe with all its inhabitants on six successive days, the last being devoted to the creation of man. An interpretation, much more compatible with the findings of geology and biology, is offered by Thomas Aquinas. Following Augustine, Thomas affirms that God, instead of creating actual plants and trees, fishes and birds, created only potential ones, i.e., only "their origins or causes." It was not, of course, a concern for the facts of biology or geology which prompted this interpretation, but a desire to affirm that man alone, of all living things was produced by God directly. As a consequence, both Augustine and Thomas Aquinas refused to maintain that man, like other living things, was created only in potency, in the shape of causes which could actually produce him in the course of natural history. Were one to extend their theory of the creation of things in their causes so as to include man as well as other living things, there would be no conflict, at this point, between the Bible and modern science. The latter does not in any way deny, any more than it affirms, that there was an act of creation. That is a question outside its interests, beyond the reach of its method and indifferent to its progress. The theory of creation, of course, has its own difficulties, and the Bible raises rather than answers philosophic questions. But it is interesting to see that, whether or not the Bible be taken as a guide, it is possible to affirm that man came into existence some time after other beings.

Aristotle and Leibniz seem to be the most conspicuous members of the opposition. According to Aristotle, man is a fixed and unalterable species which always was and always will be existent in nature. For Leibniz, every individual—not only men—is a permanent part of the furniture of the universe. Leibniz, however, offered his as a metaphysical doctrine relating to the insides of things. He did not maintain that living man was eternally part of a spatial or experienceable nature; he claimed only that his soul was a fixed component of that realm of being which permanently lay behind that nature. His view can thus be readily combined with the view that man, as possessed of an observable body, is a latecomer in the natural world.

There are some who conclude from the writings of such idealists as Berkeley, Kant, and Hegel that all of nature exists only so far and so long as men think of it. If such an interpretation of the writings of these men were correct, they too must be said to hold that nature could not precede the arrival of man. But the interpretation is in error. These idealists attempt to show that the natural world depends for its being on the exercise of thought. However, the thought on which it depends is, for them, not the thought of a limited finite being with a finite mind, but the thought of a divine, transcendent or absolute spirit with an eternal and unlimited mind. For these idealists, as well as for their opponents, man arrives after the natural world has been in existence for some time. It is Aristotle and his disciples, and apparently they alone, who deny that there is a date in the history of the world when man had not appeared. But the denial entrains so many untenable dogmas about geology, biology, the fixity of species, the nature of time, causation and chance, that there seems to be no alternative but to reject Aristotle and agree with the majority.

There is considerable evidence that man had an animal origin. He has organs, nerves, and blood, a musculature and a brain similar to those of other mammals. He is subject to similar diseases and is a host to similar parasites. He and animals feed, grow and mature under similar circumstances, react with pain and pleasure to the same kinds of bodily disturbances, and perceive by means of similar sense organs.

There are, however, signal differences between men and animals. The texture and quantity of man's hair, the shape of his nose, lips and back, the length and opposable power of his thumbs, his exclusive ownership of a chin and nonprojecting canines, the size of his brain, the nature of his foot and gait, the way he speaks and the kind of diseases to which he alone is apparently subject, mark him off quite clearly as a distinct type of being. These differences do not, to be sure, suffice to keep him out of the animal kingdom, or even to set him far apart from the higher primates. The body of a bat differs far more radically from that of a porpoise than the body of a man does from that of an ape—yet there is no doubt but that both bat and porpoise are animals somewhat akin. The differences between the bodies of men and apes are radical enough to separate them into distinct biological families, but the similarities are close enough to keep them together within the common class of beings who have highly developed, somewhat similar mammalian bodies.

A man's body is quite similar in structure and function to that of an ape's. The differences are readily explained as being the result of a process of evolution, in the course of which the traits of some subhuman being were modified until they assumed their present human and distinctive form. Biologists differ considerably in their account of how and why man happened to come to be with his characteristic upright posture, large-sized brain and his peculiarly shaped feet, teeth and jaw. But all of them seem agreed that he and his distinctive traits have an animal origin and that he, as a consequence, is an animal and nothing more.

It does not seem worth while to dispute the contention that man has an animal ancestry and came to be in the course of history. The view is supported by the independent investigations of geologists, archeologists and anthropologists. It is opposed only by the theory that man has always existed in his present form or that he is a special creation inserted within the frame of nature. It would be a mistake, however, to suppose that if it be granted that man had an animal origin it is also granted that he is nothing but an animal. Just as it is possible for a child to surpass its parents, so it is possible for an animal to pass beyond the limits within which its ancestors dwelt, and to arrive at the stage where it becomes a radically distinct type of being. It would then attain and exercise powers which it did not have before and which have no animal mode of expression. In short, it is possible for an animal to become a man, though a man is not and cannot become an animal.

2. DARWIN'S THESIS

To show that man is an animal, one must show that every trait of man, bodily or nonbodily in nature, is a developed, complex or variant form of some animal character, differing from it in degree and not in kind. An attempt to do this has been made a number of times in the course of history, notably by Montaigne, La Mettrie and Condillac. The most persuasive presentation of the thesis, however, is I think to be found in Darwin's *Descent of Man*.

Darwin maintained that man's capacity for happiness and sorrow, love and hate, his sense of beauty and of right and wrong, as well as his ability to remember, imagine and reason, were either duplicated in other animals or were present in them in a rudimentary form. Dogs impressed Darwin as not only having intelligence, but self-consciousness; he thought birds had a sense of beauty, monkeys an ability to make tools, and dogs, birds and monkeys some form of speech and moral sense. He could find nothing in man which was not duplicated, at least in embryonic form, elsewhere in the animal kingdom. As he quaintly put it, "If man had not been his own classifier, he would never have thought of founding a separate order for his reception."

Darwin erred, however, in supposing that every human characteristic is duplicated somewhere and to some degree in the animal kingdom.

Man is sometimes religious. No animal ever is. It is not to the point to say, as Darwin does, that there are men who have no religion, for one kind of being is not to be distinguished from another by virtue of an *activity* in which all the members of one group engage and all the members of the other do not. One type of being differs from another by virtue of a *capacity* which all its members and no other beings have. What Darwin should have shown is that there are types of men who *cannot* be religious or that there are animals which are or can be religious, if only in a minor way. But this he fails to do.

Animals decorate and occasionally show sensitivity in color and design. But an artist reproduces in his art the meaning of another thing, and this no mere manipulation of color or design begins to approach. The sense of beauty of an animal, and the art of which it is capable, differ not in degree but in kind from that open to a man.

Man, too, alone has science, philosophy and history—speculative inquiries into the nature of realities he never directly encounters through the senses. What animals know is what they learn from sense experience. No multiplication of such experiences could ever sum up to a knowledge of that which lies outside the reach of any sense.

And then there is man's speech, his use of symbols, his ability to pledge himself to do something in the future, his ability to cook and his ability to engage in sexual acts for pleasure rather than for the sake of reproduction.

There is no evidence that animals engage in such acts even to a slight degree. On behalf of Darwin's thesis, it could however be maintained that, though animals have the ability to engage in such acts, they do not exercise it. But we ought to say that animals are unable to do what no one of them in fact ever does, because in that way we suppose nothing beyond what the evidence warrants. It is arbitrary to assert that a dog is a man or angel in disguise, unfortunately limited by an inadequate body or a sluggish will. A sound method and a sure sense of values dictate that things be taken in the shape they appear until we are forced to view them in a different light.

It is possible to hold that dogs do not speak because they do not have the requisite equipment or inclination. But it would be more reasonable to assert that they do not speak because they do not have the ability. Similarly, it would be possible to maintain that there are no animal scientists or philosophers, either because the animals have not been properly educated or because they are not interested. But it would be more reasonable to say that animals do not pursue these subjects because they cannot. Animals present themselves as animals and nothing more. We have no reason for supposing that the evidence is insufficient.

But, on the other hand, there are also men who are dumb, insensitive and irrational. It would seem reasonable, then, to conclude that they too are without a capacity for speech, religion, art, science, philosophy and history. The practitioners of these various subjects protest. They deny that any man is completely devoid of the ability to practice them. It is a rare artist indeed who does not believe that every man has some artistic ability; theologians affirm that atheists are not only capable of religion but are actually engaged in practising it in some aberrant form; it is a commonplace with many philosophers that all men speculate to some extent. One must yield to these protests or give up the idea that these different abilities, although possible only to men, are essential to them. We ought not, I think, yield to these protests. Found in all mature, normal men, these abilities are not in the rest.

If these abilities were essential to men, they would be present in every human being. Unfortunately there are idiots, and fortunately there are infants in the world. If these are human—and human they seem to be—they must already have these various abilities, or these abilities are not essential. But we term the one an idiot and the other a child precisely because they lack the abilities which mature and normal men possess. They can be termed human, not because they have these various abilities, but only because they possess a power which, in favorable circumstances, may become expressed in these diverse forms.

Because there are idiots and children, we are forced by a different route to come to the same conclusion that Darwin does: religion, reason, speculation and art do not suffice to define men as beings of a radically distinct type from animals. Darwin obtained his conclusion by minimizing the kind of ability some men possess. We obtained it by affirming that these were abilities possible only to men, and then remarking that there were human beings who could not rightly be said to possess them. Such abilities can not therefore serve to distinguish all men from animals.

3. THE NECESSITY FOR THE BODY

What is essential and common to men is not a set of specific abilities to think or cook—for then idiots and children would not be human—but a single power which is the source of these diverse abilities. Though an infant and an idiot neither understand more nor deliberate better than a dog or a horse, mankind has rightly refused to equate infants and idiots with dogs and horses. There is a great difference in one's attitude towards those who desire to vivisect the former and those who desire to vivisect the latter. Everyone has at least a dim awareness of the fact that the child is merely too young and the idiot too unfortunate to be able to bring their singularly human power to adequate expression. Even the most highly developed of men are only occasionally rational or deliberate, religious or artistic. And they lose nothing of their humanity when they put their reason and skills aside under the pressure of affection, sentiment and misfortune. Men are human, not because some of them do things animals cannot, but because all of them have a power all animals lack—though to be sure only some of the men use that power to do things animals cannot.

If we can affirm that there is a singularly human power which is the source of all man's abilities, an important neglected truth is within our grasp: man cannot be an animal in whole or in part. Even his body, despite the many features which it shares with animals must, if quickened by a single human power, be nonanimal in nature.

A single power characteristic of man must be either separable or inseparable from his body. If separable, his definition will involve a consideration only of his "soul"; if inseparable, the nature of his power cannot be grasped without taking into account the fact that he has a body. The first of these alternatives is accepted by Plato. According to him, who here echoes something of the views of the East, and is echoed in turn by Descartes, Christian Scientists and Spirtualists, "what makes each one of us what we are is only the soul." The body, on this view, is unessential and the soul "never voluntarily has connection with it." But, theorize as much as we like, the fact is that men sit and run, eat and drink, laugh and cry, and this no mere soul or spirit could do. To deny that the body is an essential part of a man is to deny that a man can be ruined by cutting his throat, or that a man ought to have food and shelter in order to remain human.

The objections are obvious and pressing. It is no surprise therefore to find that those who try to view the body as an unessential part of man, change without apology to the view that the body is an essential but unwanted and impoverishing part of him. The main tenor of Plato's views is in this direction, particularly in such dialogues as the *Republic*, where gymnastics, the training of the body, is defined as an indispensable part of every man's education.

But this view, too, will not do. It plays havoc with the truth that a man who merely thinks about the good is not good enough, and that to be truly good he must be able to realize his ideals in fact to some degree. To bring the good about, a man needs a body; if that body is necessary for the good to be achieved, it is so far not undesirable or unwanted, but desirable and necessary. Ascetics have discovered a way by which they can avoid the evils which the body makes possible; but that way unfortunately is also one that makes them give up the goods which the body helps achieve. The nature of man involves a reference to the body as an indispensable avenue through which his power is to be at least partly expressed and his promise at least partly fulfilled.

For a desperate problem sometimes a desperate remedy must be found. To save the view that man's body is an undesirable part of him, one would have to deny that any body or bodily act could possibly be good. The good in man, we are then bound to say, dwells solely in his soul. But that denial cannot be maintained. If a body is in someone's way, it must be a good thing to take it away. Since a body is no hindrance once it is dead, we ought to be able to help a man by shortening his days. This we can do, not by retreating inside ourselves, but by using our body in gross bodily ways. Our body will then prove itself to be a good, if not to us, then to our fellows. Only because we have a body, can we perform the charitable act of helping our neighbors free themselves from the evils which their bodies entrain.

4. THE RATIONAL SOUL

The body is a necessary and desirable part of man. The power that is his cannot therefore be a soul which could be understood apart from a reference to the body. This requirement is satisfied if it be assumed that the soul and the body are correlatives which require one another in order to be at all, and which together constitute a man. This is the assumption of the Aristotelians. It has always had an appeal because it does full justice to the fact that man is a being who can both eat and think, run and introspect, build and speculate.

According to Aristotle, everything in nature is composed of two elements, the one matter, the other form. If a thing had no matter, it would be something general, not individual, and would be outside space and time, unable to change or move. If it had no form, it would be completely indefinite and unintelligible, a passive bit of stuff indistinguishable from any other. It is because each thing is both form and matter that it is at once definite in nature and indefinite in promise, permanent in essence and changing in existence, a member of a class and an occupant of space.

In nonliving things, according to Aristotle, the form is identical with the structure. In the case of living beings it is identical with the psyche or *anima*, that which animates it. In plants and animals, the form has no other function but to direct, structuralize and vitalize the matter. But in the case of man it has another function as well. Man, says Aristotle, has a reason. This reason neither is a body nor understands through the use of a bodily organ, for whereas the character of a body infects the character of the things known through its means, a reason grasps the nature of things as they are apart from one. For different eyes the world takes on different hues; for all minds, thinks Aristotle, it appears as it is in fact.

The Aristotelian soul vitalizes the body. Since that soul has the nonbodily power of understanding, a man as having such a soul is defined by Aristotle as a *rational* living being. Aristotle was not clear as to just how men could individually and as a class acquire that part of the soul which had no connection with the matter of the body. He seemed to deny that man's rational soul could originate from something lower or higher than man. Man for Aristotle just happens to have a rational soul and no further questions are asked or answered.

Thomas Aquinas, Aristotle's great Christian disciple, does explicitly ask the further question and tries valiantly to provide an answer. For him, as for Aristotle, the soul is a single indivisible form, and the reason is but one of its many powers. But Thomas Aquinas was acutely aware, as Aristotle apparently was not, that this means we must account for the whole soul in the same way that we account for its reasoning part. Now, for an Aristotelian, nothing on earth could be or could produce that which cannot alter. From this it follows that the incorruptibly rational part of the soul (and therefore the entire soul) is either an eternal or a created substance. The first alternative is unsatisfactory not only because it provides no reason why and no way in which the soul gets together with the body, but because an eternal soul is what it is independently of and without reference to a body. It is no more pertinent to one body than to another. Because each soul has an incorruptible reason and is therefore incorruptible, and because it is pertinent to one and only one body, it must, concludes Thomas Aquinas, be created for and divinely fused with that body. Accepting the Aristotelian view that a man is composed of a soul and a body, Thomas Aquinas thus goes beyond his master and, in full accord with Hebraic and Christian tradition, affirms that each human soul is a created thing, intimately connected with a human body by a divine and individual act.

The Thomistic theory, however, requires one to affirm that the soul is united with the body either at the instant of procreation or at some time after the embryo has been in existence. Aquinas adopts the latter view. But this means he must suppose that the embryo lives for a period as a kind of animal or subhuman. He must suppose too that it is killed or allowed to die at the end of the period, only to be immediately and divinely resurrected as a true human in miniature, with new powers expressive of its radically new nature. If Aquinas had taken the first alternative, he would have escaped this difficulty, but he would still have been faced with the embarrassment that, of all living things in nature, man alone would have been viewed as unable to reproduce without the help of God. On either alternative Aquinas is forced to say that though cats can produce cats, men and women are not able to produce beings which are truly human unless God has a hand in the proceedings. Were Aquinas right, men, as beings in nature, would be not superior but inferior to animals.

A recourse to God in philosophy is usually a way of multiplying embarrassments in the vain attempt to escape a self-created difficulty. Granted that God provides the "soul," the body in which the soul is inserted is one provided by the parents. God must then either divinely mold that soul in the light of the body it is to inhabit, or must allow it to acquire definiteness on being forced to live within that body. On either alternative, God would be responsible for the fact that one soul, through no fault of its own, occupied the body of a congenital idiot, while another, no more worthy, lived in the body of a normal, healthy human. Both alternatives suppose that God arbitrarily subjects different souls to different and unequal treatment—a conception unworthy of being associated with that of a good and just God. We make a mockery of divinity by speaking of God as creating pure souls and then compelling or allowing them to be perverted by bodies they did nothing to deserve.

Perhaps it would be better to say, following the lead of Origen, Augustine and Calvin, that the souls of men have different moral weights from the start, that they are not all equally pure and innocent but defective in various degrees? In this way one would overcome the embarrassment of supposing that a God traps what is pure inside bodies which are in various stages of corruption. But one would continue to be faced with the difficulty that the supposed creating God would still have to be described as ignorant or evil. A God who, instead of creating clean and decent souls, starts them off as perverted or doomed, is one who is either poor in spirit or awkward in performance, and thus far from the rank of a perfect being.

5. THE HUMAN CONSTANT

A man is not a body. He has a body, and that body is necessary and desirable. This conclusion is so obvious and inevitable that it would be hard to find anyone who consistently and explicitly denies it. Even those who underscore other interpretations of the nature of man, constantly shift their emphases and assert this last as well. There are passages in the writings of Plato, Aristotle and Thomas Aquinas which can mean nothing else, and one would be well within the main stream of traditional interpretations of these men to assert that they intended no other point than this,

. In the *Timaeus*, 70E, Plato remarks that "the part of the soul which desires meat and drink and other things of which it has need by reason of the bodily nature, is bound down like a wild animal which was chained up with man and must be nourished if man is to exist." "We can wholly dismiss as unnecessary," says Aristotle in the *De Anima*, 412b 6-9, 413a 4, "the question whether the soul and the body are one: it is as meaningless to ask whether the wax and the shape given to it by the stamp are one, or generally the matter of a being and that of which it is the matter. Unity has many senses, but the most proper and fundamental is the relation of an actuality to that of which it is the actuality. . . . The soul is inseparable from its body." "The soul," says Thomas Aquinas in Question 89, Article 1, of Part I of his *Summa Theologica*, "has one mode of being when in the body and another when apart from it, its nature always remaining the same; but this does not mean that its union with the body is an accidental thing, for on the contrary, such union belongs to its very nature." These three writers agree in holding that man is neither a soul nor a body. They are not clear as to whether a man results from the union of these two, or whether or not these two are aspects of a more basic and original unity, which is man. And one looks to them in vain for a statement of how a man could have an animal ancestry and an animal-like body, and yet be a single being possessed of powers and abilities no animal could possibly have. So far as subsequent thinkers have been content to follow the lead of these three philosophers they have inevitably defined themselves as unable or unwilling to provide the requisite information.

The problem of the nature of man is one of our most neglected problems. One clue is to be found in the fact that he is, in some sense, the self-same being from birth to death. He is not, of course, self-identical as a body. He grows vertically and horizontally in the course of his career. As an adult his appearance often differs so greatly from the appearance he presented as a child that it would be hazardous to assert that anyone could see a similarity. Even more important is the physiologically substantiated fact that his body contains hardly any of the cells that were present a dozen years or so before. So far as size, shape, skill, strength and appearance are concerned, a man becomes considerably transformed over the years, while so far as the constituent cells of his body are in question, he is almost entirely changed. Yet there is a deep and undeniable sense in which it is the same man who is adult and who was embryo or child. Unless a man is to be designated as a new being every time he loses or adds a cell, changes in strength, skill or appearance, it is necessary to affirm that there is something in him which is of his essence and which remains constant throughout his days. Despite the fact that he changes, he remains self-same, a being with a single essence and career.

Kant thinks it is possible to deny that a man is one being from birth to death. "If," he says in his *Critique of Pure Reason*, A364n, "we postulate substances such that the one communicates to the other representations together with the consciousness of them, we can conceive a whole series of substances of which the first transmits its state, together with it consciousness, to the second, the second its own state with that of the preceding substance to the third, and this in turn the states of all preceding substances, together with its own consciousness and with their consciousness, to one another. The last substance would then be conscious of all the states of the previously changed substances, as being its own states, because they would have been transferred to it together with the consciousness of them. And yet it would not have been one and the same person in all these states."

In this way it might, to be sure, be possible to explain how one might *suppose* a man was self-same for a time, and perhaps even to explain how he could remember. But one would not be able to explain how a man could be responsible or how he could change. On Kant's view, a man is a new substance at each moment.

There are men; the men change. But to be that which changes, a man must also be that which is constant. Otherwise what was before and what was later would not characterize *him*. But if he is constant he cannot be a new substance at each moment.

We know it is ourselves who change. That is why we know it is ourselves who are constant. And because we know that we are constant, we know it is ourselves who change. Because we know we are constant and because we know we change, we know we are neither momentary nor nontemporal substances.

A man is guilty of a crime he committed a year ago. His guilt is not decreased but in fact increased if he changes his face and fingerprints in the meantime. He is guilty all the while, and this whether or not he is conscious of the fact. We want him to be conscious of his guilt before we punish him so that the full meaning of the punishment will be clear. We await his awakening, not his recovery of identity. He does not lose his identity by forgetting who he is; he does not become a renewed man by remembering who he was. He is self-same all the while, in sleep and waking, but the latter alone is the appropriate time to let him know the nature of the crimes he committed. If he changes his face and fingerprints he is different in appearance from what he was. But throughout he is the self-same being. The differences characterize him; they are changes *of* him, not changes *to* and *from* or *in* him.

A man has a single, constant essence. It is tempting to suppose that this essence is the life which quickens his body. The embryo does not have a life which passes away as soon as the embryo assumes the shape of a child. The child does not die in order to become a youth. It is the same life which vitalizes the embryo and the developed body. Only one life is allotted to a man. That life relates, permeates and vitalizes every part of the body; it is sensitive to the adventures these parts undergo. One life suffuses the whole and suffuses it from birth to death.

The life of a being, however, varies in intensity, force, mode of expression and bent from the beginning to the end of his days. The vitality of an embryo is different in nature and stress from that of a man. The life in the body is a continuous rather than a constant thing. There is more to a man, too, than the life that happens to be exhibited in his body. He is equally himself when he is passive as when he is active, when asleep as when awake, though the degree of life exhibited in the body varies considerably at these different times. Only part of him is immersed in the form of a life in the body, and this seems to ebb and flow in the course of the day. A part of man's nature might be said to be expressed as the life of his body but there must be a part existing outside his bodily frame.

The life that is immersed in the body is a persistent but flickering flame. A man cannot be identified with it, for he remains self-same even while it fluctuates. Nor can he be identified with that life as together with the body which it quickens, for two changing things do not add to a constant unless their variations balance one another. The body and the life within it vary in the same direction, and to somewhat the same degree. The life in the body, no less than the body, is something which a man has rather than is.

All changes presuppose something constant. Either, then, men are but passing shadows across the face of some more constant thing, or there is within them a constant factor which is expressed as a fluctuating life in a changing body. But men act on their own and are self-same throughout their careers. There must be something in them which is neither body, the life which animates it, nor the changing composite of the two. We must look elsewhere for the secret of man's identity.

Were men merely unified bodies, everything they did would be a function of those bodies. Yet all seem to have a reason of their own. Though that reason expresses, responds and reports the things the body does and undergoes, it frequently concerns itself with other things as well. While the body feeds and grows, it thinks of mathematical truths or the scent of the rose. Though it does not operate until the brain is developed, and though it often reflects the state of the glands and the general health of the body, it is often vigorous though the body is weak, and feeble though the body is strong. The greatest intellects do not necessarily have the largest or most convoluted brains, the best physiques or the most stable and perfect bodily health.

One could then make out a strong case for the identification of oneself with one's reason. Despite the fact that the body constantly changes in shape, size and accomplishment, the reason seems to have a rather constant cast. Men seem to retain the same mental qualities and intellectual bents throughout their lives. No matter how they vary the nature of their bodies they do not seem to be able to change themselves from engineers into poets, or from poets into mathematicians. The body also distorts and limits their intentions, but the reason seems to allow them full play.

Yet the reason cannot be what we seek. The reason is a late achievement, not present in the embryo. It has a different cargo and a different destination at different times. The statement that a man is a rational being expresses the character of a hope rather than the nature of a fact, unless experience deceives us most grievously.

Nor is it the memory, as Locke suggests, which is at the end of our search. The memory splits into multiple unrelated fragments as one develops, embraces only part of what one is, does not encompass the present moment, and has little, if any, existence at the moment of birth. But what is constant in man is unitary and all-embracing, exists at the very beginning of his life, and encompasses the present moment.

The human constant might more reasonably be identified with the will than with the memory or the reason. One can will to act, to think or to remember, and so far as this is true the will must be more fundamental than these others. The will, too, seems to remain constant for quite a while. Future deliberations run along the same course as past ones, and men hold themselves responsible for those past promises and acts they willingly performed. Yet despite all this, the will cannot be that of which we are in search. The will waxes and wanes in strength and direction from time to time. It is not a constant. It is not possessed by all human beings, nor by any all the time. Infants and those asleep and unconscious seem to be without a will of any kind. A will exists only when one is willing; the rest of the time it disappears into the recesses of one's being, appearing once again with somewhat the same, though not necessarily the identical, bent it had before.

The constant factor characteristic of a man lies beneath his life, memory, mind and will. It is not the whole of him, for the life and the body, the memory, mind and will are part of him as well. Nor is it separated off from these, for he is one being and not many. A man is both a constant and a changing being. He can be both and still be a unity because his changes are determinations, because they are the possessions of a single undetermined factor which is unchanged throughout his days. That constant, undetermined unit is his *self*.

To know oneself it is necessary to know something of one's self. That self is what a psyche becomes when it is concerned with realizing not only its own good or that of its kind but also a good pertinent to others. Baby or idiot, immature or ill, a human, by virtue of his self, is concerned with some goods that do good neither to him nor even to mankind. This of course must be shown, but for the time being it will perhaps suffice to remark that the self is partly expressed from the very beginning as a life in the body and soon becomes expressed as well in the form of a will and a mind, to make man an embodied self which may eventually will and think.

The self is a constant, enabling a man to be self-same throughout his career. But because that self, from the very beginning, is expressed in and through his body, a man can change in acts, structure and powers in the course of time.

6. THE ORIGIN OF MAN

A man differs from an animal in the range and character of his sensitivity, the kind of body he has, the techniques with which that body is charged, and in the kind of freedom he can utilize in order to bring his concern and body together in perception, emotion and willing. All these differences are consequences of the fact that he has a self, partly unexpressed and partly expressed in his body. But, though different in kind from an animal, a man has an animal origin and comes to be in the natural course of generation.

An animal has an animal body; a human, a human one. The difference is not one in degree of complexity, for the body of an ape seems to be about as complex as that of a man. Nor it is one in degree of specialization. There are parts of an ape's body that are more specialized, others that are less specialized than ours. The tongue of an ape can do less, the foot can do more, than the tongue and foot of a man. The difference between the body of a man and the body of a higher animal is a result of the fact that each quickens its body by a different type of concern, the one originating from a self, the other from a psyche. That is why men can do things with their bodies that animals cannot, and conversely.

The animal's body is receptive to the animal's concern, allowing and even tempting it to spend itself entirely as a bodily power. The concern of a man, on the other hand, though it infects every part of his body, is never adequately expressed in that body. Only through the exercise of considerable art and with great effort can a man succeed in living in and through his body in the way an animal can. He is, like an animal, helpless as an embryo; but, unlike many animals, he is helpless also as an infant. He must be habituated and trained over the years before he can act with the same dexterity a quite young animal can.

It does not take a tiger long to walk and eat, to growl and leap with the natural grace that marks a tigerish body properly suffused with tigerish sensitivity. A fish takes even less time, the amoeba no time at all, to reach the stage where it expresses almost its entire sensitivity in and through its body. But it is a rare man whose body ever becomes fully vitalized. When he succeeds in making it as alive as an animal's, he succeeds only by bringing part of his concern into play gradually and over a longish period of time, and against the opposition of his body. But though a man does not express his concern in and through the body as adequately as does an animal, he is superior to an animal, as is evident from the fact that he can use that concern to enable him to think and will. His partial expression of his concern in and through his body is a consequence of the fact that the object of his concern is too rich for that body, requiring for its expression the use of at least a mind and a will.

How did man acquire his characteristic concern which he maintains and uses even though he cannot exhibit it fully in and through his body? The question is a double one, asking firstly how did man first arise, and secondly how did each individual come to be. The answers to both parts of this question are similar. Unless men were nothing more than animals and evolution a myth, the bodies of the first human embryos must have resisted their concerns in ways which the bodies of previous embryos did not. The resistance of those bodies forced those concerns to change in nature and object, thereby enabling the concerns to be more adequately expressed in and through the bodies than they could have been expressed before. Those embryos matured as previous embryos could not. They built bodies and acted on the world in new ways, making use of new concerns directed towards new objects.

The first human embryos must have dwelt within the bodies of animals. But otherwise their history must have been analogous to the history of any embryo today. Each human embryo today, though living inside a human body, takes its rise (as the first human embryos obviously did) from living cells which are not human.

Each human embryo starts as a nonhuman being, whether its parents are human or not. And whether or not the body in which that embryo dwells is human or animal, some time between conception and birth that nonhuman being gives way to a human one. Quite a while in fact before it is born it is fully human, unique, free, with its own self, rhythm and career.

The cells from which the human embryo originates were once parts of living bodies. Like other parts of living bodies those cells were, strictly speaking, not alive then. Rather they were enlivened. Bodily cells take in food, grow and develop, not of themselves but by means of the power of the body in which they dwell and ultimately through the agency of the concern which quickens that body. This is true of the reproductive cells and their parts no less than it is of other cells and their parts. None of them merely resides in a body. They are not little packets of life, stowed away in the body from the embryo on. As parts of the body they are subordinate beings, sharing the body's adventures and trials, interplaying with one another, reflecting the presence of drugs, and showing the effects of organic disturbance and shock.

Each cell has however a structure and a unity of its own. It acts not solely as the body dictates, but also in conformity with its own design. But while it is part of the body it can function only as sustained by the life which the individual provides. It is an enlivened part resisting the life of the whole in a characteristic way. To become a living thing, the cell must be separated from the body, and then freely exercise a power of its own.

Cells, which can be separated off in the course of a normal activity and which when separate make possible the rise of an independent living growing being, are properly termed "reproductive cells." They differ from other cells in the ease with which they are separated and in their ability to attain the status of actual independent living individuals. Theoretically it should be possible to separate any cell from the body and start it off on an independent career. But only the reproductive cells can initiate a state of affairs which will eventually result in a being with a body as complex and mature as those of its parents.

Separated reproductive cells look and act somewhat as they did before. But they are radically different. The act of separation provides them with true boundaries, enabling them for the first time to have careers of their own. Where before they were dependent components, now they are distinct beings, individuals in their own right. And only as separated do they deserve to be termed living sperm and egg.

Both sperm and egg, on being separated from the body, become independent living beings. Since they are cells which have none of the powers or characteristics of a human being, they are evidently not human. They are, of course, not animal, lacking animal traits and powers as well as human ones. Sperm and egg, whether animal or human, seem more like plants than like the animal or human beings which will issue from them. The conversion of them into true embryos is one of the greatest of mysteries. Little has been done to dispel it. Perhaps we ought to be content for the moment if we can find an explanation which conforms to all the facts known and coheres with the account that must be provided of the coming to be of any new being or power.

Complex living beings arise as a result of the union of a sperm and egg. Such a union is not, however, necessary. Loeb produced frogs through the mechanical stimulation of their eggs, and more recently Pincus produced rabbits in a somewhat similar way. It is reasonable to suppose that it is likewise possible to produce a human as the outcome of the stimulation of a human egg, and it is conceivable that a similar result might be obtained by stimulating the sperm instead. But the normal, more interesting case is one in which sperm and egg combine.

Sperm and egg are living beings. Should they combine, they give rise to a single complex cell. In that act they cease to be individuals, achieving the status of undivided parts of the complex cell they make possible.

The sperm and egg are quickened by sensitive concerns. The complex cell which results from their union is quickened by a power which bears the marks of both. The being that eventually comes to be, has something of the flavor as well as something of the physical properties of both parents, because the new sensitivity and new cell depend for their being on concerned cells provided by those parents.

The sperm and egg contribute part of their vitality to constitute a new cellular sensitivity; they use the remainder to constitute the characteristic resistance of the new cellular body. The new cellular body thus has a nature of its own, resisting the sensitivity which is characteristic of the new cell.

The human embryo begins its career in a state analogous to that of a low-grade living being. It is sensitive but unconscious, freely responding to stimuli in a purposive way. As it grows its body resists the sensitivity more and more. The embryo is thereby subjected to tensions which allow it to become conscious of pains and pleasures. At the moment it becomes conscious, it becomes a new type of being, a being with a psyche. It is then analogous to a higher living being. It is then a being that can bring its sensitive concern to bear on its body, thereby enabling it to feed and perceive. But this body that it has grows at such a pace that almost at once the embryo finds it impossible to exercise these functions. It is forced to change its concern, and therefore its nature, once again.

It is then that it achieves a self. It is then that it, despite its body, is able not only to feed and perceive but to control and use its body for nonbodily ends.

A self—and thus a human being—arises when an embryo, because of the resistance of its body to a sensitive concern, freely changes that concern into one which can be expressed in and through that body. The change is from a concern directed to the good of the individual or its kind to a concern directed to a good pertinent to other beings as well. It is a change from a concern characteristic of a psyche with its limited animal-like sensitivity to a concern characteristic of a self, sensitive in a new and broader way. It is a change from a being which can act sensibly into one which can act ethically, from a being which utilizes a living body so as to promote the welfare of itself or its kind, into a being which can utilize a living body so as to promote what ought to be realized on behalf of whatever may exist.

Man's first and perhaps greatest task is that of mastering his body. In this activity he parallels the activity of other living beings, differing from them primarily in the kind of concern he utilizes, in the difficulties he experiences in subjugating his body, in his ability to make deliberate use of that body, and in the extent and number of bodily techniques and habits that he acquires.

The discussion of human techniques and habits is the primary concern of the next three chapters. So far as such techniques and habits involve no supervision by mind, they are for the most part analogous to those characteristic of animals. Accordingly, a good deal of what follows in the next chapters can profitably be applied to what has gone before, thereby enabling one to complete the previous account of subhuman beings. From now on, however, our concern is with man, and the discussion that follows is important primarily for whatever light it throws on his nature and capacities.

CHAPTER EIGHT

TECHNIQUES AND HABITS

1. THE UNITY OF THE EMBRYO

THE EMBRYO begins as a single being feeding on the food its mother provides. Almost at once it becomes too large and inefficient for its own good. It must, therefore, immediately change its tactics and mode of life or be prepared to die. These alternatives all growing beings face from time to time. The lowest organisms meet the issue by subdividing into a number of similar independent cells, each with a life of its own. The animal and human embryos meet it by subdividing into a number of different kinds of dependent subordinate cells. Most of these new cells must forever cling to and remain under the embryo's sway if they are to continue and prosper; only a few of them, the "reproductive," are eventually able to exist and develop alone.

To escape death the lower organisms multiply, give way to a multiplicity of independent beings. The animal and human embryos escape by changing their structures, turning their bodies into complex unities of multiple dependent cells, with restricted powers and modes of activity, under the single control of a psyche or self. Because the parts of the body can act effectively somewhat independently of the body as a whole, the embryo no longer need directly supervise every act. The quickened parts can be allowed to perform routine tasks as though they had a life of their own. By producing specialized cells, capable of independent activity to some degree, the embryo is able to conserve its energies and devote itself to other tasks. Since its cells remain within its control, their increase in number and kind makes possible an increase in both the variety of possible bodily activities and the lines of possible growth. The embryo is a living being which develops in bodily function and dexterity as it grows.

The initial specialized parts which the embryo produces soon grow so large that they must subdivide. Like the body as a whole, they organically unite different subordinates. They become organic unities which are or will grow to be the organs of heart and lung, head, leg and hand, all subject to a single power and yet capable of many acts of their own. From embryo on, the living being is thus a unity of organs rather than of cells. It rules not like a monarch directly controlling the affairs of different cells, but more like an overlord who has allocated his power to men of lower caste and depends on their allegiance and delegated rule to prosper and to grow.

2. THE ORGANS

There is no sharp boundary separating one organ from another, or from the living body, the organism, as a whole. To extract an organ from the body is to do violence to both, creating definite boundaries and new conditions, sometimes with disastrous effects on both. A radical enough division spells death to the organism and all that is within. When a pig is quartered one doesn't get four little pigs, but pork, and ham, and glue.

Sometimes an organ can be cut away without the organism being thereby destroyed. If a leg is cut off, it is deprived of all vitality, but the organism need not die. And sometimes an organ can be isolated in such a way that it is the organism and not the organ which is killed. Recent experimenters have been able to extract a living heart and keep it beating within a glass jar. It would be easy but wrong to conclude that all they did was to change the location of the heart from the body to the jar. Were that true, the heart within the body would not be an organ of the body but a separate living thing, beating freely and irresponsibly no matter what the organism required and the psyche or self desired. The heart within the body, however, varies its acts in accordance with the requirements of the leg, the lungs and the liver, is kept alive by the organism as a whole, and can occasionally be deliberately controlled. The act of isolating the heart is an act of remaking it in part, of providing it with powers and functions it did not have before—and of depriving it of others. The extracted heart beats somewhat the same way as the heart within the body does because its structure is roughly the same. But, unlike the latter, it is a genuine, independent living being, newly produced and formed.

The heart is a vital organ, whose acts and products are essential to the continuance and functioning of other organs. But it cannot act alone. It must be fed by other vital organs and these must be fed by it in turn. The heart, the liver, the stomach and the kidneys work together. They form a kind of unity in which each provides material needed by the others. They function without supervision and make possible the use of such auxiliary organs as hand, foot, eye, ear, nose and tongue.

Neither separately nor together are the vital organs the source of life or the sole avenue through which it flows. If they were, the hands and feet would depend for their vitality exclusively on them, and there would be no psyche or self which corrected the tendencies of the body by increasing or decreasing the body's sensitivity. A living being is a single being whose psyche or self quickens and sustains every organ of the body, vital and auxiliary, though these have their own characteristic powers enabling them to do much by themselves. Each organ is an instrument for all the others, an agency for obtaining and transforming material by means of the vitality they ultimately receive from the psyche or self. Yet, throughout its career, each organ remains a dependent thing, no matter how freely and automatically it behaves.

Most of the organs can be utilized in more than one way. Hands can be used to grip and to push, the throat can serve to swallow and to cough; a man uses his tongue to taste and to talk, his nose to breathe and to smell. If each mode of activity required the use of a different organ, a man would have to be much more cumbersome than he now is, or he would have to give up doing some of the things of which he is now capable. He would require at least a score of hands if he needed one with which to grasp, another with which to lift, a third with which to push, a fourth with which to twist, etc. Because he has only two, capable of doing many different things, he is much more compact and flexible than he otherwise would be.

It is unfortunate that man is not even more compact and flexible. It would be to his advantage if he could use his flesh to enable him to see as well as to feel, or if he could taste with his teeth as well as bite. The converse is also true. Some of his organs have too many tasks to perform. Some of their functions could, with profit, be assumed by new organs. If, for example, he could acquire an organ whose exclusive function it was to smell, and another whose exclusive function it was to taste, the common cold would not prove such an inconvenience.

A man can profitably be renovated in many ways. It would be desirable if he had more organs and if some of his present organs had more functions—providing that he did not thereby become too cumbersome and could engage in the old tasks with as much despatch as before. We know that he is now organically superior in some respects to other beings because, without having become proportionately more cumbersome, he has organs, such as hands, which they do not have, and because, without becoming proportionately more inefficient, he can use organs, such as the tongue, which they also have, in ways they cannot. To the degree that it is evident that the distance between man and other beings can be considerably increased by similar improvements, to that degree it is evident that man is neither the offspring of a good and powerful God nor the highest possible product of an evolutionary movement. Man, though organically superior in some ways to others, is much less than he might be.

It will never be to man's advantage to have each organ so specialized that it can do one and only one thing. Such specialization would demand that he do but few of the things of which he is now capable, or that he be so stuffed and decorated with organs as to make it very difficult for him to move quickly out of harm's way.

A man must use some of his organs in multiple ways. This multiple use of organs, this capacity of organs to perform many functions is an advantage. It enables a man to remain compact and yet engage in many tasks. The advantage, however, entrains a double danger. If an organ has many functions, then an injury to or a loss of it will handicap its possessor in ways in which the injury or loss of a more specialized organ would not. If the tongue is injured, it is difficult to drink, eat, speak and taste. The more functions an organ performs, the more serious is its injury or loss.

The second danger is more constant though not as serious in its results. The different functions of an organ are not, as a rule, compatible. A man cannot at once drink and speak, since he has only one throat and cannot make it simultaneously swallow and expel. If the competing tendencies are of equal strength they will get in one another's way, preventing the significant use of the required organ. If they differ in strength the stronger is bound to have its way, and the weaker will fail to achieve adequate expression.

The tendency to drink and to speak compete for the use of the throat. If they had equal strength a man would neither speak nor drink, but would splutter instead. This, fortunately, is a rare occurrence. Due to the constitution of the mind and the body, the drag of fatigue, the lure of novelty and the circumstances in which a man is placed, the different tendencies have different strengths at different times, inclining him to respond now in one way and then in another. Because tendencies usually differ in strength, a man is able to express himself without much difficulty through a given organ at almost any time. And since the strength of different tendencies varies from time to time, he is usually able to express himself in multiple ways through the same organ.

Each organ has its own work to perform. Each is composed of different kinds of cells, having characteristic functions. Sometimes the cells of one organ can be transferred to another. They then usually take on the functions which are characteristic of the cells into which they are introduced. The constitution of a cell depends on the organ of which it is a part, just as the nature of the organ depends in part on the nature of the organism in which it dwells.

When an organ is transferred from one being to another it is subjected to a new economy and conditioned in a new way. There is no hope for schemes of rejuvenation, therefore, which concern themselves with the transfer of a gland or two. Old age infects the entire body and soon exacts its toll from whatever we may introduce. Every new cell would have to find its place within the old body and adjust itself to a rhythm well worn before it could get to work at all. But even if the entire body were replaced by one fresh and new, the life which animated the whole would still be old and frayed, infected by memories, emotions, moods and thoughts which would soon age and corrupt the body to bring it to the level of the one that was there before. Every cell and organ is conditioned by others with which it is joined, and by the psyche or self which vitalizes them all, as the inevitable consequence of the fact that a living being is first and last a single being and not a multiplicity.

It is possible, of course, to do things to the cells which radically affect the character and functions of the organs and the organism as well. A slight change in the constitution of certain cells can make all the difference between health and sickness, sanity and insanity, a giant and a dwarf. The good or ill health of the parts is the source of the good and ill health of the whole. But a man well or ill is in principle and source the same man still. The self he exhibits when he is in good health can be discerned in the life he leads when he is unwell. When sick his symptoms may be like those of others, yet he is sick in his own way, cheerful where another is despairing, yielding where another is not, producing a different total effect with a flavor of its own.

Each vital organ has a typical location, structure and appearance. These can be considerably modified without injury to themselves or to the whole. There are healthy men whose liver, kidneys and lungs have not the color or consistency that doctors cherish, whose hearts are on their right sides, or whose stomachs are misshapen and upside down. It would be unwise to try to change these merely because they do not conform to a norm. The norm is a rough guide, not an absolute standard. It provides no inviolable rule. It tells us the way things have been accustomed to appear and not the way they ought to be. There is no condition one has a right to impose on any organ except that it should function efficiently as part of an organic whole.

Each organ specializes and canalizes the energy it obtains directly from the organism and indirectly from the psyche or self. It works together with other organs, offering its products to them in return for theirs. Each is interlocked with every other. No one of them can assume the role of being the indispensable agent for the conversion of material for the benefit of the rest. Each is fed by the others and feeds them in turn. A leaky heart takes its toll on the lungs, infected lungs play havoc with the heart. A cure or correction of one will benefit them all, offering them material in larger quantities or in a more palatable form. One may, however, over-correct, make an organ better than it should be in the context of the rest. The life span of an athlete may be shortened if, having enlarged his heart through exercise, he fails to make adequate provision for the use of all its products or for the continued satisfaction of its increased needs. To live long and well one must provide for the expansion and contraction of all the vital organs together, and then adjust them to the needs and uses of those which have only an auxiliary function.

3. REFLEXES, INSTINCTS AND HABITS

Each organ takes time to develop and is exercised as it grows. Part of the energy it receives it uses to increase its substance, the rest it uses in order to make and transmit material others need. The constant passage through it of borrowed and transmitted energy wears down a channel in its being, a habit of activity which becomes more and more entrenched as time goes on.

There is no power in the organism designed to beat a heart, and in existence before the heart itself; there is no power to secrete bile before the liver has been formed. Nor is the energy which these organs use, specialized and prepared within their embryonic forms, biding its time until it can appear in organs full grown. A full-grown organ has a power and mode of acting not possible to its embryonic form; it is fed by other mature organs and is exercised along paths just recently formed. Nor, finally, can an organ be made to grow, unexercised and unused, and then suddenly be put to work. Everything it does is the product of the interplay of many factors, and their interrelation is only gradually and slowly learnt. A leaky heart has one way of pumping blood through the body, an enlarged heart another. If a heart could be grown full-sized but unexercised, it would somehow have to build up the kind of habit which ordinary hearts develop as they grow.

The beating of the heart is an acquired, not an innate mode of activity. Within the limits provided by the structure of the heart and the rest of the body, the tempo and form of the heart's activities can be considerably and, occasionally, permanently changed. Because its activities run along habitual routes, it can function steadily and without deliberate supervision. But for the same reason, its customary acts can sometimes, as medical histories and quite a few Orientals demonstrate, be restrained and even subjected to unusual transformations. Hearts have been forced to skip beats, to change their rhythms and to follow new patterns of behavior. The way the heart normally beats is only the way it has been accustomed to beat, not the way it must or always will.

The embryo prospers because it refuses to remain unspecialized and monotonous, because it is willing to lend but unwilling to divide the life it has. By the time it is ready to enter our world, almost all its organs are developed and attuned. There is then little more for it to do for its body beyond exercising the different organs in new situations and adjusting them to one another in different ways. The hardest and most indispensable part of its education is already far behind.

The infant's body is neither new nor untried. The infant was first an embryo, spending part of its energy in vitalizing and in endeavoring to control the embryonic body, and in habituating the embryonic organs. The heart, liver, lungs, and brain, all the nerves and tissues of the infant were in existence some time before, constantly exercised in embryonic ways. The new-born infant is an old campaigner on quite familiar terrain.

The glory the infant trails behind it is a set of organic habits, well-learned and well-grooved. These habits are ingredient within its organs, carried over from embryo. Formed unconsciously and involuntarily as a result of the repetition of acts on the part of definitely structured organs, they provide the indispensable foundation for everything the individual can bodily do. All bodily acts, no matter how new, depend on the continued functioning of the vital organs; they bring some accustomed muscles into play. Throughout one's life, even while striking out in new directions or while engaged in the performance of genuinely novel tasks, one makes and must make use of routes formed and partly fixed in embryo.

By being precipitated into daylight, the infant is forced to take account of a new environment, much more complex and unpredictable than that it was accustomed to face. The embryo was protected and cushioned. It had no occasion to listen, to sneeze, to blink or to suck. It had no opportunity to develop habits for the control of its ears, nose, eyes or mouth. Yet the infant begins and must begin almost at once to use these organs with surety and despatch. It blinks its eyes without antecedent practice, yet perfectly well and at once in reaction to something approaching close. It would seem from this that a tendency to blink the eye lay dormant within the embryo, poised and ready, awaiting merely an appropriate occasion to move the eyelid. One who adopted that assumption could, however, with the same justification, claim that the single-celled embryo has already within it firm and inescapable tendencies to mate and to jump out of the way of approaching automobiles, but that it awaits a score of years or so in order to express these tendencies with most effect.

The fact that an act is well performed on its first occasion is no warrant for the supposition that there is an innate and definite tendency to do it, which comes into the open at an appropriate time. Nor is there warrant for the supposition that such acts are merely mechanical, automatically performed by isolated parts in blind reaction to definite irritations. Though acts, well-performed from the first, may occur without thought or desire and sometimes without much effect on other bodily activities, they nevertheless depend on the continued functioning of other organs, vary in performance though the stimuli remain the same, and can sometimes be deliberately controlled. We are able to blink, sneeze and suck voluntarily as well as involuntarily, and can change the way in which these acts are performed. Blinking, sneezing and sucking are like other habitual acts. They have a similar origin, function and result. They are the outcome of a sudden and stable union of new movements and old habits, forged into unity under the provocation of the world about.

New circumstances require an organism to acts in new ways. When its acts are built directly on the habits it learned as an embryo, when they occur early in life, function only in response to stimulation independently of the requirements of the organism as a whole, and are performed from the first with considerable success, psychologists describe the being as in the grip of a "reflex." When its acts implicate the entire body and operate in greater independence of the kind of stimulation provided, they say that it is acting by "instinct" instead.

Both "reflexes" and "instinct" are habits, differing from other habits in being more useful to the organism or its kind, and in the frequency and ease with which they are exhibited. They are not always more insistent than other habits. It is possible, in fact, to forge habits in an instant which are much more insistent than those normally acknowledged to be reflexes or instincts. Thus, a shocking experience can suddenly and rather permanently solidify the habit of listening and the habit of jumping into a new habit so insistent that one is ready to jump with terror at the slightest sound. The "instincts" of loving one's parents or preserving one's life are not more insistent, are not less readily dislodged, are not more effectively carried through on their first appearance. If we are to use the term "instinct" significantly, we must take it to refer to the solidification of embryonic habits as a consequence of shocks suffered by a helpless infant. It should not require one to refer to a supposed wisdom located in the muscles or tendons, or to some supposed ineradicable innate and perfect way of acting.

Despite the rarity of its occurrence and the fact that it is usually suppressed or conquered, the habit of jumping with terror at sounds is one which could be made more common and could become more deeply entrenched than almost any practice men have been accustomed to salute as a "reflex" or "instinct." Even such indispensable activities as respiration and digestion can be accentuated and depressed more readily than those inspired by a gripping fear. Such so-called instincts as fighting or acquiring, despite their actual frequency of occurrence, could not be exhibited in as many men as could those acts which owe their rise to a sudden fearful shock. Many individuals never acquire an adequate channel or occasion for the expression of an "instinct" to fight, or for the expression of an "instinct" for the accumulation of goods; those who pursue these activities have had to wait long periods before they had a chance to engage in them.

If it is desired to distinguish the so-called instinct or reflexes from other habits, one must take account of the paths through which they run, the kind of prior habits of which they make use and the kinds of occasions necessary to produce and provoke them. Later habits are built on earlier ones, themselves learnt and not native. All depend for their possibility, rhythm and direction on the structure of that through which they move. They all come into play under the pressure of circumstance. A shock is necessary in order to root the practice of jumping at sounds firmly within one's being. Only a slight disturbance is necessary in order to have the knee jerk, the saliva run, or an act of self-protection begin. But to produce and stabilize such techniques as smoking or swimming immediately and forever, we apparently need a shock beyond our capacity to withstand.

Behind theories of instinct and reflex there is a hidden and arbitrary supposition that what a man does after a slight disturbance is a necessary expression of an irresistible tendency to act is just that way. What such activity reveals is rather how flexible a man is and how susceptible he is to his environment. It tells nothing about his essence, his obligations, his needs or his desires. A change in the environment will lead him to act differently; a change in his control will force other tendencies into ascendancy. Yet men have sometimes justified the sending of others to death in terms of an "instinct to fight," have sanction the ownership of surplus goods by an "instinct to acquire," and have explained away acts of cowardice as the irresistible product of an "instinct for self-preservation." The followers of Tolstoy know nothing of an instinct to fight, the poor rarely exercise an instinct to acquire, and heroes and martyrs easily conquer an "instinct" to look to themselves. A reference to reflexes or instincts hinders rather than helps us to find out what a man will, must or ought to do.

Habits are acquired as a result of action; this in turn is the result of an attempt to realize an object of concern. The nature of habits is determined in part by the structure of the body, for the body provides a limited number of channels through which the concern can be expressed. The nature of habits is determined in part also by the intent of the individual for he encourages the expression of some tendencies and the repression of others.

Habits are constantly being altered. Men are constantly making and remaking themselves, constantly being made and remade. A good job demands a good preparation in the form of embryonic and infantile habits, and appropriate occasions for combining and organizing them. With the surgeon's knife we can reach many of the habits built up as embryo. By changing a man's environment he can be led to bend his acquired inclinations in other directions. But throughout he retains some control.

A man's habits can be changed and united deliberately. To the extent he can deliberately change his habits, the man is the ruler of his destiny. His habits can also be changed and combined by modifying the structure of the body and the environment, and by varying the conditions which stimulate activity. Because a man is overrun with habits he can be guided down a number of specifiable paths. Because his habits can be controlled from within and are in part formed under the pressure of the environment without, each man is at once the master of his fate and a creature of circumstance.

Involuntary patterns of behavior are acquired in somewhat the same way as are fears, techniques and virtues. It is man's good fortune that some of these habits can, without serious disturbance to his equilibrium, be learned at once and permanently retained. It is his misfortune that some of them take years to acquire and readily slip from him with disuse. It is good that he so quickly and easily learns to blink an eye; it is sad that he learns so poorly and so late how to think or to be kind. But the secret of his promise lies in the fact that all of them are habits and are thus capable of being modified, coordinated and controlled.

4. THE ORGANIC UNITY OF HABITS

Conditions infect the nature of that which they condition. To provide a road along which one can travel is also to tempt one to travel and to incline one to do it in one way rather than another. City plans for relieving congestion have sometimes failed because they not only promoted further traveling but made it assume forms which had not been anticipated.

The ways in which men eat, love, fight, or acquire depend upon the fields in which they are active. Since the nature of a stimulus is defined by the response it calls forth, the ways in which men eat, love, fight and acquire define the stimulating value of the objects with which they deal. Neither the misogynist nor the child has a tendency to love in adult ways. The misogynist does not have the power to reply in such a way as to make another lovable; the child does not have the body or mind to permit it to love in all the ways an adult can.

A habit does not operate in isolation. A habit of eating, for example, works together with the habits of looking, reaching, conveying, tasting and chewing, attaining prominence usually only after these have almost come to rest. The manner in which the being organizes these multiple habits determines the import which its objects have for it. Food functions as a stimulus for it because other habits, under the pressure of hunger, have been made more difficult of access, and the habit of eating forced into focus. The frame in which something is done helps define the nature of what is done.

The things men do is a function of habits previously mastered, of their environment and the structure of their bodies, but they are also a function of the intent and kind of organization the individual has imposed on them. The hungry man's food is a stimulus for eating, not because he blindly reacts to the presence of nourishing material, but because he so organizes the dominant habit of eating within a context of supporting, partly repressed activities, that he can effectively and directly respond to one aspect of the material before him. His organization of habits, which permits of his effective response, lies in part with him. The vegetarian's stomach can handle meat, but he refuses to respond to it as food.

When a man is unable to exhibit any control or power of organization, what he does caricatures what he would otherwise do. The starved man is not stimulated by food, but excited by it. His gobbling is eating only by courtesy, an unorganized reaction which runs through and overruns, but does not utilize, the habitual grooves involved in ordinary eating. He may not even get to the stage where he digests his food; at the sight of it he may collapse, cry or ignore it. If only a few avenues of expression are open to a man they cease to be channels for the exercise of habits, and become instead the primary paths along which unorganized energy is unleashed. A structured, organic body, with its own tendencies and possessing the power to resist the expression of a concern, is necessary if a being is to be able to exhibit that concern with effect.

Habits degenerate into blind impulses when other habits are too thoroughly suppressed or are too sharply separated from them. An impulse is a habit disturbed. It is a bodily tendency expressed independently of the demands of the self, a sign of the fact that the body has its own concern which it partly fulfills in the face of the prescriptions imposed by the self.

There are blind impulses of the mind as well as of the body, in society as well as in the individual. The habit of thinking in a single way soon rides a man to make his mind the avenue for the exhibition of a mental passion as disastrous and as distressing as a bodily one. Simple intellects make a fetish of thinking. They become intrigued by a single line of thought, worshippers of some narrow method, and are soon driven by what they had planned to follow. There is a tinge of insanity in those who ride the hobby horses of limited methods, forcing everything within their confines. To preserve sanity, one habit of thought must be supplemented by others and all of them must eventually be welded with the habits which dominate the body.

The preservation of society requires each custom and organization to be bolstered by others. A proletarian dictatorship would prove as distressing as a military one. To prevent a method from turning into a mischief, it must be exercised in a context of diverse independent methods. A society which rallies only to the cry of courage, industry, patience or any other single limited type of activity is on the verge of becoming brutish or inflamed. It must bring other activities into play if only to enable those that are cherished to be prominently displayed.

A man who refuses to listen to anything while he is eating is like a man who drinks in private. Having sundered his act from those habits which might have enriched it, he is about to become a glutton, a bare impulse in the shape of a man. He can then too readily attain the state where he ignores the pressure of other habits, thereby turning himself into one debauched, a locus for the discharge of unharnessed force. The terrible thing about a glutton or a drunkard is not that he eats and drinks with animal-like pleasure, but that he is about to lose all ability really to eat or drink or do anything well defined at all, becoming instead a sequence of excitements and impulsive acts which can be held captive, for but a moment, by soothing his gullet.

5. TECHNIQUES

Techniques are unities of habits acquired slowly, and usually with difficulty. Walking, talking, painting, fishing and swimming are techniques. They presuppose practice. Thus, we learn to walk by walking. Our first achievement is an inspired stumble and a collapse. We begin awkwardly, for our muscles are not yet under control. We do not know how to coordinate the body so that our energies are united for the efficient performance of this single act. There are dispersions, wrong emphases and misplacements. Our task is to bring our bodies under greater control, to use our muscles in more effective ways, to refine the process we already initiated. Learning to walk is learning to walk better. It is an art mastered by practicing. The nature of one's walk is a function of the body one has, the place one walks, the models one imitates, as well as of the particular acts performed. The sailor's gait is different from that of the mountaineer's; the knock-kneed step of the Japanese child of the hills is different from the bow-legged stride of the Western child of the plains.

The ground for walking is laid long before we move an inch. Walking is a complicated process involving the subtle interplay of many different muscles. Without considerable preliminary use of these muscles, it would be almost impossible for the infant to employ and combine them to the degree necessary in order to take its first step, awkward though that step be. To walk, use must be made of bodily movements already under control, forcing these into new combinations. Some earlier tendencies must be inhibited and others stressed, this one must be confined and that one expanded, and all must be interwoven to form a new unified mode of activity.

Walking utilizes and transforms activities already learned. Just as a word completes a grimace, so a step completes a jerk. Walking makes use of movements which, at other times, ended in a mere stretching of the limbs. It is not a summation or an outgrowth of earlier acts, for it introduces something that was not there before—a coordination which changes the meaning and cut of the factors it brings together. Walking is a new achievement in the life of the individual, but it presupposes an earlier, successful performance of other habits whose pattern it partly follows, partly changes and partly suppresses.

Walking is a facet of a unitary organic act. A being can engage in it only by inhibiting other acts and adjusting itself to a changing environment. We do not cross our knees when we walk; we walk one way on the sand and another on the hill. The walk changes its pattern from moment to moment as the being is compelled to modify its tempo and its emphases in response to the situation in which it is. Our hearts beat faster, our arms cease to swing and our senses become keyed to a different pitch as we change a stroll into a climb. But even when we continue to walk quietly along an even path, we are forced to suppress, expand and stress different tendencies at every step. Each move occurs as a member of an organic whole, which in turn is sustained by a bodily and thus a partial manifestation of the individual's concern.

If the elements involved in the act of walking were not already interrelated within an organic unity of behavior, the act of walking would await its beginning on the chance merging of its numerous components. Instead of being the normal accomplishment of children, the act would have its full-blown inception at different periods of life. It would be a strange and surprising occurrence, coming to this individual in infancy, to that one in childhood, to another in youth, to a fourth in old age, and to another not at all. Walking, like every technique, is a stressed activity environed by a host of others.

The movement of one part of a being has its repercussions on every other, inconspicuous and trivial though the movement may be. Every act of arm and leg, of jaw and heart is a component within a wider pattern of activity. Each is interrelated with multiple other acts. Otherwise it would not be the act of a single being, changing its rhythms in terms of the others. If each act of the body were an absolutely independent occurrence, the legs would move at the oddest times and irrespective of what the individual was doing. All of us would then occasionally imitate the activities of those youths who seem driven to go to the attic or to visit a friend at the very moment the rest of the family is gathering at the dinner table.

The acts of a man are the acts of a single individual. This is a truth which must infect every remark that can be made about him, forming an obstacle to the belief that he is only a colony of isolated parts which accidentally work in harmony. It is, however, possible to exaggerate this truth and thereby obscure the equally important fact that habits have their own characteristic rhythms, routes and laws of development, persist in their expression despite changes occurring elsewhere in the body, and take place irrespective of the intent, needs and desires of the whole. A four-year-old may speak like a two-year-old, walk like a five-year-old, think like a seven-year-old and sleep like a baby.

The act of walking is interrelated with other acts, but usually with only a slight effect on its nature and course of development. The limbs have a relatively independent power and mode of behavior, a behavior which is capable of being perfected to a considerable degree without regard for the other needs of the organism. It is therefore possible to tempt a child to walk before it is at an age for proper walking, and it is possible to teach it to walk in ways not appropriate to its childish needs. A properly developed body and a decent footing, the warm encouragement and inspiring models provided by its parents and friends are needed if it is to get to the stage where, perhaps a little earlier than is wise, it makes its first attempt to stand on its own feet and propel itself by its own efforts.

Once the child has mastered the beginning of the art of preparing to fall and then putting a foot in front of itself to prevent the descent, it can proceed to perfect its mode of walking in a way that is out of all keeping with its powers to engage in other acts as well. It can rapidly gain such control over its movements that walking becomes more a point about which other acts turn and to which they are adjusted, than one of many coordinate activities.

Walking does not exhaust the nature of any individual. But it certainly is a better description of some men to remark that they are walkers than that they are anything else. They express themselves by walking more clearly and effectively than, for example, they do by thinking. The walking (like the thinking) is a specialized activity; it should be controlled by the interests of the being acting as more than a body. But for some purposes it is desirable that certain men should concentrate on such specialized activities and run the risk for a time of being unable to integrate them within a significant and harmonious pattern of behavior. A perfectly adjusted man will not be so likely to help others find the way out of a wilderness as he who can walk effectively though his throat is parched, his stomach empty and his eyes blurred by lack of sleep. Similarly, only he who has persistently pursued the art of abstract and rigorous thought can be counted on to make those intellectual contributions on which the shifts of civilization depend. He who thinks only to the degree which the state of his body warrants may attain an animal-like cunning, but it is doubtful whether he can achieve that perspective which is the heritage of useless, specialized thinking.

Walking is but one of many techniques. Like the others it is a means for making and remaking the body by using it. It defines a man as an artist or artisan of the body, for art is the use of a learned technique for making and remaking things. A man's body is a work of art, re-formed under the exercise of gradually acquired techniques. Each of these techniques is carried on without consciousness the more surely it is mastered, though none of them is ever properly pursued except so far as its course is continuously modified through the spontaneous interference of the concerned self.

Because a concern is expressed in the body, there is life in that body, and eventually habits and techniques. So far as a man is concerned with the realization of a good which is broader than the good of his body, he refuses to allow those bodily habits and techniques to be exhibited uncontrolled. He varies their direction and power spontaneously. Should the spontaneous modification prove of no avail, the man must, if he is to prosper in and through his body, abandon the attempt to act in an habitual way. He must strike out in new directions. Otherwise he will perish the more surely he has habits and has mastered techniques.

The acquisition of bodily techniques is an achievement of the body under the guidance of the self. They are mastered no better by men than by other beings. We come to understand man's nature a little better if we turn from such techniques to one which he can master to a greater degree than is possible to other beings—the technique of using signs.

CHAPTER NINE

SIGNS AND LANGUAGE

1. THE OBJECTS OF SIGNS

MANY TECHNIQUES are open to man. But there is none, the acquisition of which so distinguishes him from other beings as that which involves the use of signs. Subhuman beings use signs, but not as many, as extensively or as effectively as men; they do not know how to employ signs to constitute a language. It is because man acquires the art of using signs, and to a degree and in a way that other beings cannot, that he is able to speak, to write, to discourse, and eventually to have a science, art, religion, history and philosophy.

An inquiry into the nature of signs is an inquiry which touches on the activities of subhuman as well as human beings, but does not exhaust the essence or promise of either. A man remains a man even though he does not use signs; there is no loss of humanity involved in falling into a dreamless sleep. But only if he uses signs, and in a way that others cannot, does he make clearly manifest the humanity that is his. His use of signs does not distinguish him from other beings; being distinguished from them, he is able to do things they cannot, such as the making use of signs in a language.

A *sign* is any entity, the acknowledgment of which prompts one to attend to something else. Smoke is a sign for one who, because he sees it, looks expectantly elsewhere. It is not a sign for one who, as a consequence of his acknowledgment of it, fails to interest himself in something else. The smoke is then only a puff on the horizon which occurs in a temporal and physical relation to other things.

Smoke is usually taken to be a sign of a fire to be seen in the vicinity; clouds are usually taken to be signs of weather to come. These signs are also used for other purposes, but whether they are or not, their use brings into focus a difficulty which established theories are inclined to skirt. When clouds are used as a sign of rain, what is it to which the clouds refer before the rain has come? What if the weather clears? Nothing is a sign unless someone makes use of it, but nothing is a sign also if there is no object to which it refers. A sign is a sign of something for somebody. Eliminate the something or the somebody, and the sign is a sign no longer. But then, before there is rain in fact, what is it of which clouds are signs?

Clouds are full-fledged signs when they are used. They must therefore signify something. Used to signify weather, they can be signs only of incipient weather, of weather as now future, of weather as not yet determinate, of weather as fair-or-rainy. Or, where the clouds are rainclouds, their object is rain as now future, a rain without actual strength or duration, a *kind* of occurrence which can be specific and determinate only in the present that is to be. There is no actual rain for the clouds now to signify.

The specific occurrences and concrete objects of the world do not exist in the future that now stretches ahead. Next year is not already in existence, filled to the brim with all the realities and events that will in fact occur, awaiting only the indifferent passage of time to make its presence known. If it were, there would be nothing like becoming, action, causation. All things would then from the beginning of time already be. They would be full-blown existents aeons before they existed in the present. They would exist in the present and past just as they did in the future, irrelevantly decorated by different dates.

A sign signifies something general, indeterminate, the future as it now is. The objects that coexist with the sign can be signified only as objects which could be observed, could be utilized or could act in the future—as possibilities which have not yet been realized. The object of every sign is thus a part of the future. That future is indeterminate in nature. It is not amorphous, however. The things and occurrences in the present limit the range of what can occur; they categorize the future, making it a tissue of delimited possibilities to be delimited further by being realized and made concrete in the present that is to be.

The fox is a prospective danger to the chick, the chick is a prospective morsel for the fox. Each contributes to the constitution of the future. Each signifies a possibility by means of the other. That signified possibility is constituted by that other and is related to the possibility constituted by the signifying being. There is now a prospective danger for the chick; an eating fox is a real possibility for it now, though the fox may die before it can do harm. There is now a prospective morsel for the fox; an eaten chick is a real possibility for the fox now, though the chick may never in fact be eaten. There is room in the realm of possibility for failure on the part of the fox and escape on the part of the chick.

A prospective danger can be realized as an immediate or as a remote threat; a prospective item of food can be realized as something torn, chewed and swallowed, or as something still to be reached. The chick may achieve a momentary security, the fox may be momentarily chagrined. Whichever it be, whether or not the chick escapes, whether or not the fox eats the chick, the actual delight or chagrin, pain or relief that is in fact realized is one which never was or could, in its concreteness and detail, be signified or expected.

2. EXPECTATION AND ANTICIPATION

A sign is referred to an object through the medium of an expectation, bodily or nonbodily. The expectation is a dynamic act by which the user of the sign moves from the sign to the relevant future. It relates the sign to an undetermined but limited frame which allows for a number of alternative occurrences. The fox expectantly turns from the perceived chick to the chick as edible, while the chick turns from the perceived fox to the fox as a source of danger. Each acts with respect to the being it confronts in order to control the way in which the object of its sign will be realized. The one acts to turn the edible into the eaten, the other to turn the dangerous into a harmless threat.

All beings tend to *anticipate*, to read into the object of an expectation determinations it does not have. They tend to treat the object of a sign as though it were already determinate. The fox is overanxious, the chick is excessively timid. The former therefore reads into the undetermined future the character of being delightful, the latter reads into the undetermined future the character of being disastrous. The mouth of the one begins to water in anticipation of a meal, the other is filled with deadly fear before it is touched. A more cautious fox would have been content with the expectation that there was food readily available to it; a more courageous chick would have been content with the expectation that something dangerous was in the offing. The fox would then have been ready to act more adroitly, the chick would then have been ready to act with more decisiveness. Both could have acted as beings alive to the fact that the outcome need not be disastrous to the chick.

The future allows for the failure of the fox to eat the chick. But both the fox and the chick anticipatorily read into the expectable future the result which the one is anxious and the other is afraid to have occur. The anticipation prompts them to act as though other alternative results were precluded. It may make them act in ways not appropriate to the present which is about to be.

Errors arise when the future is anticipated and thus viewed as being more determinate than it is. It is tempting to suppose that the smile of a rogue is a sign that he will do a kindness, when it is a sign only that he will try to act as though he were a friend. By yielding to the temptation, many a man has made it easy for the rogue to strip him of his goods.

Anticipation is a basic source of error; but it also serves to help one distinguish signs that had been used interchangeably. A cloud, for example, may now be used as a sign of incipient weather; smoke may now be used as a sign of an observable event in the vicinity. Each is now a distinct sign with a distinct object. But when first used, cloud and smoke were equivalent signs, having as their object a broad future, a domain within which a number of events—rain and fire, noise and quiet, and so on—were possibilities.

The expectation accompanying the use of these signs was appropriate to both of them indifferently, not to each individually. It did not allow for the distinction of one of these signs (and its object) from the other. Such a distinction is not the outcome of an examination of the signs, for no sign reveals the nature of what will be signified by it. Any number of signs, no matter how different in nature, can be used to signify the same thing. Nor can the distinction be the outcome of a knowledge of a difference in the futures which are pertinent to those signs. As equivalent, the signs signify and continue to signify the same future. The distinction results from a refinement in the character of the expectation, or from a happy anticipation of the object which could be the terminus of a refined expectation.

Anticipation, thus, though a frequent source of error, is no guarantee of it. It goes beyond what an expectation, germane to a number of different signs, allows. But it may terminate in an object appropriate to some one of those signs. It goes beyond what an actual expectation warrants, but not necessarily beyond what a subsequent refined expectation may.

Sign-using beings start with many equivalent signs of an indeterminate broad future. But they also anticipate in line with their past experiences, add determinations to the future they expect. When they do this, they risk making errors, for there may not be a possibility having the characters they anticipate. They may anticipate what they cannot expect; they may signify one thing and anticipatorily act as though they had signified a more determinate version of it.

Sign-users may, of course, be fortunate enough at times to signify some subordinate possibility as the appropriate object of one of their equivalently used signs. Thus, instead of signifying a broad future by means of clouds and smoke, they may signify only rain and this by means of those clouds which are located somewhere near where the rain is anticipated. They will then be in a position to discover that rain is a more appropriate object for those clouds than for other clouds or for smoke to signify.

An interest in weather helps one to move to the stage where clouds and smoke are used as different signs of different objects. Similarly, an interest in kinds of weather leads one to distinguish different types of cloud as different signs of the different kinds of weather. The process of distinguishing clouds can be further refined, and clouds which are signs of heavy rain can be distinguished from those that are signs of light rain, clouds which are signs of a rain of short duration from clouds which are signs of a rain of long duration. But no matter how much one refines the process of distinguishing signs and their objects, one is always left with signs which point to a future that is never completely determinate while it remains future. An actual heavy rain has a specific strength and duration, a host of details, which were lacking and must be lacking to it as a mere possibility, as a mere object of a sign.

It is possible to distinguish different types of cloud, the cirrus from the stratocumulus, the cirrostratus from the altocumulus, and to use them as distinct kinds of signs of distinct types of weather. The process of discrimination can be continued further, but there is a point beyond which it is not worth while to pursue it. Each cloud is distinct from every other, and in fact presages a future somewhat different from the future signified by any other. Yet the future to which it points is similar to that which is the object of other clouds. It entrains the same expectations and for all practical purposes is a sign equivalent with that other. Each object is related to a different possibility, but since many possibilities are, from the standpoint of practice and even theory, not distinguished and perhaps not even distinguishable, there will always be a number of objects which are and always should be used as equivalent signs.

The desire to have a distinct sign for each possibility is a desire for excessive precision. It is a desire which cannot be satisfied except by treating every single item in the world as a sign distinct from every other, and then recognizing that no one of them could be used twice in exactly the same way. For some purposes it is desirable to distinguish different types of grass and sometimes even to distinguish one blade from another, and use them as distinct signs having distinct objects. But for the rest of the time it suffices to know the common possibility that all blades of grass signify. Except for specialists, all blades of grass should be synonyms.

So long as a number of different signs serve equally well to signify some expected result, there is no need to discriminate among them. It is just as wrong to insist that the process of discriminating signs be carried out to the limit as it is to insist that it must never be carried out beyond some preassigned point. The discriminations vary and ought to vary with our interests and time.*

*After I had finished this book, I came across the following by the brilliant Benjamin Whorf (*The Technology Review*, vol. XLII, April 1940, p. 6.): "Hopi has a noun that covers every thing or being that flies, with the exception of birds, which class is denoted by another noun. The former noun may be said to denote the class—flying class minus bird. The Hopi actually call insect, airplane, and aviator all by the same word, and feel no difficulty about it. The situation, of course, decides any possible confusion among very disparate members of a broad linguistic class, such as this class. This class seems to us too large and inclusive, but so would our class 'snow' to an Eskimo. We have the same word for falling snow, snow on the ground, snow packed hard like ice, slushy snow, wind-driven flying snow—whatever the situation may be. To an Eskimo, this all-inclusive word would be almost unthinkable; he would say that falling snow, slushy snow, and so on, are sensuously and operationally different, different things to contend with; he uses different words for them and for other kinds of snow. The Aztecs go even farther than we in the opposite direction, with cold, ice, and snow all

The need to use distinct signs varies as one's interest in distinct parts of the incipient future waxes and wanes. Concerned only with knowing whether danger looms, a man is wise to ignore signs pointing to other things, and to lump together as equivalent all signs which signify the danger. An increase in the number of interests makes desirable the use of new distinct signs; a refinement of interest makes desirable a distinction among signs which have previously been used as equivalent. He who opens up new vistas should coin new terms or use old ones in unusual ways; he who clarifies what is familiar should sharpen definitions or distinguish among familiar terms. The oracle creates new terms; the logician has resort to distinctions. The one is concerned with a neglected facet of the future, the other with a neglected difference in what is familiar. The philosopher is concerned with both; he must be suggestive as well as precise. He is a poet pointing to realms previously unnoted, by means of new signs or by making use of old ones in novel settings; he is also a grammarian who inserts new boundaries in familiar fields and remarks that fact by multiplying distinctions, thereby making technical use of accepted signs.

3. SALUTATIONS AND OCCURRENCES

Signs are used by subhuman as well as by human beings. Both act in public ways while moving from signs to objects *via* expectations. The public act may or may not have relevance to the object which is being designated by the sign. If the act is not relevant, it is an *occurence;* if it is relevant, if it has bearing on the object expected, it is a *salutation* of the accompanying sign of the expected object. A sneeze which happens to accompany the act of signifying rain is an occurrence, having no bearing on the expected rain. The act of closing windows while signifying rain is a saluta-

---

represented by the same basic word with different terminations; ice is the noun form; cold, the adjectival form; and for snow, "ice mist'." I am grateful to Mrs. D. D. Lee for having arranged to have Whorf's published papers sent me.

tion of whatever sign is being used to signify that rain, if the windows are being closed in expectation of rain as capable of wetting and spoiling the floors.

An unintentional act may prove to be an excellent salutation. The look of terror which unknowingly sweeps over the face of a frightened child is a salutation of a sign of something dangerous. Another being could use that look as a sign to designate the danger the child is expecting.

A given salutation need not be used more than once. Although a man may put on a raincoat only once in a lifetime, the act could nevertheless be an excellent salutation of a cloud, enabling another to designate the rain. Nor need a given salutation always accompany the use of some one sign. At different times one can act with respect to future rain in different but equally pertinent ways. One can salute the clouds sometimes with a shout, sometimes with a bow and sometimes by a run for cover. Where a specific act constantly accompanies the use of a specific sign, however, it makes it possible for others to become aware what the being is signifying by means of that sign. Were men to wear raincoats only on seeing one type of cloud, put on rubbers on seeing another, run to the cellar on seeing a third, they would be exhibiting the fact that they had, on these different occasions, three different kinds of expectation which were directed to three different phases of the future, and that therefore they were using the three types of cloud as three different types of sign. The constant use of any one of these particular forms of salutation makes it easier for others to learn what is being signified. But it is not essential to the being of a salutation that it be employed more than once, or that it be the constant accompaniment of some particular sign.

The act of putting on a raincoat can be a salutation accompanying the use of a cloud as a sign. It is then an act which reveals that the individual looks forward not merely to weather, which is the object signified by the cloud, but to rainy weather. If he had stopped his act midway and thus had moved to or looked towards the raincoat without attempting to put it on, his salutation would, as capable of being completed in many ways, have been a salutation of the cloud as a sign of possible weather, of weather that may or may not be rainy. An appropriate salutation is one which is capable of being completed in many ways. Only such a salutation has a sufficient degree of indeterminacy to make it a proper accompaniment of an expectation; only it is appropriate to that undetermined future which alone can be the object of a sign.

Every completed act, performed in anticipation of a future situation, is more determinate than the signified future warrants. The vice of excessive caution is expressed in the shape of completed salutations. It is determinism in practice, revealing the error of supposing that the future is more determinate than it is. A salutation ought to be as incomplete as a signified object is indeterminate; otherwise it will not only prove inappropriate at times but will lead others to miss the object that is in fact being signified.

There can be many equivalent modes of salutation. Instead of looking to one's raincoat, one might run towards the house, begin to close the windows or look troubled. Salutations, moverover, are modes of expression open to beings other than men. As the sky darkens, the birds fly for cover, the hens begin to squawk, the roosters crow, and the dog quiets. In their different ways they are all equally saluting the same phenomenon.

4. WORDS, CALLS AND CRIES

Subhuman as well as human beings can use the salutations of others as signs. They can use the salutations to signify the future *acts* of those others or to signify the *objects* which those others are signifying. This is possible because the concerns of beings, particularly of the same species, converge. Their expectations are intertwined.

Living beings form close knit groups, not because they begin with the acknowledgment of a common body of signs or even of common objectives, but because they feel with one another and so can use the public acts of their fellows as signs of what their fellows expect or will do. The mother may not be aware that her face betrays her fear; the infant without knowing why the mother is afraid and without having fear itself becomes aware, by using the look of alarm as a sign of danger, that its mother is afraid of something. The infant becomes afraid, not because it sees something to fear, but because it feels that its mother is afraid of something. Like many other fundamental emotions, its fear is acquired by contagion, not generated by an awareness of objects to which the fears are pertinent. We all become afraid at times even when we have nothing to fear for ourselves, because we employ the act of a frightened neighbor as a sign pointing to something of which that neighbor is afraid. We are not usually clear as to just what it is that frightens him, but we are quite clear that he is frightened by something.

The contagion of emotion makes for solidarity. That is not enough, however, to make communication possible. Communication requires that one individual use his own salutation as a sign of the prospective acts of another, and that the other use that salutation as a sign of the object to which the former is referring. Communication thus requires that a salutation be used as a sign by two beings, the one referring to the acts of the other, the other referring to the objects signified by the first. If we refer to the acts of another and he does not in turn use our salutation as a sign, we are attempting to but not succeeding in communicating with him. If he uses our salutation as a sign but we do not, he signifies what we do but not because we attempt to communicate something to him.

The salutations used in communication may have many forms. The extending of quills, the pawing of the ground, the baring of teeth are salutations which make excellent signs, and may be effective instruments for communication. Vocal salutations are, however, as a rule and particularly with human beings, better for the purpose of communication than any other. An act which requires an eye to observe must await until the eye is turned in that direction; one which requires an ear in order to be noted compels attention. A visible act awaits an observation; an audible one intrudes. The norm of human communication is that which signifies by means of vocal salutations, precisely because they are intrusive. Man is master of the art of using his own sounds as signs, of signifying while he intrudes.

The ability to make sounds does not mean that a being is more perceptive or more intelligent than one able to act publicly only in nonvocal ways. Nor, granted the questionable supposition that vocal organs are better instruments for the expression of intelligence than others, does it follow that they exist for that purpose. Not every organ of a high-grade being performs a high-grade function. The ability to make sounds is like the ability to smell; lower beings may have the ability to a greater degree than higher ones, though the higher can, of course, make use of the ability in ways the lower cannot. Dogs have better noses than men, and birds have a larger repertory of sounds than such comparatively highly developed beings as whales and cows. Sign-users who are unable to make sounds are superior to vocal beings who cannot make use of signs.

Only high-grade beings use sounds as signs, because only these are able to use signs at all. The ability to make sounds is an incidental ability which they may achieve as the outcome of the acquisition of bodies of a certain kind and degree of complexity. The ability to make sounds is more like a chance variation than a purposive or useful power; the ability to use signs with intelligence is a significant achievement, the result of the high-grade ability to be sensitive to the concerns and objectives of others. Once the power of using signs has been acquired, it can be applied so as to make the vocal organs important instruments of signification.

The mooing of a cow, the bleating of a lamb, the screech of an eagle seem to be on a level with the acts of browsing or the beating of wings. Both the former and the latter are occurrences, the one vocal, the other not. They are produced by beings who do not then use signs, or they are irrelevant to what might be signified by those beings.

Vocal occurrences are *outcries*. They contrast with *calls*, which are vocal salutations accompanying signs of the expected possible acts of others. The cluck of the hen and the whimper of her chicks are calls. Each vocalizes while signifying something and while expecting the other to engage in some act relevant to what is signified. Since neither uses its own sounds as signs, neither communicates. Each may, of course, learn something from the other by using that other's call as a sign of what that other will do or of what it is signifying, and thus be ready to act concordantly with or to satisfy that other. The chicks not only hear the cluck of the hen, but treat it as a sign of the next move of the hen and sometimes of the object she is signifying. The hen not only hears the whimper of the chicks, but treats it as a sign of the food they want and sometimes of what they are about to do. The chicks tend to move with the hen, the hen tends to satisfy the chicks. The hen does not, in this case, cluck because the chicks whimper, the chicks do not whimper because the hen clucks. Each calls independently of the other.

The calls of the hen could have bearing on the calls of the chicks, and conversely. One of them could call in expectation of the call to be provided by the other, and that other in reply could call to the first in a similar way. They would then *exchange calls*. They would seem to be communicating, to be speaking to one another, to have a language. But they would not be communicating, for they would not be saying anything. They would be talking *at* or *to* but not *with* one another.

Because the "speech" of birds is an interchange of calls, birds cannot, strictly speaking, be said to have a language—except in the sense in which angry disputants may be said to have a language. A bird, like an angry disputant, calls out to others in expectation that something will be called out in return. But there is nothing which it signifies by means of its sounds. Its sounds accompany its expectation that other sounds will be forthcoming; they do not themselves serve as signs of those subsequent sounds.

To speak to another one must turn calls into *words,* change the vocal accompaniment of a sign into a sign of what is expected. The words will continue to have the same sound as the calls. But by virtue of their different sign-function, they will be radically distinct from them.

In echolalia we seem to employ nought but conventional words. Yet we say nothing; our sounds express cries, not words. In addressing a dog we make the same sounds as those we make when we speak to one another. We are, however, not using words—nonsense syllables would have done as well—but are calling to the animal. It is one thing to swear at things, another to swear at animals, and still another to swear at men. The same noises can be made all three times, but they are different in import. We cry out at things, call to animals, and use words with men.

Because cries, calls, and words can all be expressed with the same sounds, it is to be expected that there will be theorists who understand human language to be only a tissue of cries or calls, and that there will be others who see the cries and calls of subhuman beings as words in an animal language. Those who take language to be but cries or calls, unwarrantedly overlook the fact that sounds can be used as signs by the beings who produce them. Those who think that animals use words, unwarrantedly suppose that all sounds are used as signs by those who produce them. We know that we use our own sounds as signs; the former theory denies what we know of ourselves. It is often hard for us to know whether our fellows are using words; the latter theory knows more about animals than we usually know about our fellow men.

5. *EXCLAMATIONS*

The most elementary and perhaps the first of words is the exclamation, a salutation used by the speaker as a sign of an expected nonvocal act to be performed by the listener. "Look!" is an exclamation, signifying another's expected act of attention to the object one is signifying. "Watch out!" is a word used in expectation that he will act with respect to an incipient danger. They contrast with such a call as "Oh!", a salutation not itself used as a sign. Separated from the expectation of the acts of others, both the exclamation and the call are outcries which disturb but do not refer to anything.

An exclamation by itself is a condensed sentence. It states in brief, "I expect you to deal with this interesting occurrence." Referring another to something I have signified, the exclamation is thus not only social in meaning but serves to convey to another what position I expect him to take towards what I have signified. The exclamation does not make evident the objects or acts that I, the speaker, am expecting. It ought to be expanded.

The nature of the object to which the listener is being directed or the character of the act we await from the listener is made clear through the use of subordinate terms, articulating the intent of the exclamation. When this is done we have a language. Language is exclamation expanded.

The effect of an exclamation on the listener is primarily to prompt him to attend to that to which the speaker attended. The effect on the listener must be and is intended to be different from what it is on the speaker himself. The speaker has already responded or is now responding; the listener is expected to respond. The former responds apart from the exclamation; the latter is expected to respond because of it. The speaker expects the listener to attend to what he has noted, but does not usually expect him to act as he himself does. When we exclaim, "ouch!", we expect another to note that we are in pain; we do not expect him to withdraw, writhe or weep, though we may. When we exclaim, "Look out!", we signify another's possible exercise of caution. One or the other of us may be quite out of danger.

An exclamation is a sign accompanied by an expectation that another will attend to that to which we have attended, but will act with respect to it in a different way. The speaker responds and the listener is expected to respond; the one responds before or while he exclaims, the other is expected to respond after the exclamation has been heard. So far as they respond in similar ways, it is usually by attending and then at different times; so far as they respond at the same time, it is usually through actions and then in different ways. It is the error of such theories as Mead's to suppose that discourse requires the use of similar sounds and similar activities on the part of both speaker and listener, leading to the paradoxical result that—as Mead himself affirms—the lion's roar must intimidate the lion a little, since it must, on Mead's theory, tend to react to its own roar as others do.

6. NAMES, PREDICATES AND METAPHYSICALS

The different words men use in conventional discourse can be viewed as components of elaborate exclamations. They enable the listener to locate the object which interests the speaker, or they help clarify the nature of the sign and expectation which the exclamation accompanies.

The unit of language is the sentence. It makes explicit the whereabouts and nature of that about which we are exclaiming. Its parts are exclamations which together serve to clarify the more comprehensive exclamation conveyed by the sentence as a whole. "Look out!" is clarified when expanded to "There is a sniper," i.e., to, "I expect you to look there, to note the threat there exhibited and to act accordingly."

The sentence as a whole is exclamatory. Each word in it is ultimately exclamatory in intent. As parts of the sentence, the words are of course only potential exclamations, and this whether or not they originally functioned as isolated exclamations. Taken out of the sentence each word can be elaborated by means of connected subordinate exclamations. There are thus no irreducible words. Each can function as an exclamation in the form of a condensed sentence, to be elaborated through the use of other words. The meaning of each of these last words in turn is to be explicated, as the dictionary makes evident, through the use of other words and so on.

A language can be conveniently analyzed as making use of three and only three kinds of words. Some languages, to be sure, have fewer and others more kinds of words. But those that have fewer either make one word perform multiple functions, or supplement its use by bodily gestures, actions or grammatical constructions; those that have more, specialize and refine the basic divisions. An adjective, for example, is a noun in a subordinate position, and together with a regular noun forms a single term, one of the three basic divisions of language—*names*, *predicates* and *metaphysicals*.

Names are exclamations which serve to mark out an object as standing over against one, and to which another is expected to respond or is to signify through other signs. Names can be subdivided by virtue of their specificity of reference into denotatives, pronouns and proper names. *Predicates,* on the other hand, record the structure, relation or nature of that which one confronts. They are of two kinds, common nouns and descriptions, the latter being a more explicit version of the former.

Names and predicates require one another. The former alone would tell where to attend but not what it is to which one should attend; the latter would tell what it is to which we should attend, but not tell us that it was available for attention. Were a language completely dead or self-enclosed, there would be no need to go beyond the use of these. Artificial languages can be created in which there are, in addition to predicates, only names for the subjects of those predicates. But then the reference of the sentence as a whole would be nowhere remarked.

A complete expression contains a term which remarks what it is to which the sentence as a whole is to be referred. Such a term may be called a *metaphysical*. Works like "is," "and," "or," most metaphors, and the metaphysical categoreals, "being," "substance," "causality," etc., are metaphysicals. The latter and some of the former refer to the concrete being of which the referent of a name and the referent of a predicate are aspects.

Metaphysicals appear in discourse usually in the form of names, predicates, connectives between them, or as components of larger signs. It is primarily when metaphysicals assume the guise of verbs and connectives that it becomes most evident that our discourse refers to a real, substantial world beyond itself. In any case, without metaphysicals, explicit or implicit, there would be subjects in a language but no sign of a subject matter; there would be predicates, but no reference to a predicatable object. Metaphysicals refer to the unarticulated being which the subject and predicate together articulate, and to which as their unitary locus they are referred. When we say "this is red," we do not mean that it is the object as a "this" which is red, since it obviously isn't, but that an object, referred to by "is," is the source and locus of the referents of both the "this" and the "red."

The recognition of the role that metaphysicals play, makes it possible to understand how it is that one can create a fiction and describe it as being "true" or "false." A metaphysical relates to an indeterminate being which a fiction imaginatively determines in one of many possible ways. The truth of the fiction is one with its consistency—with the way it follows out the implications of its own determinations. The great virtue of idealism is that its coherence theory of truth allows it to do full justice to the logic of fictions. Its great limitation is that for it all assertions are treated as referring only to fictions.

We learn much about man from reading the *Pickwick Papers*. Yet when we speak of "Mr. Pickwick," we are not referring to any existent man. The *Pickwick Papers*, like other works of good fiction, specifies in a possible and plausible way some feature characteristic of everybody. "Mr. Pickwick" refers to the potencies to be found in *any* man, and what is said of Pickwick is a way of imaginatively realizing those potencies. To say that "Mr. Pickwick is gentle yet not a fool," is to use "Mr. Pickwick is" as a metaphysical for a vague set of potencies pertinent to man, and "gentle" and "not a fool" as arbitrary, connected determinations of those potencies. The whole statement would be somewhat more accurate, though more prosaic, if it read: gentleness and foolishness are not necessarily linked in man.

Artists provide plausible, consistent determinations for indeterminate realities. We learn from them what things promise and what follows if the promise is realized in a certain way. Art is more flexible than history, more profound than science and has a richer vocabulary than philosophy. Like the others, it too tells something about the world as it is, but unlike them does it by concentrating on one that is only possible.

All discourse has its metaphysical component, or—what is the same thing—all metaphysics is empirical. The object of metaphysical inquiry is the concrete reality which provides discourse with subject matter, content and truth. The philosopher attempts to understand what that reality is capable of, though as apart from nonessential and transient details. The artist is concerned with a portion of it as revealed by details. The scientist is concerned with expressing it in a precise way by interconnecting details.

The artist restricts his range more than the others but probes deeper. He interrelates his terms in novel ways to express better the depths of being which are vaguely adumbrated in daily life. The scientist has a more rigid and universal grammar in which he expects every detail to find a proper place. The philosopher concerns himself with everything as the object of the term "is." He contrasts with the artist whose object is confined within the area marked out by some name, and contrasts with the scientist who is interested in conceivable objects which would account for the predicates being what they are. The three types supplement one another and none gives all the truth alone. But the philosopher attempts to encompass the truth of the others in somewhat the same way as the body encompasses the acts of the heart and the lungs.

The object of a name is a being as a mere "it" and thus as at a possibly infinite distance; a predicate has as its object the traits of a being as infected by the contributions which the knower makes to that being; the object of a metaphysical is the substance of a being as articulatable in a number of possible ways. The three together, as forming a unitary portion of discourse, are symbolized by a sentence, a single sign of the object as something to which another may be directed. The sentence may refer to a present object, the thing before one, but only on the implicit or explicit supposition that it is something to which another might attend. We need no signs to acknowledge what is present, but we do need signs in order to represent what that present thing may be for others.

7. CONVENTIONAL DISCOURSE

Few words are forged by any one man or in any one epoch. Most of them are part of one's inheritance. As a group they are as much beyond the control of either individuals or society at any one time as are the conventional practices of worship or technology. They rise and pass away as gradually and almost as imperceptibly as these others usually do.

The meanings of most words are slowly modified in the course of history. Occasionally, however, some powerful individual or group, some crisis in thought or fact, compels men to change the signification of the words they have been accustomed to use. Plato turned the term "sophist" from one of praise into one of contempt.

Aristotle took the ordinary Greek words for timber and shape and made them into the philosophic "matter and form" with new and wider meanings. The calendar now in use is properly called the "Gregorian" after Pope Gregory XIII, who introduced it and led men to put it in place of the "Julian" calendar they had been using. The humanists converted the name of the great scholastic philosopher, Duns Scotus, into "dunce," so that a name for wisdom became a sign of stupidity. It is perhaps they who were responsible for turning the solemn "hoc est corpus," "here is the body of God," into the silly "hocus pocus." A revolution in the practice and spread of education and learning converted the important scholastic "trivium" of basic studies into "trivial," and helped change the meaning of "vulgar" from "popular" to "boorish". In feudal days a "villain" was a free villager and a "blackguard" was a menial servant in a great household. The abandonment of the Aristotelian cosmology helped debase the word "quintessence," so that instead of referring to the fifth and heavenly element of the medieval universe it now refers to a "concentrated extract." Some words, on the other hand, retain somewhat the same meaning while they undergo transformation in shape or spelling. "Brief" is English for "brevis," "space" is English for "espace," a "drawing room" is a "withdrawing room," "to maim" is to commit "mayhem," and "algebra" is English for "aljabr."

Despite such changes in the meaning and character of words, most of those we use today are inherited and have almost the same meaning and nature for us that they had for our immediate ancestors. The first and longest linguistic lesson the child has to learn is to recognize the established signs and to use them in the ways they have been previously employed. The words, manners and taboos of a group are signs which men must adopt if they are to find a respectable place within that group. Every trade and enterprise has its own set of signs, whose gradual mastery and eventual automatic use the apprentice spends his time attaining. Part of the task of the farmer, sailor and aviator is to make use of the established signs of the state of the incipient weather. The medical doctor is not accredited as a reliable practitioner until he has learned to identify the established symptoms and has come to know what other doctors say they signify. He may later diverge from his fellows, but to enter the practice he must first agree with them on how the signs are to be used. Part of almost every Ph.D. degree is a reward for using arbitrary signs according to established conventions. "Doctor," medical or otherwise, is a title which may in fact designate the master of little more than a technical vocabulary.

That words and other signs are habitually used and that they seem to have definite referents to which the individual is always expected to refer by their means, may lead a theorist at times to write as though there were entities which functioned as signs apart from any user. Because they have been forced to learn that a red glow is a sign of fire, danger or the sun, and clouds a sign of fair weather, rain or dust, men tend to suppose that the glow and the clouds signify their respective objects apart from any sign-user. Sometimes they even go so far as to hold that the very words they use have a natural affinity for definite objects, and that the words by themselves designate those objects. "Ding dong" seems for them to be, by its very nature, the sign of a ringing iron bell; "babble" they view as a term which itself intends to mark the sound of a running brook. No other word than "God" they think points so evidently to divinity.

Some words, to be sure, are similar in sound to the objects they signify; others are causally related to their objects. But there are words which are similar in sound to objects they do not signify, and there are words which do not refer to the things to which they are causally related. "Sun" has the same sound as "son," but the one does not designate the other. "Impotence" obviously designates that which could not have caused it. There are words, too, which are similar to their objects or are causally related to them but which also signify objects to which they are neither similar nor causally related. Though "babbling" approximates the sound of a brook, it does not necessarily repeat the mumblings of the demented which it equally signifies. A cloud is causally related to rain and serves as a sign of it, but clouds have also been used as portents of events to come in human affairs.

A causal connection or similarity between words and objects is what perhaps led men originally to employ those words to designate those objects, though this is by no means evident or well established. In any case, there are many words like "impotence," which could not be caused by the objects they signify, and words like "nonverbal," which could not possibly be similar to their signified objects.

Every entity, and thus every sign, vocal or nonvocal, is related to some future possibility which may be termed a natural object for it to signify. But it does not signify that object unless someone uses it as a sign of that object.

8. THE NATURE OF LANGUAGE

The primary use of words is to designate expected things, acts or words whose possibility is provided by something other than those words. Words are essentially conventional signs, signs used to designate something to which they do not "naturally" point.

Words are signs of other words and of things or acts. All other signs employed in communication—religious symbols, railway and traffic signals, monuments, conventional gestures, facial expressions, etc.—can be treated as words having a different grammar and a different medium from those employed in discourse or writing. Conversely, all verbal and written discourse can be treated as a variant of some other mode of discourse which makes use of different kinds of signs and relates them in different ways. Words come late in the history of the race and of the individual, but some nonvocal signs, such as traffic signals, come later still. It is indifferent therefore whether we say that words are vocal salutations used as signs, or whether we say that other salutations are the silent words of bodily or social discourse.

Words, or other signs, do not make a language. A language presupposes a grammar, a structural representation of the type of word, act or thing expected to follow the use of a given word. We speak grammatically and use a language when we make an habitual, conventionally established use of words as signs of words or of other things which have an established structural function in relation to those words. When, for example, in English, we begin by employing a subject term, we prepare ourselves to make use of a copula and predicate. A language of words is not, however, a complete language; it is but a more flexible and complicated tissue of connected vocal signs to be employed for the sake of signifying acts and things.

A language is shared. It always has the form of a dialogue, though that fact may be obscured. He to whom one speaks may be silent and his reply may be silently provided by the speaker. The speaker may even merely imagine a listener and may answer for him as well as speak to him. Or he can act the part of both listener and speaker, presenting a dialogue as though it were a monologue.

The speaker may use his signs only to signify that the listener will also use them as signs. If the sign the speaker offers is then used by the listener to signify other items in a language, language becomes a medium of discourse. There is a language of chants, of polite and diplomatic discourse where grammatically structured units are passed back and forth and may not refer to anything beyond. A man says "How do you do?" and thus seems to ask a question of another. The other does not answer the question and, to make matters worse, puts the same question to the speaker. On the surface nothing could be more impolite, though actually the reverse is the case. Neither has in fact asked a question; neither wants the other to talk on the state of his health. To answer the apparent question with an account of one's health is to be unmannerly. The speaker uses these words as an accompaniment of a nonvocal reference to the other as one acknowledged to be in the same social situation with him. He offers the words to the listener as a sign by which the listener can refer to him as also an acknowledged part of the social situation. Neither points to anything beyond the two of them; they may dislike one another or may have nothing further to do with one another. But for the moment they have made social contact and used a language together. They have engaged in the verbal counterpart of the act of smoking a pipe of peace, of breaking bread, of bowing and so on. Theirs is an interchange of words, a discourse not a communication. Each uses his own words as a sign of the momentary equal social status of the other, and expects the other to accept the words that have been offered as a sign that the speaker is peaceably inclined.

A full-grown language is more than a shared act of grammatically related terms interchanged by speaker and listener. It refers to some third thing beyond both. We speak to another about something. He understands what we say, not when he views our language as a sign of what interests us, but as a sign by means of which he can refer to what we signify. We offer words to be used by others as signs of the things to which we are referring apart from those signs. If our offer is accepted, communication is achieved.

The sentence is the grammatical unit. It is a single sign which the speaker offers to the listener to use as a sign. Language is thus not merely a set of grammatically related terms, but those grammatically related terms unified and used in expectation that the listener will also make use of the unity as a sign. We communicate by means of a language when we use shared sentences to signify realities beyond them. In ordinary prose a sentence ends at a full stop. In poetry a sentence may be as long as the entire poem; its subject may be what in prose would be a sentence. The grammar of poetry is quite different from, though illustrating the very same principles as ordinary prose. Its grammarian is still to be born.

9. *FREEDOM AND LANGUAGE*

Signs may be used unconsciously or by intent. They may be already available or may be produced on the required occasion. They may have the form of things or public acts. They may be used singly or in interrelation, as isolated terms or as parts of a shared language. It is as parts of shared language that they most evidently are elements employed in a technique of expression and communication.

A technique is a tissue of habits exercised with freedom. It is the past ingrained in the body, making probable some limited course of activity which is filled out in unpredictable ways. Viewed from the perspective of the speaker, the technique of language is a barrier to be vitalized, retreated from and transcended. It is vitalized in living speech, retreated from while one reflects, and transcended by insight and action. Poets are masters of the art of vitalizing language, mystics of retreating from it, and speculators and philistines of transcending it occasionally.

Like all other beings, man points beyond and deals with things outside the signs he uses. But only he can be aware of what signs are. He alone can therefore make an effort to stay inside language at the same time that he attempts to break through it to its object, and recapture that object in language in another way. In its most highly developed form, as communicable speech, language is the past as ingrained in one's body and one's fellows. It is a barrier, to transcend which is to be face to face with reality. Since only man has a developed, communicable language he alone is able to go beyond it.

Dialecticians and sophists confound language and reality. They forget that language is a barrier through which one must peer in order to get to know one's fellows and the world. They are mastered by language; they take what is said as though it were the duplicate of or the very thing of which something was said. By concentrating on language they deprive themselves of the opportunity to have something to say.

Only man can be a philosopher and this to the degree that he formulates the meaning of reality inside language and observes that the reality still stands outside. He makes use of an inherited grammar as though he were two men who alternate in supplying the requisite terms. His philosophy is a dialogue in solitude, by which he unites himself with others and orients himself to a world which he before but dimly knew and incoherently expressed. It differs in degree of achievement and clarity of purpose but not in kind from the intent of all his other honest attempts at communication. More than any other communication, however, his philosophy has to be thoroughly rehearsed in private before it is expressed in public, for it has strength only as far as it uses and is not used by language.

A man has something to communicate only if he has first made contact with something. And he can communicate with someone only if he has first communed with himself. The language he uses in his communication should be used in an individual and fresh way if he is to escape from the binding forms of conventional practice and thought, and help his fellows do the same.

Man lives primarily in a world of words and other signs, submitting more to, and ruling more by, threats and commands, assertions and denials, hints and promises than by any force which may be available. The fetters of economics and technology are like straw when compared with the fetters which language imposes on him. Yet language enables him to be free. Language forces him outside himself; it directs him and his fellows to a world beyond, which otherwise might not have been noted.

A language is a technique which takes time to master. It differs from other techniques in its degree of complication, its public utility and its relevance to intents and expectations. It serves to make public what one has in mind, but it can be and is often used, and with accuracy and effect, when the mind is not at work. Conversely, it is possible to have a mind before one has a language. A child seems to think long before it is able to speak. It evidently and quite often thinks beyond the reach of its vocabulary.

It is possible to say what one does not mean and to mean what one does not say; it is possible to speak significantly and yet not have a thought behind the words. Speech involves the use of signs, but one does not need a mind in order to be able to use a sign. In fact, just as men stop at a red light from habit, so they frequently speak and even communicate with one another without thinking. Man's ability to use signs, verbal or nonverbal, provides no clue to the existence or nature of his mind. To know what mind is and does, we must leave bodily techniques behind and consider an entirely different side of his being.

CHAPTER TEN

THE NATURE OF MIND

1. MAN'S FOURFOLD BOND

LIKE THE REST of the beings in nature all of us are held captive by our pasts, our bodies, our fellows and the world about. These form a fourfold barrier, standing perpetually in our way. They limit what we could possibly and actually be, have and do.

We are creatures of experiences already lived through. What we did days ago plays a part in our acts today. The past keeps us moving within narrow grooves, turning us into biased beings who concentrate on one prospect rather than another, sometimes even to our detriment. It forces some tendencies to the fore and keeps others repressed, though our needs may require a different stress. The shape of our tomorrow we molded all yesterday.

Our bodies have requirements, drives and modes of acting which can be controlled at times, but never entirely defied. Possessing their own structures and habits, those bodies have rhythms and make demands to which we must submit whether we will or no. Those who have often exhibited fear by running, find it hard to avoid a frightened run even when they would prefer to be at rest. Before a timid man has a chance to say what he would like to do, his legs are on the move, precipitately carrying him from the scene. Anyone else, in the same circumstances, might also have been frightened. But some would have had their bodies so well keyed that it would be hard to discern a move. If we demand of the brave that they do not budge when startled—a common, though not easily satisfied demand—only those can be brave whose bodies have been properly trained. Whatever praise they deserve is earned then and there by their bodies alone, though credit is also due them, as distinct from their bodies, for past practice and control. Whether trained or untrained, the body leaves its mark on whatever we do.

All of us have been shaped by our societies. We act as social beings even in solitude. The lives of other human beings constantly interplay with and intersect our own. From birth on, our neighbors drive us subtly but surely along paths we never chose. They provoke certain acts and the repression of others; they stand in the way of our efforts and of the effects which those efforts would otherwise produce; they force us to occupy ourselves with problems we would have preferred to ignore, and then they compete with us and force us to forego resolving the issues they raised. Our attempts and our achievements bear unmistakable signs of the pressure exerted by our fellow men.

We are parts of a universe, beings in nature, as well as members of a society. No matter how aloof we try to be, we always yield somewhat to the demands and force imposed by nonhuman beings. At every moment, we are compelled to take account of them as having natures and careers not in harmony with our own, and we constantly shift our emphases in the endeavor to subject them to some control. They help fix the boundaries of our future; they alter the shape our acts assume in fact. The world that lies ahead is structured primarily by what lies alongside.

There is no real escape from our fourfold bond, struggle as we may. If a man could free himself from his past, his body, his fellows or the world, he would be without roots, a language or a home: in the world and yet not part of it. He would be alone and ignorant, untaught and untrained.

Something can be said, in fact, for those who recommend that we passively submit to all our bonds. The more a man yields to the conditions which hem him in, the more secure and stable he often is, the more definite is his future, the more routine and easy is his life. Those who persist in battering their heads against a wall are caught as surely as are those who passively yield. And in addition they lose the peace that comes from the acceptance of the conditions that prevail. They also soon batter according to a pattern, thereby revealing how much they are under the influence of habit, the demands of the body, the pressure of their fellows and the character of the wall. Professional rebels are conservatives in disguise, breaking the fixtures of thought and existence in a somewhat steady and tedious way. They are trapped as surely as others are; their judgments and acts are no less dated and are no less predictable than are those of the quietest conservative. The heresies of today are the prelude to the dogmas of tomorrow. Rebellion at bondage is but a preparation for being bound again, sometimes even more firmly than before.

Yet each man does and must avoid being a creature of any one of these four bonds. Otherwise he would be dead in spirit and in body. He would do nothing, but would have everything done to and for him. Those who pride themselves on being stable steadily recede into the background. The defenders of the *status quo* are now in the process of becoming part of the *status ante*. "I am a man of my times," is the birthcry of an antiquarian. To be alive is to master the fourfold ring of conditions in a manner all one's own. And this every man does to some degree. None is wholly passive. All subject their bonds to some control. We differ from one another primarily in the extent to which we master our bonds while we submit to them.

We are never completely bound by the past. Nor do we ever free ourselves from it entirely. To be sure, we can reform. Yet we cannot reform ourselves completely at one fell swoop. A complete reform would take a lifetime to perform. By the time it was completed, the earlier stages of the reform through which we had gone would be solidified into constraints as effective as those from which we had escaped. The most radical reform touches but facets of a man's nature. Though he change the bent of his interests, forget what he has learned, defy the lessons of his experience, develop virtues where he before encouraged vice, he will continue to act somewhat as he did before. There is a common signature signed to all acts before and after a reform. In opposing the demands of his past, a man inevitably yields to it in other ways.

Nor is anyone completely under the dominance or completely in control of his body. We can master the body's rhythm, break its habits, enliven and constrain it despite its demands. We can, to some degree, even change its tone and structure through drugs, exercise and surgery. All but the most drastic changes are quickly caught and absorbed within the body as a whole, which continues with almost the same strength, insistence and direction it had before. Like a surging sea which may be successfully fought at every moment but never defeated, the body reasserts itself no matter how often it has been denied. No man can rightly claim that he is the master of his body, but only that he has mastered it at various times. The way to escape from the thrall of the body is to control it again and again. And since men must eat and sleep, drink and breathe, each must constantly submit to his body in some respects in order to be able to resist it at all. To control the body we must yield to it, if not in one way then in some other. And every gain that is made must be recovered the next day.

Nor need men quietly submit to the pressure of their fellows. There have been and there undoubtedly always will be a number who resist beyond any assigned degree. Social defiance, however, is but another way of expressing a submission at the same time. Men do not change their societies; the most they can do is introduce changes within them. They cannot cut themselves off completely from their fellow men, but must act in terms of what their fellows produce and intend. Revolutionaries and criminals work inside the frame of an established social whole, differing from others and from one another in the way they treat the good and evil others have made possible. Both opposition and conformity to society presuppose a social field which determines what is respectable or criminal, conservative or revolutionary, reasonable or foolish, promoting security or disorder.

Finally, men do not quietly submit to or really try to escape from nature. They struggle with her, yielding to her in one way while mastering her in another. Men have always struggled with nature, but only in our age has the struggle been buttressed with strategy and accompanied with an acute awareness that we will yield in the end, though not without having made some gain. Our scientists and engineers force nature along unaccustomed routes by following her at the same time. They made the airplane possible, not by ignoring but by yielding to the fact of gravitation. They conquered nature by infecting her with their own demands, which she then proceeded to carry out without their aid or encouragement.

All four barriers are forever in our way. We are always trying to subject them to some control. As a result of our efforts they take on the contours of our intentions and we, though still trapped, often do what we want. We are in fact free beings, for we can and do initiate acts, and can and do assert ourselves—sometimes with considerable success—while firmly bound.

2. MAN'S THREEFOLD FREEDOM

No barrier can come so close that it can prevent our being free. If it could it would destroy us as independent beings and would as a consequence have nothing to constrain. We are able to be trapped only because we stand over against any possible bond.

We are free—independent beings who act on our own—in a threefold way. Each of us independently initiates acts in the endeavor to realize some privately isolated objective. And when those acts encounter the opposition they inevitably must, we freely call upon unused reserves in the effort to achieve the result we were on the verge of losing. Finally, when the opposition is too great for us, we freely occupy ourselves with new objectives in terms of which we may be able to act and struggle with more effect. Our freedom is a triply employed power by which we endeavor to realize objectives, initially regardless of, then in the face of, and finally tangentially to the opposition we happen to encounter. It turns our barriers firstly into fields of operation, then into more or less effective means for the realization of our ends, and finally into occasions for acting in new ways.

Freedom is a power by which the indeterminate is made determinate, the general specific, the abstract concrete, the possible actual. It is most perfectly expressed when we initiate actions designed to convert a result intended into a result attained. Each of us has a characteristic way of focussing on the future, of interpreting it from his own perspective, of treating it as an objective, as a possible good to be made into a good that is real. As intended, the objective is more determinate than it was, but it is not yet entirely determinate. Action is required to make it fully determinate, to give it definiteness and substance.

In origin our acts are means for re-forming ourselves and perhaps other beings so as to make concrete and present what is now abstract and future. Produced from within, they are free sources of the determinations by which we attempt to convert possibilities into realities .When they encounter the opposition they inevitably do, we must, if we are to realize our objectives, express ourselves spontaneously, thereby exerting additional effort. Though none of us can break through any of our barriers, all of us can and do vitalize them, shape them anew, spontaneously reply to the opposition which they offer to the realization of our objectives. We thereby master the past, the body, fellow beings and the world to some degree.

Sometimes our barriers are too much for us. They effectively prevent us from realizing our objectives. We are then prompted to make an effort to isolate and realize new objectives. Only if there were—as there is—an ultimate objective, an end to whose realiza-

tion we are necessarily pledged, would we, despite every defeat
and regardless of all appearance to the contrary, always strive to
realize it.

Because only men have ultimate objectives, only they are unable
to change into superior types of being when they encounter insuperable obstacles to the expression of their human concerns.
When they encounter resistance which effectively prevents the
expression of a concern for their ultimate objectives, they try to
change the nature of their acts. Like other beings they are, despite
an inability to change in nature, always free to meet defeat with a
new adventure, feeble and unsuccessful though this may prove
to be.

Each of us initiates acts. Each of us struggles with all four
barriers. Each of us spontaneously shifts his emphasis in the face of
defeat. Most of us concentrate our energies, however, on only one
of these three enterprises, and are inclined to struggle more with
some barriers than with others. But a man is somewhat less than
a man should be, unless he employs his freedom fully in all three
ways and takes adequate account of all the obstacles he confronts.

A man must master bodily techniques to be free while bound.
But he never becomes as free as he can be until he freely acquires
and uses a *mind*. That mind of his is not a gift. It is achieved. To
know how it is achieved is to take a first step in grasping what it is
and what it can do. Only then will one learn how one can know
the world in which one is, and what man's ultimate objective and
duty may be.

3. THE ORIGIN OF MIND

It is generally agreed that there were no human minds before
there were human bodies. Democritus, Plato, Plotinus, Descartes
and their followers, who claim that the mind is a separate, eternal
substance or part of one, constitute only an apparent dissenting
minority. Their claim relates to a frozen mind, a mind which is a

reservoir of perfect, eternal truths—not to a fallible, fumbling mind, pertinent to the contingent, changing facts of daily experience. These writers, no less than the others, are agreed that mind in the latter guise does not and cannot exist before there is a human body. The opposition between the minority and the majority does not relate to the question as to whether or not the mind is an integral part of a living being. It relates solely to the question as to whether or not there is another mind, superior to the former and capable of existing and functioning apart from anything in nature. All thinkers seem agreed that there were no human minds before there were human bodies. It would be possible but foolish to suppose otherwise.

It is possible to admit that human bodies are presupposed by human minds, and still misconceive how minds arose. To minimize this prospect it is helpful to remind oneself that man and his powers are a product of a natural evolution resulting from the exercise of freedom in an environment.

Men acquire their minds as the outcome of an exercise of freedom. It is not inevitable, however, that freedom should be exercised so that mind should be its outcome. It is not necessary that there be minds. The acceptance of this last proposition forces a clean break with Hegel and his school, including those who, like the Marxists, turn the Hegelian idealism into a materialism. The Hegelians subscribe to the theory that mind and everything else in nature is the necessary product of a relentless historic movement which nothing can stay or redirect. But that movement is a movement *for* the things in nature and not *of* them. It is a cosmic juggernaut which alone determines what does and can occur. For Hegelians, of the right and of the left, the things in nature are impotent puppets, pulled by invisible strings. No one of these things really develops or comes to be; rather, all are precipitated out of an infinite maw which acts according to a logic of its own, unaffected by the efforts or inclinations of finite beings. The Hegelian view does not account for the existence of individual human minds. These have their source inside and not outside nature; they arise as a result of the activities of specific beings, exercising powers of their own.

The mechanistic, deterministic view which was so popular in the last century has appeared to some to be the only alternative to Hegelian idealism or materialism. But there is little difference in principle between them. The latter, like the former, denies power and activity to individual beings. In addition, the latter supposes that whatever occurs is an inescapable consequence of some previous cause—a supposition which Hume clearly revealed to be without warrant and which is in fact, as we have already tried to show,* internally incoherent.

Hume thought his analysis implied that there was no causation in fact. He overlooked an alternative: there is causation, but it is not the production of a future effect by a past cause. Man and his mind arrive late on the cosmic scene, but not as a result of compulsions exercised from on high or from the past, nor as a result of a blind chance movement of things. Man and mind are the outcome of intelligible yet unpredictable activities on the part of natural beings.

Were there no causation, as Hume maintained, there would be nought but a sequence of independent and irrelevant occurrences, each one a miracle, impotent and inexplicable. No rational explanation of anything would be possible and it would be necessary to cancel out the evidence of daily experience and the possibility of intelligent practice.

Hume's theory, like the theory it opposed, defeats itself, though in a different way. The more firmly one holds to it, the more surely one must affirm that its denial is equally reasonable. A theory which asserts that the past and future are completely independent, must allow that the future may be entirely unlike the past. Accordingly, it must allow that, after a time when events followed

*pp. 4ff, 24ff.

one another in a meaningless procession, there can come a time when they are related causally and rationally. The more one disconnects the events of the future from the past, the more one allows for the possibility that all events are intimately connected in that future.

Hume thought his principles required him to deny that there was any causation in fact. If that conclusion followed, it would mean that the future was independent of the past. If, then, there was no causation in his day, it could still be true, on Hume's own principles, that there could be causation today. But Hume drew the wrong conclusion from his analysis. There was causation in his day just as surely as there is causation in ours, but it is not an act by which past "causes" reach out to control and compel a present effect. The past is dead, impotent, perished. It cannot produce anything. It is by agreeing with Hume on this truth that we can, in consonance with the evidence of daily experience, affirm: the past and the future are causally connected, but the past does not necessitate the future.

The difficulty which Hume underscored and misconstrued is not avoided by giving up mechanism and accepting a theory of teleology in its place. Teleology supposes that causation is the exhibition of an irresistible power exerted by the future on the present. But, like the mechanism it opposes, it maintains that effects are already determinate before they actually occur. Teleology is mechanism in reverse. Rightly maintaining with Hume that nothing as past can be active in the future, the teleologist falsely supposes that the productive cause of things is something not yet in existence, and perhaps beyond anyone's power to observe, limit, or control. The value of his theory is largely that of a purgative. It eliminates mechanism but puts nothing better in its place. The future on which it rests its hopes is just as impotent as the past which mechanism glorified.

In order to account for what occurs, it is not necessary to suppose either some distant powerful future thing which pulls all existents irresistibly forward, or a finished past which somehow continues to work in the present. The past conditions the future as a limited but not yet determinate realm within which a range of occurrences can take place. A concrete course in time is necessary in order to determine and thereby realize that future. The result can be known in advance as a possibility, not as an actuality. It is actual only when the free and unpredictable concrete course terminates in it.

Minds are an outcome of the exercise of freedom. Like consciousness and language, they first appeared after the world had been in existence for some time. The minds belong to and originate in individual men. Since a mind is not a palpable thing passed on from generation to generation, each man today must acquire his own mind, and this in somewhat the same way that the first men did.

It does not seem that there ever were grown men who were without minds of some sort. The most primitive men of which we have any knowledge had their mythologies, religions and art. They speculate, they discover, they invent. The primitive adult is neither idiot nor infant. When he was born he was human; as he matured he must have acquired a mind in somewhat the way we acquire minds today.

It is, of course, possible that in earlier times the minds of men were less developed than are minds today. There is no justification for dogmatism on the point, however. We have no data which would justify us in saying that the minds of men at other times were inferior to ours. The most we have a right to claim is that their minds were perhaps different from ours—characterized by different habits and exercised at a different tempo.

So far as the problem of the origin of our minds is concerned, it makes no difference whether they are similar to, better than, or different from the minds of our ancestors; the problem of the origin of our minds is still the problem of how and why each one of us acquires his mind. The initial appearance of our minds or of dimensions of them is but a special case of the appearance of mind in any human being. It presupposes intelligence, the ability to relate what it perceives to what it sensitively discerns.

A being can, as a rule, be intelligent only when calm. When excited by others, it always will if an infant, usually will if an animal, and sometimes will if an adult, abandon its intelligence. Either it uses the perceived as a sign not of what it expects but of what is expected by others, or it treats the sensitively discerned not as though it were the object of its own but as though it were the object of another's concern, or it ignores both the perceived and the discerned. On hearing an insistent cry, excitable beings move from what they perceive to what their neighbors expect, look to what is sensitively discerned as though it were the object of their fellows' concern, or put aside both the perceived and the sensitively discerned to point blindly to a future whose nature they do not know. By treating their perceived neighbors as a sign of what those neighbors fear, they tend to act with fear when they are with those neighbors again, despite the fact that there may be nothing then to fear. By treating what they sensitively discern as though it were the object of the concern of others, they act with fear towards what are irrelevant possibilities. By ignoring both what they perceive and what they sensitively discern, they give up the guidance that an individual sensitive concern could yield, and instead participate, like unconscious beings, in the dynamic act of dealing with a fearful but unknown future from the base of an unobserved present. In these three ways they infectiously share the emotions of others. They thereby abandon their intelligence, giving up as it were the concern as sensitive for the concern as purposive.

By abandoning its intelligence, an individual both gains and loses. It recovers the use of its concern as vitally and intimately related to the concerns of others, and thereby frees itself from the narrow individual perspective characteristic of its sensitivity. But then the teachings of its own experience are distorted or ignored. It has the wisdom of the lily of the field, or of the sparrow with her young, but no longer knows the world it encountered when calm and in which it lived as a separate individual. A being ought to be both vitally and intelligently concerned, at one with its fellows and yet a being apart. If it is both, it is in a position to have and use a mind.

Minds are acquired in infancy. They presuppose intelligence. They are possible only to infants who have grasped the meaning of some of the items they encounter through the agency of their senses. That it is intelligent, the infant of course does not know. It does not know what it expects or that the expected is pertinent to what it perceives. It connects them without knowing what it does or why.

The infant must also, if it is to acquire a mind, be part of a social group. Minds are possible only in societies. To be able to acquire a mind the infant must be able to participate in the vital life of its kind. Since what it intelligently grasps are not the goods with which others are actually concerned, but those goods as relevant to its own good, it must, to be truly social, direct itself towards a good other than that which it intelligently grasps. A mind is possible only for an infant whose individual intelligence is rendered useless by the activities in which it vitally participates with others.

No infant can acquire a mind unless it is at once intelligent and in a position where its intelligence is useless. These two conditions are necessary, but they do not suffice to make mind possible. There are subhuman beings which are intelligent but which cannot use their intelligence because they are so vitally involved in the affairs of others. They do not, however, acquire minds, for though they are forced to sacrifice what they intelligently grasp in order to live in the herd, they are unable to recover what they sacrifice.

Only a man can at once live with others and apart from them. He alone can acquire a mind because he alone can, in the face of a vitally shared experience, insist on remaining intelligent. A mind is man's reward for being faithful to his own intelligence while living as a vital member of a group.

Mind is intelligence reinstated, made pertinent to vital activities, given body and driving force, enabling a human being to be at once an independent individual and a part of a social whole. It is intelligence employed despite and in the face of the demands of group existence. It is the agency by which the individual overcomes the resistance which the infectiously shared concerns of others offer to what it intelligently and sensitively discerns.

The sensitively discerned is the object of an intelligent use of the perceived. Irrelevant to our concerns as purposively intertwined with other concerns, it is made relevant by means of the mind. Mind, because it makes what we sensitively discern pertinent to the concerns of others, is a means by which the sensitively discerned is given a double meaning, turned into a metaphor. It is the agency by which the sensitively discerned is treated as having a different weight for others than it has for us. For us, what we sensitively discern is a good whose realization depends on how we act; it is an object of mere intelligence. For others, it is at best an unknown good related to the objects of their concerns. Our minds enable us to grasp it as a possibility relevant both to others and to us, as a good which is an object not only of our concern but of the concerns of others, though in a different sense and with a different value. Apart from mind either we would intelligently refer to it as individuals, or we would ignore it in order to live vitally with others. By means of mind we give it a double value, see it not only as having an intelligent meaning for us but also as having an emotionally grasped meaning as the terminus of the concerns of others.

4. LEVELS OF MIND

Mind is the power of treating content as having one significance in one context and another significance in another context. It is first employed when the perceived is treated as pertinent to the sensitively discerned, as at once something we expected and something another expects. By being related to the sensitively discerned as having this double meaning, the perceived acquires a double import, signifying a future as at once pertinent to us and to other beings.

When the intelligent infant feels the agitation of its mother, it views her as a perceived being concerned with an objective it sensitively discerns or is accustomed to expect. The infant is contagiously agitated perhaps while expecting the milk it is accustomed to await when perceiving its mother. It thereupon infers, perhaps wrongly, that she is agitated with respect to that milk. Instead of passively awaiting the milk or being agitated with respect to something unknown, it treats the expected milk as though it were the object which agitates its mother. It has no knowledge, of course, of the nature of milk; yet it has a mind as a consequence of the fact that it turns to the milk as a sensitively discerned possibility which is not only signified by means of the percept of its mother but is pertinent to the agitation it shares with its mother.

A higher level of mind will be attained by an infant which can grasp the nature of the mentally acknowledged possibility. Using the mentally acknowledged possibility as a focus, the infant will then be able to forge connections between it and new perceptions. The new perceptions will thereby achieve the double role of being relevant to the infant and to a perceived, concerned being. The original possibility will then not only enable the infant to connect new perceptions with what it expects but to treat perceived beings, in whose concerns it does not vitally participate, as beings concerned with what it expects. New perceptions, and the beings to which they pertain, thus permit the infant to know the possibilities on which it focussed, as possibilities pertinent to other perceptions and to other beings. By referring new perceptions and beings to the milk which it intelligently and agitatedly expected, the infant thus comes to know them, though only in terms of milk.

The infant knows whatever it confronts to be somehow and in some way related to milk, but knows nothing more. Its undeveloped mind knows merely that the possibility of milk is pertinent in some way to what is now perceived and what now exists. To develop its mind it must grasp the different senses in which the milk is pertinent to all types of experience and being.

A limited possibility, such as milk, can serve as an appropriate focal point for any number of diverse perceptions and concerns. But then it must be subjected to radical interpretations. To view everything from the perspective of milk requires a grasp, beyond the power of an infant, of the different ways in which milk is pertinent to different perceptions and beings.

An infant is able to develop its mind because it is involved in the concerns of multiple beings in multiple ways. It has multiple objects which it intelligently expects. If its intelligence were restricted to but one possibility it could do nothing more than use that one possibility as a focal point for everything it encounters and thus subject it to radical interpretations so that it becomes somehow pertinent to everything.

A multiplicity of focal points make it unnecessary to give strange meanings to a single possibility in order to make that possibility pertinent to different beings. But so far as a being has multiple focal points it has multiple unconnected thoughts. It must connect its diverse focal points, find a means of inferring from one to another.

A scientific mind is acquired so far as one forges a connection between different perceptual items, and infers from that connected whole to a principle by which different focal possibilities can be related one to the other. The inference of which science makes use, the principles of transformation scientists employ in order to move from one perception or focal point to another, are the material of mathematics. Mathematics is in search of a principle which can transform the different limited principles of science into one another. Both science and mathematics ignore the bearing percepts have on real objects, and how those real objects are concerned with possibilities. To know these one must have the mind of an artist. It is the function of the artistic mind to generate metaphors, to bring together diverse perceptions into unities which are revelatory of all the beings to which those perceptions belong. It is the further function of cosmology to generalize this effort, to extend the artistic metaphor to all beings and make evident how it is to be interpreted from case to case. A grasp of the nature of all beings from the vantage of a comprehensive metaphor makes it possible to relate all objects to a single objective. That objective, acknowledged to be nothing more than an objective, is one of the main things a philosophy seeks to know. Philosophy is Godless cosmology. This is true even when its discourse is pious and its ostensible topic God.

The philosophic mind senses the unity behind different inquiries. It attempts to formulate a grand metaphor encompassing all that is. It presupposes the existence of the artistic, the cosmological, the scientific and the mathematical. But it does not wait for them to complete their special tasks—granted that their methods allow for a final result. The knowledge of how their tasks differ provides sufficient material to philosophy to make possible a characterization of the kind of results they will reach. Starting with any item, the philosophic mind frees it from the details which obscure the fact that every actuality is finite and is concerned with a possible future good. From then on, there is nothing more for a mind to do than to get richer and richer ideas of the nature of the good and of the actual, and of the concern which relates the two.

Just as no man need give up his intelligence to have a mind, so no one need abandon his interest in science, art, or cosmology to have a philosophy. The object of philosophy is the unitary truth which all beings and activities exhibit, not a truth opposed to them. The unity which it provides is a unity which not only allows but requires a multiplicity of diverse mental activities.

Various levels of mind come to be for the same reason that mind itself arises. The diversity of experience stands in the way of the use of established connections. It thereby drives the individual to divide his enterprises and ultimately himself, or to find a higher ground in terms of which he can bring the separated items together. The mind is stretched to the utmost limit if it can reach the stage where it is able to interrelate all that is to an ultimate all-comprehensive ground. Beyond that point there is no need and no place for it to go.

5. INFERENCE

Every concept and idea, every item of perception and sensitivity, has different meanings in different situations. Each is a principle of inference by means of which we can move from the case where it is pertinent in one sense to a possible different application in another. The work of mind is inference. When we affirm that what we perceive is relevant to an object beyond, our affirmation is the inference that because the perceived has one meaning in relation to us, it has another meaning as apart from us and as ingredient in that object. Such an inference enables us, while sharing the vital concern of others, to view those others through the agency of what is perceived. A similar inference, exercised with reference to a possibility, discerned or conceived, makes it possible for us to grasp the meaning of others as vitally concerned with the objects with which we as intelligent beings are also though differently concerned. On all its levels, the mind makes use of the material of intelligence (or of what can be derived from that material), as a principle of inference, and thus as having one value for us and other values for other beings.

Inferences are of two kinds: contingent and necessary. An inference is contingent if the premise does not suffice to warrant the conclusion, and thus if the conclusion must obtain at least part of its content from the principle of inference. The conclusion "It will rain" is obtained from the premise "The sky has begun to darken" by means of some such contingent principle as "If the sky darkens, there will be rain" or "If rain is promised, rain will come." The conclusion does not follow from the premise alone; content implicitly or explicitly in the principle makes the conclusion what it is.

A necessary inference differs from a contingent one in that the premise alone suffices to warrant the conclusion. In a necessary inference there is only a logical relation between premise and conclusion; there is no principle which provides content for the conclusion. Such an inference is derivable from a contingent inference by treating the contingent principle as a premise. C. S. Peirce* seems to have been the first to discover this truth. "Let the premises of any argument," he said, "be denoted by P, the conclusion by C, and the principle by L. Then if the whole of the principle be expressed as a premise the argument will become L and P ∴ C. But this new argument must also have its principle which may be denoted by L'. Now, as L and P (supposing them to be true), contain all that is requisite to determine the probable or necessary truth of C, they contain L'. Thus L' must be contained in the principle, whether expressed in the premiss or not. Hence every argument has, as portion of its principle, a certain principle which cannot be eliminated from its principle. Such a principle may be termed a *logical principle*." Every principle of inference, Peirce's observation makes clear, contains a logical principle by which one can rigorously proceed from a premise and the original principle to the conclusion. Any result in nature or mind, therefore, is a necessary consequent of some antecedent and of some course which starts from that antecedent and terminates in that result.

*Collected Papers, 2. 465-6.

Of the two modes of inference, the contingent is the more original, the more common and the more basic. Necessary inference is a deterministic ideal rather than a fact, of interest after vital but contingent inferences have been completed. They are occasionally approached and imitated in the postulate systems which logicians offer as portraits of the nature of mathematical thought, in neglect of the truth that mathematics is, with mathematicians, a creative enterprise using contingent principles to move from contingent starting points to contingent results.

The work of mind is inference. It is not common, however, to speak of all the results of mental activities as conclusions, and any attempt to speak of mind as engaged in inference is therefore bound to meet resistance.

Firstly, we are accustomed to think of conclusions as logically necessitated by premises. This, however, is little more than the result of the pressure of specialists. Ordinary men constantly "conclude" and say they do, where logicians would see only inadequately grounded results, unworthy of the name "conclusion." To draw a conclusion it is not necessary that the premise should necessitate it. The principle exhibited in the process of drawing the conclusion contributes to the determination of the conclusion in the same way that the course of reaching an effect determines the nature of that effect.

Secondly, we are accustomed to think of conclusions as results affirmed; yet we do not affirm but rather entertain the results of many contingent inferences. It is arbitrary, however, to view conclusions as necessarily results affirmed, as points to which one deliberately reasons and at which one rests. It is a rare conclusion in fact that is reasoned to deliberately; most intellectual results, even those widely acclaimed as the termini of inference, are obtained without preparation and are rarely affirmed, serving merely as momentary perches at which the mind rests in a series of inferential leaps.

Thirdly, men are not as a rule aware of how they reason. Nor do they acknowledge the perceived or the discerned as principles of inference. It is not necessary, however, to know how one reasons in order to reason, nor necessary to acknowledge a principle of inference in order to make use of it. Just as men speak grammatically without knowing how, and use a term as a subject or predicate without acknowledging it to be one, so they move to conclusions by means of principles whose function they do not remark.

Fourthly, it is customary to speak of premises and conclusions as propositions which may be true or false, and to refuse the designation to mere terms. Yet what is an isolated term but a condensed proposition? Or, where a term is a component of a proposition, what is it but that proposition partially filled out, a premise pointing to a possible conclusion? An isolated term has a different application to different objects and is thus a proposition of the form: "This X is other than that X." As a component of a proposition, it specifies "this X," and points to "that X" as an object which another term of the proposition is to specify. In either case it can be a conclusion of an inference.

As a consequence of this quadruple disinclination to recognize a conclusion as that to which men actually conclude, men—particularly if they are logicians—are sometimes tempted to speak as though they possessed two minds. One would suppose from their accounts that they were in possession of a divine pure reason, which necessarily and alone moved noiselessly and perfectly from premise to conclusion, and that in addition they had an imperfect, psychological and human mind which haltingly and illegitimately hopped from one detached idea to another. But there is only one mind, making use of countless contingent principles of inference.

6. *MIND AND FREEDOM*

If a man could, like a medieval angel, have his whole being concentrated in his mind, he would be unable to learn anything from the world outside. He would have no body and thus no life, no pain or pleasure, no intelligence or emotion, no images or concepts, and no work to do.

A man is not a mind; he has a mind. That mind embodies but part of his nature. It is capable of exhibiting but part of the freedom characteristic of him.

His mind is a barrier analogous to that of his body, though it is one which he himself, in part, erects. It is good that such a barrier should exist. A man who had no mind would either be subjected to the restraints which particular things happen to impose, or he would have retreated so far from them that he would have lost himself in a mystical enjoyment of his or their private beings. The mind is the self external to itself, the individual as organized and restructured apart from the body and in part as a result of his own activity.

Since the mind is a barrier, the individual is forced to take account of it. He must vitalize it at every moment, converting it from an habitual set of inferences into individualized activities exhibiting the essence of his concern. The inferences in which he engages must be fresh and novel at every moment, reflecting the effort of the self to make the mind conform to the self's intent.

No man thinks all the time, though Descartes and Kant assure us to the contrary. We retreat from the mind when awake and when asleep, recovering ourselves as beings with a unitary promise which no particular mode of expression can exhaust. A man who always thought would not be a man who thought for a purpose, but at best one who exuded thoughts as another might odors. Men can, do, and at times ought to avoid making use of their minds. They can, do, and at times ought to dismiss the most perfect chain of reasoning, in perfect accord with the world, as not important. They can, do and sometimes ought to dwell in quiet solitude, peacefully and imperturbably. Because they then retreat from the mind and not from the world, theirs is a retreat not to the unintelligible but to what is beyond the intelligible. It is an enjoyment of the self as being more than mind, rather than as being alienated from the world.

Every man breaks through a barrier in the form of mind in order to concern himself directly with the things he has in mind. His actions, then, instead of being only the direct expression of himself as filtered and structured by his body, reflect also what he has in mind. They are planned actions, actions which are intelligible to him but which are more than what he has made intelligible. He breaks through the barrier of the mind, too, in flashes of sympathy by which he reaches to the being of objects as substantial, independent, not entirely understood.

We are aware that there is more to the world than that which we get into our minds because even while we use our minds we transcend them and touch the beings which lie outside. Intellectuals run the risk of losing touch with reality, but once they become concerned with reaching it by passing through the barrier of the mind, they are able to reach it as that which they not only know but also understand. The sympathy of an animal is without reason, the reason of an intellectual is without sympathy, but a full man sympathizes through reason.

The conclusions towards which the mind actually moves are conclusions which are possible for it because of its past, and are made probable because of its acquired habits. A habit of thinking in certain ways leads to the derivation of one kind of conclusion from a given set of premises rather than another. The mind, however, is not a slave of its past. It reconstitutes itself as it goes along. In an actual inference it vitalizes the possible result which its own past defined and its own habits forced into focus.

The mind is faced by a body having its own habits. That body is a barrier. It provokes the mind to entertain images and concepts relevant to the body. As Spinoza remarked, the idea that Peter has of Paul tells more about Peter's body than it does about Paul. To avoid this it is essential to retreat from the body and thereby have a mind uninfluenced by that body. Only then will it be possible to derive conclusions regardless of the needs or demands of the body. A truly intellectual being thinks in ways and attains results which are not in exact conformity with the course and interests of his body.

The mind's direction is also determined in part by other beings near and far. In moving to a conclusion the mind isolates and quickens a future partly determined by them. But to be a mind at its best, a philosophic reason, it must retreat also from such barriers and move to objectives and ideals which portray a world that might and ought to be, but may never be in fact. It then moves beyond what nature for the moment is, but not beyond what it intrinsically is and may actually become.

It is a commonplace that to think is to be free. Like many a commonplace, it contains a truth and an error. By means of the mind one effectively escapes the limitations of the past, the body, the environment and even the whole of the existent world. Yet the mind has its own habits, limitations of its own. It can serve to hold one within monotonous and outworn patterns; it can lead one to submit to the demands of other beings more than one otherwise would. A mind to make one free must first free itself from arbitrary constraints, and must then freely constrain itself in conformity with an ultimate bond. It must break through the barriers of past, body, neighbors and world, and then construct a final barrier of its own in the form of an idea of which everything else is an illustration. Then and then only will it be a mind as free as a mind can be, a mind which freely forces itself to be constrained only by the good and the true.

7. *THE MIND-BODY PROBLEM*

The operations of the mind make a difference to other activities in which a man might engage, for the mind has natural roots and natural fruits. There are professed materialists and naturalists, however, who think that the mind has no role to play in nature. Huxley, for example, was a good Darwinian, and Santayana has spoken of himself as the only materialist now living. Yet both of them view a mind as little more than a domicile of idle dreams. They affirm that mind has a natural origin. They deny that it has a natural goal. They are naturalists on the way up, not naturalists when they arrive.

Theirs is the converse of the neo-Platonic view which took matter to be a product of mind and refused to allow that this product had any effect on the mind which mysteriously generated it. According to the neo-Platonists, matter is impotent, a shadow thrown across the wastes of emptiness. The Huxleys and Santayanas reverse the roles which mind and matter play in this account. The defects characteristic of the one are therefore to be expected in the other, though in opposite corners. Thus, just as for the neo-Platonists there are no laws or habits which matter embodies and no power which it can exert, so for the halfhearted naturalists there are no habits or laws to which the mind submits and no difference which it can make. Motion is a mystery for the one, logic a mystery for the other. For both there is no way of affirming the evident truth that the state of the body often makes a difference to what one thinks and that the nature of one's thought sometimes makes a difference to what one does.

Mind has a role to play in nature. But it would be driving this point too far to affirm that the mind is nothing more than an instrument for the pursuit or use of things in nature. Dewey's statement that "knowledge is a mode of practical action" formulates a program. It does not describe a fact. It asks us to make our knowledge significant in practice. It would express a falsehood if it meant that all knowledge was already significant. N-dimensional geometries are not plans for changing the course of the world. It would show little submission to the facts to deny that most of the truths learned at second hand have an inconsequential role to play in the lives of those who hear them. The mind is but one of the factors in an organic pattern of activities in which it is sometimes dominant, sometimes coordinate and sometimes recessive. The truths of which it is aware sometimes, as in the case of the fanatic, disorganize and confound. Sometimes, as in the case of the indolent, they serve only to adorn a passing mood. It is a professor's delusion that mind is power, all primed to work and then only for the good.

Nor is it true that the mind concerns itself exclusively with the phenomena of daily life. It reaches at times beyond the here and now, and sometimes even beyond the particular details of nature. If mind did not, it would be impossible to think some such truth as: "Natural things and events are in a constant process of change," which is what most naturalists intend. That proposition does not restrict itself to what is happening here and now; it applies to all of nature. It necessarily goes beyond any evidence we directly have or can obtain. No experience is wide or long enough to include all the facts it embraces. So long as such assertions are significant—and they must be significant if the affirmation or denial of naturalism makes sense—the mind cannot be defined as nought but an instrument for the solution of practical problems.

There are times when occurrences in the mind merely reflect the occurrences in the body or conversely; there are other times when mind and body condition one another. A depressing thought may occasionally paralyze the body, a diseased gland may corrupt the mind. But it is also true that the thought of glory can force weary legs to keep on running, and weary legs can make sweet the thought of rest.

Though there are times when the mind and body go along parallel paths, there are other times when they move in different directions. Sometimes we think of food while we are hungry, but we can also think of crackers while we are thirsty and can move our legs while we contemplate the muscles of our arms. The vitality and direction of the mind or body can be varied independently. When the body is at rest, the mind can begin to move and when the mind becomes quiet, the body may be most active.

The mind and body are thus related to one another somewhat as are walking and breathing. They are different phases of a single being, capable of working together, of benefiting one another and of operating in independence of one another. But the one comes to be before, and is a precondition for the existence and exercise of the other. Though we primarily and initially express ourselves through the body, we can come to express ourselves through the mind.

One can get along for a time with a theory that the mind is a changing pattern of ideas which somehow keeps abreast of events happening elsewhere, that it is an offshoot of bodily processes, or that it is a kind of aptitude or function of the body. These theories do not satisfy—that is why there is still a "mind-body" problem. But even if they were perfectly coherent and did succeed in accounting for every property and act of mind and the way it functioned with respect to the body, they would be adequate to only a facet of the human being. From them one could learn nothing about the nature and function of the self, the constancy which characterizes it, or its power to vitalize and yet transcend the body and the mind.

A "mind-body" problem is permanent and insoluble if the mind be viewed in isolation from a wider self. The mind is then not only treated as distinct from the body but as something which could not be owned or be linked to the body. It is easy to create insoluble problems of this kind. Thus, if we neglect the fact that there is a child involved, we can create a "finger-mouth" problem, and ask ourselves how a finger, which is other than and separate from a mouth, could ever get into and out of it. The problem is not merely soluble but solved as soon as we bring in the child. The finger gets into and out of the mouth because the child puts it in and takes it out. Similarly, there is no problem of how a mind can be distinct from and yet cooperate with, influence, be influenced by and act independently of a body at different times—once it be recognized that one being owns them both and connects the content of the one to the other in these different ways.

Though both mind and body go their own ways to some degree, they can never be completely sundered from one another. They are normally related by *emotions* which reflect the tension provoked by differences in their content, rhythm and direction. The emotion fills out the gap between them, thereby infecting them both and modifying their activities.

An emotion is possible only to a being with a mind whose acts are not entirely in accord with those of the body. It arises when the activities of the body and mind diverge, becoming most evident when an individual, without intellectual preparation, suddenly changes the direction of his bodily acts. As the James-Lange theory of the emotions suggests, if one goes through the acts of a man in anger one will have an emotion of anger, providing—it is important to add—one does not then think of what one is doing. An emotion can also be provoked, however, as the James-Lange theory seems not to allow, by sending our thoughts careening in one direction while we habitually and bodily continue in another. It is possible to provoke a flush of irritable anger by entertaining some alien thought while engaged in the pursuit of familiar tasks in routine ways.

No man is ever free of the emotions for long, for none has a mind which is in perfect accord with his body for more than a few moments together. But the emotions are rarely noted unless they are violent, forced to fill in an unusual and large gap due to a sudden change in the course of the activities of either body or mind. And, since the emotions infect both the mind and the body which they relate, sooner or later they lose their warmth and intensity. They then become steady emotional states which define the temper of one whose mind and body continue to have a somewhat constant bearing on one another at a fairly constant distance.

The mind and body are also discordant with respect to the objects with which they deal. While perceiving one thing, men think of others. The world with which their bodies are concerned diverges from that towards which their minds are inclined. To overcome the discrepancy, the individual charges his thoughts with a spontaneous *mental desire* to make them applicable to the objects his body confronts, or spontaneously charges his bodily acts with an alien *interest* or *bodily desire* in an attempt to force them to deal with the things he has in mind. Our thoughts are spontaneously turned towards the world even when they are deliberately forged to help us escape, and our bodies are spontaneously impelled to turn where our thoughts point even when we are most anxious to be immersed in what is present and immediate. The truth in pragmatism is not that mind does or should concern itself with the practical but that, when it does not, it is possible that it will be made practical spontaneously. But it is also possible that a spontaneous mental desire will force the body to submit to the guidance of the theoretical. Which will occur is beyond any man's prevision, being the result of an adventure in freedom which experiments first with the one solution and then the other.

The emotions and desires await the occurrence of a discrepancy in the objects or activities of the mind and the body. They provide momentary ways of harmonizing the two. It is possible, however, to harmonize them more permanently through the use of the *will*. This concerns itself with objectives pertinent to both mind and body, directing them, despite divergencies in momentary content, to work in harmony.

The will has many grades, many degrees of adequacy. In its most elementary form it fastens on the object of the body or mind and forces the other to conform; in its highest form it is a *creative* will which fastens on the good and controls both the mind and the body in the light of it. Like the emotions, it presupposes the existence of a more permanent relation between the mind and the body, expressive of the fact that both are possessions of a single undivided self. We begin to move to the core of man's nature when we deal with the will and the self which makes that will possible.

CHAPTER ELEVEN

THE WILL

1. EMOTION AND DESIRE

ACTION IS required to make what is in mind fully determinate. If the action produces the result envisaged, what is in mind attains the status of an empirical truth, and the individual adjusts himself to the world about. But action also occurs regardless of what is in mind.

We often, all too often, act nonrationally. What we have in mind fails to conform to what we are prepared to bring about as bodies. While thinking of one result we are frequently keyed to act so as to bring about an entirely different result. To make a truth of what is in mind, we must control the body and other beings. If we cannot do this, we think idly, or we provide ideas which stand in the way of the correct apprehension of what does in fact occur.

A man's body is usually prepared to act in consonance with the tendencies and habits which external conditions and internal economy force to the fore, regardless of what he has in mind. His bodily acts are primarily ways of modifying the state of his body in relation to the things about and of modifying the things about in terms of the needs of the body. Hungry, he reaches towards food; shivering, he turns from the cold. At one time the state of his body may be more responsible for promoting a tendency than the provocations offered by the world; at another time the latter may have a greater influence. Even though food is not available, hunger pangs may force the tendency to eat into ascendancy. The pangs keep other tendencies repressed, prompting a man to look for food, to move towards the place where food is usually found, to chew what he can put his teeth into. On the other hand, a man well-nourished can be provoked to eat by tempting odors, flavors, and colors, by threat and custom. These can force the tendency to eat to the fore, though the internal economy of the body may require that the tendency be restrained for a while.

Similarly, ideas in the mind are a function of the nature of the mind and what the mind confronts. At different times one or the other of these conditions takes a dominant role. A chemist thinks about iron, water and oxygen in somewhat similar ways; the sight of a triangle starts the ruminations of a mathematician in a way it does not the poet's.

The mind and the body have their own habits. They respond independently to different external conditions. Both are vitalized and possessed by the concerned self. That self spontaneously brings them into accord by altering both, thereby enabling them to converge on a common objective. This double infection of mind and body by the self, with its consequent reference of them to some single objective, is felt by the self as an *emotion*. Emotions direct the individual, despite diverse mental and bodily tendencies, to think and act concordantly.

An emotional being has a mind and a body which are in consonance, but only because both are denied independence and the results they can independently produce are made impossible. The mind and body of an angry man are in accord. He is a unified being, his emotion infecting and altering the tendencies of his mind and body. He may continue to act on the being to which he was bodily directed or he may continue to think of the object he had in mind. But as in the grip of the emotion his action will take a different turn from the one it normally does and his thought will have a different content. The object of his anger, though physically in the path of his body or intellectually before his mind, will at the same time be made to sustain what he tended to think or what he tended to do. As an object of both mind and body, the object of his anger will usually have no other reality than that of being angrily referred to by means of his emotionally coincident mind and body.

No man can persistently accept an emotional solution to the problem of making his mind and body cohere. The emotions are exhausting; they testify that the mind or body or both are functioning improperly and may have been made to converge on something not actual apart from that emotion. They direct a being to think and act so as to bring about results he did not envisage and may not want. Only the emotion of love, and then only when directed to the self of another, is partly free of these defects. Love synthesizes the object of a mental inference and a bodily tendency so as to make what is observed serve as a guide to the nature of a real being beyond. The lover recognizes the emotional object to be constituted from within by a self analogous to his. He knows another as lovable. But the object of his love, like the object of any other emotion, he may misconstrue. The other is lovable, but he may not have those virtues which the lover lovingly bestows on him. Not even love is an altogether satisfactory agent for making the mind and body cohere.

Some men free themselves from the grip of the emotions by acquiring habits of thinking in consonance with their bodies; others free themselves by acquiring bodily habits of acting in consonance with their thoughts. Such men are sane, excessively sane in fact. They are sane by habit, purchasing their sanity by subordinating the mind to the body or the body to the mind, thereby depriving themselves either of a free and independent mind or of a vital and independent body. The main difference between the two types is that the noses of the one are usually red and of the other blue.

The mind and the body have their own goods; to make one of them permanently the model for the other is to do injustice to that other. Also, there are novelties in experience for which our habits are not prepared. Those who are sane by habit, therefore, cannot avoid an occasional conflict between the demands of their minds and bodies. Fortunately, most men are more sensible, and unite mind and body through desire instead.

A *desire* is the means by which we offer an object of mind or body to the body or the mind. It shares something of the character of an emotion, since it infects and alters the nature of the mind or the body. It shares also something of the character of an act by which the mind is subordinated to the body, or conversely. It is unlike either an emotion or a subordinating act in that it allows either mind or body to function without restraint, and can so operate that whichever one was once subordinate can become superior.

Desire does not exert a force on the body or the mind. It merely offers the object of the one to the other. If I desire to plant a tree, what I have in mind is referred to some perceived site where, as a component in the percept, it can provoke those bodily tendencies which are appropriate to the planting of a tree. If I desire to eat, the food towards which I tend is treated as a possible conclusion, and can then serve to provoke thoughts appropriate to eating.

Desire is an act, not of the mind or the body—for it makes use of these—but of the self. It takes an object of the mind or the body and offers it to the other. It is through desire that an object of bodily hunger is granted an opportunity to alter the trend of the mind; it is through desire that an object of curiosity is granted an opportunity to alter a bodily tendency.

Both the mind and the body offer resistance to desire, for each has its own objective. In order to have a mind and body in harmony, a desiring man must therefore at one and the same time present the mental objective to the body and the bodily objective to the mind. He is, as a consequence, driven in two directions; he is beset by conflicting desires. Hungry, he still is curious, curious he still is hungry.

Desire provides no adequate solution to the discrepancy between mind and body precisely because it provides two solutions. It also fails to direct the mind or the body. It presents but does not refer objectives to them. It provides possible provocations for the mind or the body; it is not always capable of provoking one of them to conform to the other.

It is always a question as to whether what is desired can be sustained by the body or the mind. Though we desire food we may not be able to think of any thing relevant; though we are curious about the nature of the stars we may not be able to act in any way that will make those stars more available. An adequate resolution of the opposition between mind and body requires that what the mind conceives the body can perform, and what the body wants the mind can conceive. A will provides the requisite means.

2. THE NATURE OF THE WILL

Desire presents to the body or mind an object towards which the mind or body is directed. It presents a bodily object to the mind or a mental object to the body, whether or not they are capable of attaining it. *Will*, in contrast, presents to the body or mind an object towards which the mind or body is directed, but only so far as they are capable of attaining it and in such a way as to provoke a bodily or mental movement towards it.

We will objects by provoking the mind or body to deal with them. We desire objects by viewing them as possible objects of a will. Having desired, we may fail to will; having willed, desire is in part at least fulfilled. If we think of food as that which is to be eaten, we only desire it. We will to eat it when we make the food, as an object of perception or thought, function as a determinant of a bodily tendency to eat.

What is in mind is willed when it is referred to something actual for the sake of eliciting some not yet expressed bodily tendency. Conversely, that to which the body tends is willed by being presented to the mind for the sake of eliciting a thought about it.

Will thus refers an object to the mind or body as capable of responding to it. We will, however, without knowing how to make the will effective. We do not know what the required bodily or mental act is, or how it is to be brought to the fore. And we may fail to bring it to the fore, because our wills may be weak. But so long as a bodily tendency is aroused by something we think of in order to arouse it, we are exercising a will, and making it possible for the body to act in conformity with what is in mind. So long as the mind can be made to think of an object focused on for the sake of making us think, we are exercising a will, and making it possible for the mind to act in conformity with the body.

What is in the forefront of the mind is by will referred to what is not yet in the forefront of the body, and conversely. We will to eat when we are not keyed to eat; we will to think when we are not ready to think. We exercise our wills by thinking of food as impertinent to the dominant tendencies of the body but pertinent to some not yet expressed and perhaps not even understood bodily tendency; we exercise our wills too by treating the food for which we hunger as that of which we ought to think in the face of a present thought directed elsewhere.

We normally will, not to change the direction of our minds, but the direction of our bodies. We then "say" to the body that there is something it ought to do. This "saying" is in part a mental act and in part transcends the powers of the mind. It is mental so far as it fastens on an object as that which ought to be pursued. It is not mental so far as it refers that object to the body so as to incite the expression of an appropriate bodily tendency.

3. CRITICISM AND OBJECTIONS

The will is an expression of the self. It does no physical work nor does it think. It does not transform itself into physical force and thereby translate ideas into acts, nor does it change itself into mental energy and convert a bodily tendency into a thought. The body does physical work; the mind thinks. The will neither moves nor thinks. It has no other task or power but that of offering objects of the mind to the body and objects of the body to the mind so as to make the objects of one into provocations for the other.

To views like these it is tempting to object that there is no such power as will, or that the account of it repeats the very question it was designed to answer. The first objection has two forms—one of which was stated by Spinoza and the other by Hobbes. According to the Spinozistic view there is no separate power of will. Its supposed activities are nought but activities of the mind. According to the Hobbesean view there is also no separate power of will, but for the opposite reason; the will's activities are supposed to be nought but activities of the body.

The mind and body, for Spinoza, run along independent routes, each constituting a distinct domain, independent of but concordant with the other. By maintaining that the mind and body are perfectly concordant, Spinoza obviously rules out any *need* for a will. A concordant mind and body make a will unnecessary since the only task of the will is to bring mind and body into accord. By treating the mind and body as correlative but independent powers possessed by no one, Spinoza in addition rules out the possibility that there could be a will to relate them. If a man were a mind and a body and nothing more, it would be but a tautology to say that he had no will.

Staying, however, within Spinoza's system and recognizing that his denial of the existence of an independent power of will is not intended as a reaffirmation of his distinction between body and mind, it is evident that he is at pains to deny that there is a power in man by which he can voluntarily accept what is false or reject what is true. So far as an idea is true, Spinoza thinks, we must affirm it; so far as it is false, we must deny it. "Volition and idea are one and the same." What is before the mind determines, for him, the nature of the attitude we take with respect to it.

Putting aside the question as to whether or not it is correct to speak of affirmation and denial as acts of will rather than as acts of preference or choice (which they seem to be), it is perhaps sufficient to remark that affirmation and denial are neither identical with nor produced by ideas in mind. They are the result of a union of ideas and tendencies to affirm or deny. Spinoza, by concentrating on the content of the mind, confounds one of the conditions for affirmation or denial (mental content which is true or false) with the effect that such content makes possible (mental content affirmed or denied to be true or false).

What is important in Spinoza's theory is not his *a priori* exclusion of will and his treatment of affirmation and denial as identical with or as effects of objects confronted, but something quite different. Spinoza's important thesis is that there is no faculty of will, but only specific acts of willing. That thesis I think is correct. It affirms in another way that there are no instincts or reflexes, no separate potentialities or capacities, but only a single concern which is subdivided and distinguished in the course of being realized.

A man is not stuffed with a set of invisible springs all coiled and ready to spring out towards some fixed objective. His potentialities, his tendencies, are distinguished by becoming actualized. As merely potential, as capacities or faculties, they merge into one another and have no fixed and separate ends. A man's potentiality to eat is conjoined with and merges imperceptibly into his potentiality to grasp and chew. Just so, a man's power to will is conjoined with and merges imperceptibly into his power to be tense or to be passionate. It is only when he is resolving a conflict between his mind and his body that he has a will. The will is a distinct power only while exercised. When not exercised, it becomes lost within the self, without distinguishable traits, location or meaning.

According to Hobbes the will is the last bodily tendency which comes to the fore as a consequence of a preceding combat between a host of bodily tendencies. On his theory it is that bodily tendency which has won a victory over competitors; it is a physical not a mental power.

Like Spinoza, Hobbes, under the name of will, is obviously dealing with something else. His theory explains how a tendency, provoked by the will, comes to the fore. Instead of accounting for a will, his theory presupposes its existence. We need a will to confront the body with entertained objectives, and thereby provoke that body to act in one way instead of another. The tendency that is expressed is, as Hobbes remarks, stronger than others, but it is stronger in part because of the will.

Where Spinoza deals with ideas and does not relate them to latent mental tendencies, Hobbes deals with bodily tendencies and takes no account of the objects which provoke them. Without a will there would be the ideas of which Spinoza speaks, but no thing by which judgments of those ideas were elicited; or there would be the bodily tendencies of which Hobbes speaks, but no thought which made them appear. There is no gain in giving up the Spinozistic error for the Hobbesean, or conversely. One must be a Spinozist and a Hobbesean together, supplementing their respective half-truths by one another and applying the result to both the mind and the body. In this way one will be able to achieve an understanding of the will as referring an object to the body or to the mind in order to make the two concordant.

The present view is somewhat like that of William James. His account, however, is essentially nineteenth century in temper. It is framed in terms on a sensationalistic theory of knowledge, a mythology that all ideas strive to realize themselves in fact, an acceptance of a theory of instincts and reflexes, and a tentatively adopted determinism. Once these suppositions are put aside, the present theory and his will prove to be quite similar.

James' view, and the present as well, seem to attribute all the energy, all the effort by which we appear to be impelled to act when we will, either to the body or the mind. Ours is apparently a theory in which there is no work the will can do. But this seems to go counter to the facts. To will is to do something. One wills only if one makes an effort—sometimes a tremendous one. There is, however, no difficulty in holding that we make an effort when we will but do not thereby expend physical or mental energy.

When we will to lift our arms we do not infuse physical energy into the appropriate muscles. We do not know what those muscles are or how they function. When we will to lift our arms we use the prospective result of lifted arms as a provocation for the body to act in a way it is not now acting. Until we have actively willed the lifting of the arms, the tendency to lift the arms is not to the fore; it is not yet a distinct and definite mode of acting. It comes to the fore only as a result of an internal physical redistribution of the energy of the body, under the provocation of the idea of lifted arms. There is an effort made when one wills to act, but this is bodily effort, not an effort of the will. If by work and effort we mean physical work and effort, this is always beyond the capacity of what, like the will, is not a body.

We attribute strength to the will when the body has strength to respond in the required way. If a favored bodily tendency and act are actually elicited, the will is said to be strong; otherwise weak. There is bodily work done when one wills, work which has observable effects. But the work is work of the body, not work of the will.

However, if by effort we mean to refer to an individual's insistence on some objective not now favored by a bodily or mental tendency, there can be no doubt that every act of will requires effort. Effort is necessary to present a prospective result to the mind or body in the face of established provocations. The willed objective must crowd out the other objectives which are now being furthered by the mind or body. The drunkard wills to abstain, but the drink before him forces his thirst into focus. He needs all the energy of his being to keep the glories of abstention before him. This last is but one of many possible mental objectives and one which the circumstances do not favor. He must insist on it in the face of a tendency to think of the drink. If he is successful in his offensive against the provocative thought of drink, he must go on and institute a defense to protect his new thought of abstention from being displaced by others (e.g., by the thought of being congenial) which the circumstances might favor. Only then will he be in a position to favor a nondrinking bodily tendency and thus defy his thirst.

The successful conclusion of a willed activity may be prevented by the upsurge of some repressed tendency. Men rush off decisively in one direction and suddenly stop themselves under the influence of objectives they had just put aside. They must exert an effort to keep the willed objective steadily before them in the face of inclinations to favor something else, for to have willed one thing is not to have demolished all inclination to act otherwise. A willed objective competes against objectives furthered by the circumstances and against objectives which could have been willed. Nothing less than a continued recognition of the superior value of a willed objective suffices to keep it in the foreground against the competitive pressure of rejected objectives.

It may be contended, however, that an objective, so far as it is understood, is in the mind, and that an act of relating such an objective to the body must be an act of moving to the body from the mind. The present theory would then be one with those which suppose that something mental exerts a physical influence on the body. It would then be no more satisfactory or intelligible than the classical and established views that preceded it.

The objection would be valid if all we knew were inside us, and if what we knew were willed into the body in somewhat the way a hammer impresses itself on stone. But we know objects outside the mind. And the will, instead of putting pressure on the body, only provides that body with new provocations. Thus, when a man wills to eat the food before him, he regards the food as a terminus of a possible bodily act of reaching for it. The food elicits the bodily act of reaching for the food in somewhat the same way as a house seen in the distance elicits an act of walking towards it.

There is no more mystery in the fact that a man can willingly walk towards a seen house than there is in the fact that he can thoughtlessly walk towards it. When he perceives, he refers perceptual content to an object to make that object a perceived thing, thereby disturbing his present bodily activities as a matter of course. When he wills, he thinks of the perceived thing as that which ought to disturb his present activities. In both cases, an object as perceived, without exerting any force, conditions his bodily activities.

A man can willingly act in terms of perceived objects. He can willingly act also in terms of objects which do not now exist. He can will to build a house as well as to walk towards one. Once again the analogy with perception holds. It is possible to have a perceptual content which purports to be of a house when there is no house in fact. That perceptual content will, in an erroneous perceptual judgment, be attributed to something other than a house. A man will, as a consequence, thoughtlessly walk towards the object erroneously supposed to be a house. Somewhat similarly, a man can evaluate a site as having the prospective value of a house, and thereupon willingly walk towards the site as a site for a house, or can begin a series of acts to terminate in the building of the house on that site. In erroneous perception, perceptual content is referred to an irrelevant substance. A man then acts as though the percept and the substance were a unity. In willing what is nonexistent, a man refers a possibility to a perceived thing. He then acts to make them a unity. In both cases, an unrealized possibility is related to some actuality, and there serves, without exerting any force, to condition bodily activity.

It is not an idea in mind that makes us walk, thoughtlessly or deliberately, but an idea as referred to some substantial reality. In referring the idea to the reality, we alter our status with respect to that idea and to the reality to which it is referred. We thereby affect our equilibrium, though not necessarily in a way that favors the successful attainment of the objective.

There is no will to will and no will not to will. If there were, there would, for the same reason, be a will to will to will, a will to will not to will, a will not to will to will, and so on. To engage in a simple act of willing, one would first have to move backwards over an infinite regress and then progress infinitely downwards, all in the space of a moment. But if there is no will to will and no will not to will, a man cannot willingly employ or withdraw his will. He cannot will an act of willing.

Without the will there could be prospects envisaged and actions performed. But without the will the actions would not be elicited by the prospects envisaged, and the prospects would not be insisted on in order that the acts be elicited. The will brings a possible objective into relation with the body or mind. It thereby voids some actual objective and thus alters the way in which the body or mind will behave.

The will is hemmed in by limits which are not of its choosing. It is exercised inside those limits as the outcome of the self's endeavor to overcome an opposition between its mind and body. It is free and must be free, since its entire function is to give mental objectives a physical meaning and bodily objectives a mental meaning, and thereby provide those objectives with determinations they otherwise would not have.

Like every other free activity, the will vitalizes constraints, provided by the past, the body, neighbors and the world. It is constrained by the past, which brings different objectives to mind. It is constrained as well by a body which tends towards objectives not willed. It is constrained also by the future as stressed by neighboring things. It is constrained too by the world, for the world determines just what objects there are with which the mind and body can and ought to deal, and therefore what it is that the will can and ought to insist upon.

4. GRADES OF WILLED OBJECTIVES

Nature is more a temptress than a mother. She constantly provokes bodily tendencies and mental inclinations, and keeps them to the front, though others would bring greater relief and more satisfaction. We are frightened by snakes that are harmless, intrigued by fruits that are poisonous, beset by dangers in the guise of prospective pleasures, and confused by pleasures in the guise of possible dangers. The human mind seems to have a natural attraction for the false. We become mature when we oppose the temptations of nature by inserting willed objects between those which she stresses and those that are favored by our dominant mental or bodily tendencies. Man first stands erect in nature when he recognizes that he must free himself from the tensions which arise because the mind and body have too readily followed her recommendations—recommendations which drive the body in one way and the mind in another He must dangle before himself the prospect of acting or thinking in new ways in order to escape from that conflict between mind and body which nature promotes.

Initially, men use their wills to provide an immediate specific resolution of a conflict between mind and body. But it is not long before they employ their wills to get themselves to the stage where they can act *well* habitually, sometimes in the face of present demands. As far back as we can go in the history of the race, and quite early in the history of the individual, the will is employed to discipline the body by making it the locus of *techniques*—means for acting well habitually so as to reach objectives mentally envisaged.

There is little pleasure in setting about to master a technique.

One must first concentrate on its different component movements and steps. Then one must firmly relate them by going over them in sequence again and again. But there are compensations. While the technique is being willingly mastered, the body and the mind are in accord, for a willing mastery of a technique requires that one keep in mind what one is doing and keep one's body from disturbing the intent of the mind. And so far as nothing arises which provokes the mind or body to work in opposition to the acquired technique, the technique promises a fairly enduring resolution of the conflict of mind and body.

Though techniques enable a mind and body to work together for a considerable time, they tend to force the one or the other into a groove. The more a technique is mastered, the greater the risk that one will be too inflexible to overcome those oppositions between the mind and the body which are inevitable when the differently structured mind and body confront a novel situation. Not until men are ready to will the good are they able to use their minds and bodies independently and yet in harmony. It is only the good that encourages collateral but independent mental and bodily activities.

Men are not pure spirits and thus uninterested in immediate objectives. Nor are they so engrossed in the immediate and beneficial that they are not concerned with an ultimate good. They *attend* more or less unconsciously to the achievement of techniques, to limited objectives and to an ultimate good. But they ought to go further. They ought to *will* the good, techniques and limited objectives together, for complete men are willing men, at once ethical, disciplined and practical.

The study of men as beings who ought to will the good apart from and together with other objectives must be left for the sequel. Now it suffices to observe that techniques, limited objectives and the good are never completely in fact and ought never in theory to be sharply separated. At every moment men are concerned with all three, though at one moment they may stress one of them and at another moment another.

An error men frequently commit is that of willing one objective in a way which is not in consonance with the willing of others. They will to obtain something now, but in such a way that the ultimate good is obscured. Or, they are fairly clear about the good and misconceive what they are to will now to obtain it. The practical man has his ideals no less than the theoretician; the latter lives a practical life as surely as the former. But the one keeps the good in the background and often wills in ways which oppose his real concern. The other keeps the good in the foreground but often in such a way as to prevent him from making use of present conditions and techniques. Men are at once theoretical and practical, but they are rarely both to the degree they can and should be.

Man is a *self* before he has a will or a mind, and as soon as he has a body. It is the concern of that self which is exhibited in the acts of all three. His self needs the help of reason in order to be able to know the demands of the good, and it needs the help of the body to realize that good in the world that now exists. The self also needs a will. The self, under the stimulation of a conflict between mind and body, expresses itself as a will to bring that conflict to an end.

Through body and mind the self expresses its concern in diverse and partially adequate ways. When it employs its will to focus on the good, it provides a means by which the body and mind can function as independent but collateral agencies for the realization of that good. The self employs body, mind and will to realize the ultimate good, which is a permanent and appropriate object only of a self's concern.

Cut away a reference to the mind and body as requiring harmonization, see the will as directed towards a single, permanent objective—a good relevant to all there is—and almost at once the unmistakeable outline of the self becomes apparent. Before we deal with ethics, we should try to grasp what that self is. Not to know it, is not to know what it is to which some of our basic ethical judgments refer. Only a self is guilty or innocent, willing or unwilling, inescapably obligated and radically free. All judgments of responsibility and blame, of duty and human right, at least tacitly, take account of the self; they ought to be grounded on a mastery of its nature.

CHAPTER TWELVE

THE SELF

1. THE SELF AND THE BODY

A man is not a mind, a body or a will. Nor is he all three together. He is a self, a self that is necessarily expressed in and
through the body and may eventually be expressed as a mind and
as a will.

The self is not a body. If it were, it would have to be located in
space, and it would be possible to push it out of place and get it
inside other bodies. But the self has no bulk and is the self of that
being and no other. Also, were the self a body, it would be limited
to the performance of physical actions and there would be nothing
to wish or to think the theory that it was a body—but it is the self
which makes it possible to wish or to think.

There is something pathetic in the attempts of spiritualists to
weigh the self by subtracting the weight of the organism immediately after death from the weight it had just before. Any discrepancy they might find would indicate the loss of something
material; yet that of which they are obviously in search is a self
which has nonbodily powers and a supernatural destiny, a spiritual
and not a material thing. The same mistake is committed by those
more honored scientists who try with all their being and equipment to peer into the brain for traces of mind, will and emotion.
Ideas, ideals, decisions, approvals, disapprovals, commands, like
self-identity and intentions, are nonmaterial; they cannot be
found by looking into a material brain.

A subtler and more cautious view is one which maintains that the self is not a body but a state of the body as a whole. He who holds that view can deny the self is corporeal, and yet can affirm that it characterizes or qualifies the body. By denying that the self is corporeal, he avoids the foolish supposition that the self is a body with nonbodily functions; by affirming that the self qualifies the body as a whole, he makes a needed place for a theory of the self as that which enables the living body to be a unity.

This view, still popular today, is rather an ancient one. About twenty-four hundred years ago, Pythagoras and Empedocles defined the "soul" as a harmony or proportion between the bodily parts of a living being. Since "harmony" and "proportion" are esthetic and mathematical ways of referring to the character of the unity of the body, theirs was but a special form of the theory that the self was a state of the body as a whole. Their particular theories were brilliantly refuted by Plato in the *Phaedo* and by Aristotle in the *de Anima*. Implicit in those refutations is a reply to any view which tries to identify the self with some pervasive trait or organizing relation of the body. Unfortunately, Plato couched his refutation in such a way as to compel the acceptance of a belief in the pre-existence of the self and in the possession of knowledge before birth, whereas Aristotle put most of his stress on the way the theory conflicted with other beliefs of its defenders. Plato's and Aristotle's more significant points have often, as a consequence, been overlooked.

In saying that the self or "soul" is a state of the body, one might mean that it was the state of the body at just that time, that it was the unity of just those parts or elements which, for that moment, make up the body. But then the self would not only depend for its existence on those elements, but would change or cease to be when they were increased or decreased in number, or even merely rearranged. The self would also be unable to control the body, and in addition would be unable to engage in the nonbodily act of judging. Self-identity, self-discipline, and self-criticism would be impossible.

To allow for self-identity, one must affirm that the self is more than a bodily state at a moment. The least that could be maintained is that it is a state of a unified body, a state which continues unchanged despite bodily changes in content and arrangement. The self would then be identified, not with an aspect *of* or a relation *in* the body, but with a form *for* the body, i.e., with something which was to be distinguished from every particular transient state which the body actually had at any one time. To allow for self-discipline one would then have to go further and affirm that the self had powers which the body itself did not have, and by which it could act on the body. Finally, to make room for self-criticism, one would have to attribute to the self the nonbodily power of knowing. As a consequence of these three concessions one would have gone beyond the theory that the self was a form of the body, to the view that it had a being and status of its own.

2. EXPRESSIONS OF THE SELF

Though the self is not a body, from the very beginning it comes to expression in bodily ways. From the first it exhibits itself in the form of life in and through the body. That body has a structure and needs of its own. A man eats, not because his self needs food but because his body does. Yet it is the self which quickens the body so that it can eat.

The self is expressed in and through a body. It may also be expressed in and through a mind. That mind is not necessarily coordinate with or in harmony with the body. It goes its own way, sometimes in defiance of what the body requires or provides. The self is not a mind, but the fact of mind makes evident that though the self is expressed in and through the body, it also stands outside the body with powers and interests of its own.

An individual is a single being. Even when his mind and body are most discrepant, he possesses them as one and together. He relates them by emotion, by desire and by will. But these ways of relating are subsequent to the existence of a discrepancy between the mind and the body. The self is more than the emotions, desire or will. These are expressions of it, serving to relate those other bodily and mental expressions of the self which happen to be discrepant.

The being and task of the self are not exhausted in the act of relating a discrepant mind and body. If they were, the self would be without objectives of its own. It would not have a motive for desiring or willing other than that of relieving the tension which a discrepant mind and body provoke. It would be without interest in the rest of the world, and like an Aristotelian God or a Leibnizian monad, which is that God in miniature, would forever revolve about its own orbit. It would stand outside time, coming into it only in order to rectify the diverse expressions it itself made possible. But like every other being the self, through the agency of a concern, reaches from the present to the future and strives to make that future present. The self is more than and other than the mind, body or will, because it has a concern of its own which it manifests in and through, and thereby controls and possesses each of them.

3. THE FREUDIAN VIEW

No one in recent times has stressed more strongly than Freud the fact that there is a self, and that it tries to manifest itself in order to satisfy its concern. Unfortunately, he too often confounded the concern of the self with one of the ways in which that concern is manifested.

Freud is a complex figure, and the movement he founded has many dimensions. I shall extract from his diverse statements the thesis which many of his followers have also taken to be central, obscured though it has been by Freud's multiple qualifications and shifts in position. It is their view that the self provides the impetus for all the things men do. At the same time they think that the self seeks and obtains full expression through the performance of a sexual act. But it is not possible to have it both ways. The self, as providing the urge behind everything that is done, cannot be identified with the self as interested in a limited and special activity or goal.

Were the concern, or "libido," as the Freudians call it, the source of a host of different acts and nothing more, it would not be correct to describe it as having an objective of its own. But it also would not be correct to treat it exclusively in terms of only one of those acts. Yet it is so treated, (even when the term "sex" is used in a broader sense than usual) when it is said that the essence of the self is a sexual impulse. The provocation, rhythm, field and goal which are essential to a sexual act are other than those involved in other acts. To describe the aim of the self as sexual is therefore to describe it in terms of one of many possible and independent modes in which a single concern can be exhibited. The self is too inclusive in its concern to be restricted to a sexual impulse; a sexual impulse is too limited in its form and goal to be identified with the source of the different things men do.

Freud himself often slipped from one interpretation to the other. He tried, at one and the same time, to be a physician and a metaphysician. His preference for sexual terminology indicates the inclination of the physician to investigate the nature of a limited though powerful strain of activity; his stress upon the existence of a single concern indicates his metaphysical interest in that which lies behind every specific mode of activity. By trying to be both, Freud was able to delve deeper than most physicians and to keep closer to the facts than most metaphysicians are wont to do, but he thereby also failed to note where observations ended and speculations began.

Freud was better as a physician than as a metaphysician. It was due to his careful investigations as a doctor that we today have become so aware of the fact that men are seriously frustrated and corrupted at times by the repression of acts which center about their erotic zones. But, due to his inadequacy as a metaphysician, he led his followers and almost an entire generation to believe that the heart of a being was to be sought in a sexual impulse. His facts revealed that a sexual impulse could be repressed, difficult and dangerous though such repression was; his metaphysics affirmed that the impulse was irresistible and was bound to appear in a new form if prevented from appearing in an old.

It is only limited modes of expression that are repressed, only the self that can have variable modes of expression. The expression which is repressed never achieves a new expression, for each expression is distinct, usually with its own channel and sometimes its own goal. An act of repression does not turn one mode of expression into another, but forces the self to find another avenue of expression. Prevented from going through the door, one might try climbing through the window. Climbing through the window is not a variation or corruption of the act of going through the door; it is an alternative expression of the desire to get into the house in some way or other.

There is danger in repressing any act, not merely one which is directed to sexual ends. In order to exhibit one tendency, it is necessary to repress another, and if we repress it in the wrong way, no matter what its nature or goal, the repression may have serious repercussions. The taking of what does not belong to one is, at least in early life, urgent and hard to restrain. Certainly its repression has had sad and permanent effects on many individuals, leaving them with dreams of conquest, and with feelings of frustration and hatred that distort their lives. This shows, not that it is wrong to repress the tendency to steal, but that it must be repressed with care. It is not so much what is repressed as the manner in which it is repressed that breaks a man's spirit and twists his mind. A denial of a mode of expression must be conjoined with the opening up of a new avenue in which the concern of the self can be exhibited with the same strength and success.

By being improperly restrained, a harmless mode of expression can be made to give way to one that is dangerous and desperate. This is true even though the object is unimportant. An apple has little value. Yet by being prohibited from eating an apple, bluntly and without suggestion as to what else he might do with it, Adam was doomed to lose paradise in fact and in spirit. If he obeyed the command not to eat, his interest in the apple would still remain. But it would be dammed up within him, acting as an excitant corrupting his other interests and perverting his judgment. Adam should have been told to spray the forbidden apple regularly, to make pictures and reproductions of it, and to salute it whenever he came in sight of it. His concern, partially and momentarily directed to the apple, did not have to be expressed as an act of eating. Being denied that mode of expression, he ought to have been given another, equally satisfying. God should have known better.

Every object in the universe has some pertinence to the self. The self ought to take account of every thing that exists, in some way or other. An arbitrary taboo, denying all right and opportunity to deal with some one object, provides but an occasion for dealing with it in surreptitious and perverted ways.

A prohibition to act in a certain way does not destroy a mode of expression; it merely prevents it from being exercised fully and in the open. But it does not follow from this that if a prohibition is obeyed and another mode of expression opened, the latter is only a variation of the prohibited form. Spraying an apple or drawing pictures of it are not new or distorted ways of eating it. They are different and independent limited modes of expressing the concern of the self—a concern which, though making use of, is directed quite beyond apples and what they involve.

Every prohibition ought to be accompanied by a suggestion of a new channel and goal. Otherwise the prohibition runs the risk of serving as a means for focusing on the object, and almost inevitably involves the individual in the conflicting attempt to carry through and repress the same activity. A prohibition can perform its function of depriving an object of its capacity to act as a certain kind of stimulus only if it also promotes a new kind of response.

The teacher who told her pupils not to put ink in their hair taught them a new game, as she soon discovered when she left the room and looked through the keyhole. In the interval between the issuing of the command and the leaving of the room, she provoked a tension which made them fidget. The fidget was a psychoneurosis in minature, indicative of the incompetence of the teacher, not of an irresistible impulse on the part of children to use ink in novel ways.

Diplomats blunder in the same way the teacher did, but on a larger scale. They impose a punitive peace, cheating an entire nation of its opportunity to live and prosper, and then are dumbfounded to find that the result is chaos and revolution, or new and perverted ways of running a state.

A sexual impulse, of course, is much more insistent and widespread than an impulse to ink one's hair or to crush a state. As a result it is much more difficult and dangerous to restrain. The growth and development of most men involves the production of a sexual impulse so powerful that it can be repressed only at the risk of creating a new mode of expression which deals with the same objects in inadequate ways. Instead of being repressed, a sexual impulse ought to be supplemented by other modes of expression to make a single pattern of activity in which the sexual act is but one factor. And this is what many adults succeed in doing. They satisfy a sexual drive in the course of a wider effort to create a permanent bond with another human being, and they control and restrain it with benefit to both. Don Juan and Casanova failed to supplement their sexual desires with others; they were not lovers, but frustrated spirits constantly seeking an occasion to love. They failed perpetually in their attempt to love, for they never understood that the sexual act is to be carried through only within a context of regard and concern for the good of another.

Some adults force their sexual interests to the periphery of their lives without appreciable injury; others put it completely yet safely aside. Sexuality is not the predestined or only satisfactory mode of expression open to a man. Men find satisfaction in the pursuit of art, science, business, war, contemplation and public service. According to some Freudians, these are but perverted or inadequate ways of exhibiting sexual impulses. The view goes counter to the fact that there are celibates in these fields whose lives are richer, healthier and happier than the lives of those who devote themselves to a round of bodily pleasures. The most that could be urged is that the sexual impulse is so strongly intrenched that it requires occasional satisfaction, and that happy celibates would have been even happier had they occasionally expressed themselves in sexual ways.

The concern which is of the essence of man has sexuality as but one of many alternative though important modes of expression. It is much more central and flexible than the Freudian libido could possibly be, being directly exhibited in acts of sexual restraint and sexual indulgence, in ethical and nonethical behavior, as mind and will, in nonbodily and in bodily ways.

Historically, the fact seems to be that it was his discovery of what appeared to be a sexual impulse in children which led Freud to hold that the sexual impulse was at the root of all human activity. But from an analytic standpoint—one might perhaps even say, from a psychoanalytic standpoint—the explanation goes the other way. By confounding a sexual impulse with the essential concern of man, Freud was bound to suppose that sexuality was at the root of all his activity. He then had no other alternative but to view the activities of a child as anticipatory or variant sexual acts.

This is a highly questionable conclusion. The child's acts have not the same urgency that an adult's have. They are prompted on different occasions and by different stimuli; they end in different ways and with different results. Freud brought into the open the fact that the child indulges in many practices which have a sexual coloring, and that there is more than one kind of sexual expression, utilizing different channels. But the fact that any one of these channels is utilized by the child does not mean that the child is performing the same type of act which adults perform when they utilize such a channel.

One man reads a book, another uses it instead to stop a draught. Only one is interested in literature. Similarly, the fact that a child and an adult may both occupy themselves with sexual matters does not mean that they are dominated by a common sexual interest. The child acts in one way, the adult in another. So radically diverse are the effects and intents of the two, that one is compelled to say that the one has a nonsexual and the other a sexual interest in sexual matters.

Even if one grants that all acts of the child are miniature, partial expressions of the very impulse which is eventually realized in the sexual acts of an adult, one would still be far from a justification of the thesis that every act of the child can be accounted for in terms of a sexual impulse, or even of an interest in bodily pleasures. A theory has begun to stretch far beyond the limits of credulity when it begins to affirm that sneezing, riding a bicycle, asking questions, skipping a rope and combing one's hair all play variations on the erotic theme.

It is particularly hard to believe that childish play or curiosity are nothing more than variant or perverted expressions of sexuality. Play and curiosity are normal, healthy and significant occurrences, with their own objectives. A child can bounce a ball by the hour and ask questions without end. He thereby exercises muscles which have nothing to do with the sexual act and may eventually find a satisfaction which has a spiritual as well as a bodily quality.

Play and curiosity may at times be sexually motivated. They

may also be nonsexually motivated. They may at times offer obstacles to the expression or satisfaction of a sexual impulse. A man can play so strenuously that he weakens his power to engage in sexual activity, and curiosity can so grip him that he becomes impotent to act rather than impelled to pursue. There is nothing in curiosity or play which requires them to be understood as the natural predecessors, consequences, perversions or instruments of a sexual drive or act.

Embarrassments of this kind led Freud's disciples, Adler and Jung, to assign to sexuality a much less important role than that ascribed to it by Freud. But in compensation, they brought forward other limited impulses and tried, just as Freud did with sexuality, to view them as of the essence of that central and self-identical concern which is at the core of every man. There is more to be said in favor of a view which accepts neither Freud's theory nor a modification of it, but instead interprets sexual activity as a variation of a fundamental impulse to play. In childhood the urge to play is almost irresistible, and one could, without straining overmuch, interpret all its acts as outgrowths or perversions of an attempt to utilize everything in a game of some kind. Moreover, the child plays with inanimate as well as animate things, and plays a good portion of the day, whereas the sexual interest is primarily directed towards the living and then only some of the time. The desire to play seems much more deeply rooted and much more variable than the sexual, and can be readily interpreted as having even the adult's sexual activity as its natural outcome.

An even better alternative would be to interpret all acts as the outcome of an impulse to engage in social activities. Children are constantly acting the parts of policemen and firemen. They perpetually interrupt adult conversation and make countless miniature and sometimes major experiments in social adjustment. It is not difficult to view them as having an insatiable urge to participate anticipatorily in the adult activities of social welfare, social discourse and social adjustment. Since the adult sexual act is overladen with social meaning and implications, it would be a natural corollary from this theory that children should exhibit an early interest in sexual matters.

Here is a theory that provides an explanation for play and sex, curiosity and conversation. It has no more difficulty in accounting for sleep, suicide, and asocial acts than does a theory which stresses a sexual or a playful impulse. It also has the signal advantage of accounting for the sexual act, which is possible only to some individuals some of the time, in terms of an impulse which can be exhibited by everyone and for longer periods. There is some justification for viewing a social impulse as of the essence of human beings, for it is evident early and universally. There is no justification for treating a sexual or playful impulse as of the essence of human beings, for these impulses occur only in some men and then rather late and spasmodically.

But the social theory is, in the last resort, as unsatisfactory as the others. Like them it confounds a specific expression with a concern which lies behind it and behind other and even opposing modes of expression. As a consequence it is forced to misread the activities of the child as anticipations or perversions of an adult's, and to suppose that some one limited group of objects could satisfy the concern of a human being.

4. THE CONCERN OF THE SELF

The self has a concern, as the Freudians so clearly and persistently affirm. But as their various attempts make apparent, and as the history of philosophy, psychology and religion confirm, it is very difficult to see and to say what it is with which the self is concerned. Progress in this direction can be made, however, if one can overcome the habit of dealing with men as though they were natural beings incapable of obligations, or as though they were ethical beings incapable of a natural existence.

The self is a self of a natural yet ethical man. It is (1) constant,

(2) active, (3) concerned, (4) unique, (5) beneficial to the body, (6) responsible, and (7) sensitive to values. These different designations trench on one another and converge on the same truth. One or more of them have, however, often been slurred or denied. We must insist on them all, or abandon the hope of understanding the nature of the self and its concern.

1. A man remains self-same over the years, despite changes in his body, temper, memory, virtue and thought. His identity could be accounted for on the supposition that he was nought but a self, and that that self was an unalterable substance, an ultimate, concrete self-sufficient being. But then it would be irrelevant whether or not a man had a body or what nature that body had. No matter how the body changed or whether or not it existed, the man would be affected in no way. But a man is a man only so far as he has a body. What he does to and with that body is vital to him. He is more than a self; the self does not exhaust his nature. His self is a unitary source of diverse, bodily expressed insistencies and of a single concern for an all-embracing good; it is the private responsible inside of which his body is the public outside. Infinitely insistent and infinitely responsible, it is absolutely constant in nature, distinct from but not separated from the body, enabling a man to be self-same over the years.

Guilt is attributable to the self, not to the will, body or mind. Because that self is constant, a man can continue to be guilty indefinitely. Men, however, become guilty where before they were innocent. It would seem, then, that the self, though it could be constant once guilty, can change from the state of innocence to the state of guilt and is not, therefore, a real constant. Were guilt a defect in the self like a fault in a rock, this would be a just conclusion. But it is the very same being who was once innocent and is later guilty. While innocent and while guilty a man has the self-same self. But then guilt, obviously, though attributable to the self, cannot alter its being.

Guilt is not a predicate of the self. It is attributable to the self in the same way as distance is attributable to things far apart. It expresses the nature of a relation which the self has to the good; it does not refer to some transitory trait possessed by the self. A man changes from innocence to guilt, not by changing his self but by so acting that the good with which his self is concerned is not realized to the degree that it can be. He is guilty to the degree that he prevents the infection of what is by what ought to be. It was his task to bring the ought to be to bear on the world. If he so acted as to preclude this, he is a being who is guilty for having held apart what belongs together. He remains guilty so long as the bad situation he made possible is not altered.

2. The self is active. It acts to realize a good which lies beyond it. Its actions are manifested in the form of bodily and mental changes. These are to be evaluated as more or less desirable in the light of the degree to which the good is realized by their means.

A self which was not active would either be indifferent to all that exists, or would be intruded on by others and made to reflect the nature of their efforts. But the self is the responsible, innermost core of man. It is the ultimate source of all his acts. And because it is the inside of him, it is that which nothing else can direct or determine.

An active self is a self in time. Since nothing can exist at the very next moment unless it is possible for it to exist then, there must be a possibility which the self can and does realize at the next moment. That possibility must continue to confront the self at the moment after the next, at the moment after that and so on, for otherwise the self would, at some point in its career, change in realizing the possibility it confronts. The constancy of an active self requires that the self, at every moment, confront and realize the self-same possibility of itself.

Subhuman beings may either be confronted with, or fully realize the possibility of themselves. But if the one is possible, the other is not. The future is constantly changing in character and every attempt at realization is countered by opposing efforts on the part of others. When subhuman beings are confronted with nought but the possibility of themselves, they can realize it only in part. Their reappearance at a later moment in the same guise they had earlier is the result of a partial success in realizing a different, broader possibility. Their persistence is the result of a failure to be different. The self, in contrast, despite changes in the constitution of the world and the nature of the future, is faced with a possibility of itself which it can and does realize fully. Otherwise its constancy would be an accident, the result of a steady failure to realize some greater possibility, and the self would be a being capable of change, even if it as a matter of fact did not change. A man, however, is self-same not because he fails to be different but because his self is that unalterable source and base to which all his changes are ultimately to be ascribed. That self is a constant in time, for no matter what else may occur and what else it may do, it successfully acts to realize its own possibility again and again.

3. The self renews itself at every moment. But this is not what it primarily seeks to do. It is concerned with more than the realization of the possibility of reappearing again. If it were not, responsibility would be impossible, regret would be meaningless, hope, happiness and duty illusions.

Like every other being, the self is concerned with more than the mere possibility of itself. Like others, too, it cannot entirely realize the possibility which is the object of its concern. But unlike them, it always succeeds in fully realizing the possibility of itself while attempting to realize the possibility which concerns it. When other beings reappear it is because they fail, in some one way, to realize the possibilities with which they are concerned. But the self realizes its own possibility fully, no matter how and to what extent it realizes the possibility with which it is concerned. It does not reappear because it fails to realize the object of its concern; it reappears because its object of concern is always realized as the self, whether or not it is also realized in other ways.

The self is constant while in time because it is concerned with

a good which it steadily realizes in the guise of the self. That good
is a possibility realizable as the self. As more general, as broader
than the self, that good is a possibility realizable also in other ways.
It is in fact a possibility pertinent to everything whatsoever, for
the self differs from the psyche primarily in that it is concerned
with a universal, not a restricted good, with a good which is
relevant to all and not only to some beings. At every moment, the
self realizes in itself and perhaps elsewhere an absolute, ultimate,
universally relevant, possible good.

The good which is the concern of the self, is pertinent to all
other beings. The self partially realizes that good through the body
and to some degree in that body. That good cannot, in fact, be
entirely divorced from the objective which concerns the body.
If it could, the self would be a separate substance. As such it would
not only have a separate objective, but would therefore have a
separate inside and outside and would stand apart from and be
externally related to the body. But the self is the inside of which
the body is the outside. That body, as a physical thing, has its own
inside and its own objective. But as quickened and sustained by
the self, it is the outside of which the self is the inside.

The body is concerned with an objective which must be realized in some way and to some degree when and as the self acts to
realize the universal good, for the acts of the self are in part modes
by which the body is prompted to realize an instance of that absolute good which concerns the self. The attempt of the self to
realize the good at once assures the self of constancy and the body
of continuance.

4. The self is unique, unduplicatable. My self is distinct in being
and nature from yours and remains so no matter how similar we are
in feature, act and intent. The uniqueness of our selves is not due
to our bodies, for the nature of an inside cannot be determined by
an outside. Nor can the uniqueness be due to the nature of the
good with which the selves are concerned. If it were, there would
have to be as many goods as there were selves, and men would be

ethically incomparable. Men are justifiably judged in common terms only so far as there is a single good which concerns them all. Nor can the uniqueness of selves be found in the character of their concerns, for if each self were directed to the good in a different way, they could not be innocent or guilty in a similar sense and for similar reasons. Nor, finally, can the uniqueness of selves be due to the presence in them of characters which are possessed by no others. Unduplicated traits are conceivably duplicatable, thereby making possible the identification of different selves. But selves are absolutely unique, forever and ever distinct and different. I am not you and you are not I; we cannot become one another in theory or in fact.

One self by itself would have the same concern and objective as any other. It would be just self, with nothing to differentiate it from any other. But selves do not exist by themselves. They are completely other than one another because they are inseparable from bodies. From the very start each self is directed to a universal good, as that which is relevant to all beings but primarily relevant to the objective of its body. It is because selves approach a single, universally pertinent good as *primarily* pertinent to the objectives, i.e. to the limited possible goods, of their bodies, that those selves have uniquely determinate natures.

A self is concerned with the good as absolute, abstract and unlimited, pertinent to all beings. It itself is that good realized in a limited way, and thus as concrete, determinate and relativized. As a concrete form of the absolute good, each self is a unity of which all objectives are independent, partial illustrations.

When the absolute good is realized as a self, it continues to exist apart from that self. As so existing, it is a universal good pertinent to all that exists. The self always tries and always succeeds to some extent in realizing that absolute good in its body, for the absolute good is, through the self's concern, inseparable from the objective of the body. The self does not, however, always try or always succeed in realizing the absolute good in other beings, for the objectives of those others are separable from, even though they illustrate, the absolute good that concerns the self.

5. That is good which unifies, harmonizes. Since elements are unified by that which is less concrete than and by that which is at least as concrete as they are, there must be two distinct types of good, the abstract and the concrete. An abstract good is a form, a universal, a structure serving to interrelate more concrete entities which have a status and power independent of it. One such abstract good is greater than another the broader its range, the more elements it can synthesize to form a single unity. The highest of such abstract goods is the *absolute good*, the most comprehensive of forms, the future as a single possibility of which all other possibilities are subordinate, compatible illustrations. A concrete good, on the other hand, is an existent unity. One such concrete good is greater than another if it embodies a greater abstract good than that other. The greatest of concrete goods, therefore, is the self, since, as we saw above, the self *is* the absolute good, though in a special determinate shape.

The absolute good is not itself a great good. It is only the possibility of such a good. It becomes better when made determinate, and thus when indirectly realized in the shape of delimited concrete realities, or when directly realized as a self.

The absolute good is the total future as a form of harmony distinct from but related to what is to be harmonized. It is related to the limited possibilities which are the concern of specific things, as color is to red and blue, where color is understood to have a being and meaning apart from these specific modes. As a pure, separately existing form, it is eternally the same, a fixed standard in terms of which all existents and acts can be evaluated. As realized in the shape of a self, it is a concrete existent which all other beings partially, indirectly and independently realize, a value in terms of which all existents can be measured.

The self, since it is a self of a body, is not concerned with the absolute good as it exists by itself, with the good as a radically indeterminate, all-embracing future. It is concerned rather with that good as pertinent to the body and thus as made partially determinate and enhanced in value by the body's objective. At the same time the self, by quickening the body, relates the object of the body's concern to the absolute good, and thus enhances, by means of that good, the value of that body's objective. The body, under the influence of the self has, therefore, a different objective than it otherwise would.

6. The absolute good and the good of the body impose prescriptions on one another, thereby enhancing one another's value. The good, however, has universal applicability. It is the harmonizing form of whatever objectives there may be. The self, concerned as it is with realizing the good, not only refers it to the objective of the body, but refers it to the objectives which concern other beings. To the degree that those objectives are receptive of the absolute good to that degree are they enhanced in value, and the absolute good is made determinate.

The objective of the body is receptive to the good. The living body, the body quickened by the self, has as a consequence an objective richer than what it would otherwise have. Other beings, however, are independent of the self. Though the absolute good is pertinent to their objectives and though it can enhance and harmonize them, those objectives are not often receptive to the good. Most beings, accordingly, concern themselves with objectives without regard for the fact that those objectives can and ought to be enhanced and harmonized with others within the frame of an all-embracing unity. Largely because of the resistance their objectives offer to the enhancing influence of the good as focused on by the self, the future of other beings is less hopeful than it could be.

Because the self refers the absolute good to all objectives, that good becomes pertinent to them all, as a good which *ought* to be exemplified by every one of them. The self does not know what it does; a long and arduous intellectual voyage is necessary before one comes to the point of seeing that there is a harmony which is pertinent to, is referred to, and ought to be integrated with the particular futures of all there is. But whether it knows it or not, for every self the world is one in which the objectives of particular things are approached from the vantage of a universal good, in terms of which those limited goods ought to be enhanced and made concordant.

The self provides all objectives with the opportunity to have their values increased in harmony. It offers them the all embracing form of the good in terms of which they can convert the prescriptions they reject and accept from one another into subordinated and internal qualifications, thereby enabling them to recover some of the value they lost by mutual limitation. Thus, were a being concerned with the possibility of ruling all others, its possibility would limit and defy the possibilities open to those others so as to make them into possible subjects, or it would defy and be defied by those possibilities so that its and their conjoint realization would result in conflict. The self offers those objectives the form of the good in terms of which they can be harmoniously enhanced in value. If accepted, that good converts the possibility of being a ruler of subjects into a ruler who is also a subject, and the possibility of being a subject for a ruler into a subject who is also a ruler.

The self is concerned with the good as relevant to all objectives. It tries and ought to impose that good on those objectives and thereby enhance those limited goods in harmony. If those objectives do not accept the offered good, the beings which concern themselves with those objectives will fail to deal with the greatest goods possible to them. The self, however, is concerned with the absolute good; it tries and ought to make that good as determinate as possible. It therefore tries and ought to act on behalf of others so that what is realized in them is their objectives as enhanced by the absolute good. Other beings ought to be receptive to the absolute good; but whether they are or not, the self must act with and on those other beings so as to realize that absolute good in those beings. Its task is to enhance them in the same way that it enhances its own body, by realizing enhanced versions of the objectives which concern them.

New values, such as that of the self, come into the world with the arrival of man. For this a price is paid in the form of a responsibility to realize the greatest degree of good everywhere. The self has the responsibility of giving universal embodiment to the absolute good. To fulfill its responsibility it must try to know just what that good demands, and for this purpose must make use of a mind. To bring what is in mind to pass it must make use of a will. The self is thus driven to use its mind and will to fulfill its duty towards all that is, including its own body.

The self always fulfills its obligation towards its body, though not always to the extent it should. It is unavoidably biased towards its body and realizes the objective of its body, as enhanced by the absolute good, to some extent and in some way. Still, it may at times promote the enhanced objective of another at the expense of its own body. The self may fulfill its responsibility towards its own body only to a minimum degree, and prevent a further fulfillment by virtue of the way it acts to fulfill the obligations it has towards other beings. As a rule, however, the self does greater justice to its body than it does to others.

7. A self is superior to a psyche. That superiority consists in part in the fact that a man is sensitive to values that necessarily escape an animal. An animal is sensitive to some of the possibilities that are relevant to its welfare or the welfare of its kind; a man is sensitive to some possibilities as related to the good. He is sensitive that some objectives reject and some accept the prescriptions which the good provides, and thus is aware that there are things he ought to do on behalf of others. His is an ethical sensitivity, a sensitivity to the value of the objectives of others as having accepted or repelled the good. When a man perceives, is intelligent or

uses his mind, he sees more clearly that he is concerned, not with possibilities as pertinent merely to his individual welfare or the good of men, but to possibilities as related to a single, enhancing, absolute, though abstract good.

The idiot and infant, no less than the normal adult, have selves. But neither the idiot nor the infant is sufficiently sensitive to the values its self makes possible. They are not sufficiently sensitive to the value which the self gives to the objective of the body, and as a consequence they are also not sufficiently sensitive to the value which the self provides for other objectives. No self ever attains the stage of being sensitive to all objectives. But the more sensitive it is, the more mature it is. And the more able is a man to act and know in terms of the values his self makes possible.

The self changes the future for the body and perhaps for others. But it does not always act to realize those changed prospects, since it does not always sense the difference its presence makes. Growth in sensitivity depends on the self's ability to hold onto the absolute good as distinct from, though brought by it into relation to the objectives of others.

The self is at once selfish and selfless, concerned with the good of its body and the good of others. And it can be both because it is self-same, approaching all beings from the vantage of an absolute good pertinent to them all. What concerns it, is the future as a good other than but pertinent to the objectives of other beings, a possibility restricting and restricted by the objectives of others in a way different from that in which they restrict one another. The self always partially realizes the good in the form of a self, i.e., as an existent constant of which the rest of the world is a partial and separate manifestation, and it always partially realizes it as an enhancing principle by which the objective of its body and therefore the body itself are increased in value. Sometimes it enhances the objectives and sometimes even the being of others. Only then does it begin to do all it ought.

5. *NATURAL RIGHTS*

The maximum good a being has a right to attain is that which would result from the enhancement of itself proportionately to its present value, in consonance with the proportionate enhancement of the rest. To make more for itself is to cheat others; to take less is to cheat itself.

The right each man has to enhance himself is inseparable from a responsibility to enhance others. It is only by fulfilling his responsibility that he is able to get what he has a right to get. The degree to which he can interest himself in the good of others measures the degree to which he can perfect himself.

The inanimate do not take sensitive account of others. The maximum to which they can be enhanced, while remaining inanimate, is defined by the value they now have and the degree to which this allows them accidentally to benefit others. Those living beings which can take sensitive account of the requirements of some others, but only blindly, are the subhuman. The maximum to which they can be perfected is defined by the value they now have and the degree to which this allows them to live with the others they benefit. It is *man* alone who can deliberately enhance his own worth by deliberately setting himself to increase the values of all. The maximum worth to which he can be enhanced is defined by the degree to which he can concordantly increase the values of the rest.

Man differs from other beings in having more rights and responsibilities. His actions, unlike theirs, are always quickened by the future as an absolute, universally pertinent good. Whereas inanimate beings realize a part of that good in themselves regardless of the benefits they bestow on others, and whereas animals act to realize a part of that good as pertinent to a few, men are obligated to realize it as a single good pertinent to themselves and all the rest. The common form of the future as pertinent to all is for man the ultimate object of concern. And man alone can will to realize it.

In contrast with subhuman beings, all men have the same intrinsic rights and responsibilities. In comparison with one another, they have, above this minimum, different degrees of acquired ethical worth, living up, as they do, to their responsibilities in different degrees. To be a better man than another is to be a more conscientious one, to have tried to do more to help others to be as perfect as possible in a perfected world. The more of their rights one acknowledges others to have and the more one strives to fulfill them, the more ethical worth one has.

The better a man, the more ethical worth he has; but also the more responsibilities he acknowledges. The subhuman are unconcerned with what other beings need in order to be perfected; their endeavor to fulfill their concerns is limited to acts pertinent to a few neighboring beings. It is of the essence of man, in contrast, to endeavor to help all others to be as perfect as possible in consonance with the perfection of the rest, thereby extending their rights to the limit.

All beings change in nature to the degree that they are excessively constrained, unless perchance they perish. It is not until man arises that there is a being who can change others by venturing towards the whole future as a good pertinent to all, and who must take it as deserving to be realized within the body of all that is. He alone is obligated to perfect all there is in the world.

6. THE TASK OF MAN

No matter how insignificant, servile, impotent or vicious a man, he has a unique value, unduplicatable, unrepeatable and irreplaceable. He may look like, behave like and think like others, his power may be weak and his productions trivial. His character may be contemptible. He may be less good that he ought to be; yet he has a value that cannot be reproduced or replaced and which is greater than that possessed by any other type of being.

The birth of a human being ought always to be an occasion for rejoicing, for nothing so deserves celebration as the coming to be of a new value. One may, to be sure, pay a high price for it. It may prove to be the occasion, then or later, of the loss of other equal values. There are times when joy must be restrained; there are other times when it can be nothing more than a tinge to a sorrow deep and lasting. It is tragic that there should be infants crippled in mind and body, orphaned, starved and diseased, or that they should be born in times of famine and pestilence. These are poignant occurrences because they produce new, fresh and precious values in such a way as to subtract from the totality of the good that could have been. Looked at in their setting, as having distorted or inadequate bodies and minds in environments which tend to make them worse, their presence may sometimes be so regrettable that it might be thought wise and charitable to destroy them; taken by themselves, as human beings infinitely rich in value and in potency, they are to be appreciated as new, infinitely precious goods which never were before and never can be again.

What occurs in or outside the body or mind can have no effect on the nature of a man, but only on the things he can think and do. Nor can any reform be so complete that it severs his career in two. A person can reform only himself and must do it in his own way, leaving on the new result an impression of the self to which the cleansing is due. These limitations provide no justification, however, for resignation or fatalistic despair. The fact that an individual remains essentially the same in sickness and in health does not extinguish the fact that in the one case he suffers and in the other he rejoices, and that he can evaluate and react to these states in multiple ways. A change in external circumstances makes possible new and different activities, the pursuit of which make a great difference to the value he has and will obtain as a being in a public world. When he reforms, he gets a different hold on his objective, changing thereby the meaning that it has for himself and the meaning that he has for others. The constancy of his nature does not preclude an endless variety in the kind and value of the things he can do.

No man is a mere creature of circumstances. He molds them in a characteristic way. Changes in his cells or organs, or the conditions which hem him in from without, make possible new acts and enterprises otherwise beyond his reach, enabling him to develop and exercise new talents, and prompting him occasionally to undergo a radical reform. Yet everything he does bears the self-same signature, written though it is on different things, at different times and in different ways. Each makes and mars in his own individual way.

Given equal health, fortune and opportunity, each man, it would seem, should be able to achieve what every other can. Men begin to diverge, however, from the very start, for as embryos they already live in different environments, are fed by different foods, and inevitably lay the ground for patterns of expression and activity which cannot readily be dislodged or radically changed. Not all can be professional athletes, mathematicians, or political leaders, for as embryos they have already set individual limits to what they can attain as mature technicians of mind and body. No change in health, opportunity or determination will suffice to turn one into a violinist of distinction if his gifts do not lie in that direction. Free and unlimited though a man's promise is and always remains, it is yet bound irrevocably at the beginning of his life, for the individual works in new contexts from the standpoint and with the equipment of the old. Though there is nothing which is not in principle open to everyone equally, from the first much that a man might do is excluded beyond recall, and as he grows, more and more is outside his possible reach.

Each man can, to some degree, control the activities of most of his organs, individually and together, for the good of his body. He can also interrelate them for an end beyond. His problem is to move from the state of living in and through his body to the state of living by means of it in order to benefit others as well as himself. It is his task to remake the world, to realize to a maximum the good with which he is concerned. Only so far as he succeeds, does he fulfill his duty. Only then does he exhibit himself as one not bound by things as they are. Only then does he do what he ought—improve the world by making it the embodiment of the absolute good.

Man is a natural being with a fixed core, directed towards a good which is pertinent to all that exists. And he has a responsibility from which he can never escape. It is the primary function of his body, mind and will to help him live up to this responsibility. Trapped though he is by the bonds of past, body, society and the world, he is free to act and thus is accountable for his every failure to realize the good fully in fact. Even if he could not possibly master those bonds, he would still be responsible. He has infinite value because he has an infinite responsibility, and conversely. To deny him the one is to deny him the other.

A man's fundamental right is the right to be good. This requires him to realize the good. Whether or not, and to what degree it can be realized is therefore a vital problem. It is in fact a central problem of ethics. A man, because he is responsible, owes it to himself to plumb the foundations of ethics and make evident to himself what he ought to do. Only then can he make himself the man he ought to be.

INDEX

Ability, 125, 126, 127, 128, 177
Absolute, 35, 37, 40, 45, 47, 48, 49, 52, 53, 201, 256, 258, 260f., 267
Abstention, 234
Abstract, the, 6, 11, 15, 16, 17, 47, 53, 258, 260
Abstraction, xxii, 13, 14, 49
Absurdity, xviii, xx, xxii
Account-taking, 39ff., 55, 195, 215, 247, 263
Action, v, 32ff., 36, 51, 55, 57, 58ff., 62, 65, 67, 68, 75, 83, 87, 94, 95, 99, 103, 113, 114, 125, 136, 154, 158, 191, 197, 216, 224, 265, 266
  acquired, 152, 156
  and signs, 173, 176, 178
  and tension, 95
  anticipatory, 170, 175
  atomic, 33
  bodily, 113, 114, 117, 129, 153, 221f., 224, 241
  change in 37, 69f., 156, 200, 221, 265f.
  correction of, 69, 70, 71, 103, 119, 221
  determinateness of 33, 191
  divine, 131. *See also* Omnipotence
  division of 32
  effective, 58, 66, 70, 96, 101, 103, 112, 113, 114, 116, 117, 120, 140, 154, 160, 161, 164, 169
  ethical, 144
  free, 26, 31, 33, 62, 67ff., 69, 101, 198, 199, 200, 236
  function of, 199, 224, 235, 261
  good, 86, 87, 129, 237
  habit of, 152, 158
  habitual, 154, 196
  human, 23, 27, 67, 128, 136, 163, 200, 263
  impulsive, 18, 160
  innate, 152
  individual, 38, 99, 163
  kinds of, 58
  man of, 63
  mental, 213, 220, 221f., 229
  of children, 249ff.
  of inanimate, 67, 69
  of organs, 147, 152, 154

Action—*Continued*
  of self, 254f.
  of will, 230ff.
  organic, 162, 219, 248
  perfect, 58, 66, 70, 155
  planned, 216
  random, 35, 92, 98, 113
  regular, 18, 69, 70, 118, 154
  source of, 254
  specialized, 164, 245
  spontaneity in, 69, 70, 71, 76, 116, 199, 200
  stable, 98, 152
  stretch of, 33
  terminus of, 235
  unity of, 33
  values in, 23
  voluntary, 114, 200, 235
Actuality, xii, 6, 17, 18, 20, 30, 228, 231
  and possibility, 15, 17, 18, 32, 199, 203, 235
  determinateness of, 32, 171
Adam, 86, 87, 247
Adaptation. *See* Adjustment
Addition, error of unwarranted, xvi, xvii
Adjective, 182
Adjustment, 83, 117, 120, 153, 162, 164, 224, 251
  self-, 58, 59ff., 62, 65, 67, 68, 72, 74
Adler, A., 251
Adult, 134, 205, 248, 249
Adumbration, 50, 51, 52, 53, 183, 184
Adventure, 19, 200, 222
Affirmation, 107, 211, 213, 219, 230, 231
Age, old, 99, 150
Agent, 33
Agitation, 28, 209,
Aims, 63, 65
Altruism, xiv
Amoeba, 85, 140
Analysis, xix, 9, 13, 14
Anger, 221, 225
Anima, 130
Animals, 21, 67, 100, 137, 142
  ability of, 119
  action of, 119
  and intelligence, 205

Animals—*Continued*
and language, 178, 179
and men, xiii, xv, 120, 121ff., 127,
128, 133, 134, 139, 140, 144, 148,
166, 264
and plants, 100
body of, 100, 139
dangerous, 90
defective, 90
domesticated, 90, 93
form of, 130
freedom of, xviii
good for, 87ff., 97
origin of, 71ff., 100ff., 120, 121
useful, 87, 90
sensitivity of, 114
wild, 93
wisdom of, 91f.
Animate, 64, 67, 71f., 74, 84
Anguish, 107, 116, 117
Antecedents, 9, 18, 20, 21, 22, 212
Anthropology, 124
Anthropomorphism, xvi, 88, 90
Antagonism, 95, 96
Anticipation, 8, 10, 30, 31, 119, 158,
169ff., 251
Apes, 100, 123, 124, 139
Apprenticeship, 186
Approval, 241
Aquinas, St. Thomas, 121, 130f., 133
Archaeology, 124
Argument, 7, 8, 25
Aristotle, xii, 32, 55, 59, 72, 83, 97,
122, 123, 129, 130, 131, 133, 186,
242, 244
Art, xi, 64, 65, 98, 118, 125, 127, 128,
164, 166, 204, 249
and other disciplines, 184, 185
function of, 117
mastery of, 161
Articulation, 183
Artisan, 164
Artists, 64, 118, 184, 210
Asceticism, 129
Assertion, 24, 25, 192
Association, 113, 114
Astronomy, 43, 90
Atheists, 126
Athletes, 151, 266
Atoms, 22, 33, 45
Attention, 177, 180, 181, 182, 238
Attitudes, 95
Auden, W. H., 61

Augustine, St., 121, 132
Awareness, 108, 115, 127, 176, 214

Barriers, 57, 62, 68, 76, 120, 191, 199,
215, 216, 217, 236, 267
final, 217
intellectual, ix, xii
the four, 194ff.
See also Obstacles
Beauty, 65
sense of, 124, 125
Becoming, xxi, xxii, 3, 6, 7ff., 10, 11,
19, 28, 30, 36, 37, 38, 54, 167, 201
of necessity, 29
possibility for, 34, 54
Beginnings, xvii, xxii, 6, 18, 32
Behavior
involuntary, 156, 157
of animals, 84, 85,
organic, 162, 163,
perfection of, 163
right, 85, 249
standard for, 85
Beings, xix, 6, 39ff., 53, 95, 116, 183, 226
and knowledge, 51, 185
and nothing, 46
aspects of, 39ff., 56
beyond nature, 122
capacity of, 125
defective, 90
division of, 42
finite, 54, 201
graceful, 98f.
healthy, 86
inanimate, 43, 64, 67, 84
independent, 31, 145
indeterminate, 183
individual, 38ff., 200ff.
intelligent, 119
living, 64, 67, 71f., 74, 82, 84, 85, 116,
121ff., 143, 145, 146, 147, 150
natural, v, 4, 121ff.
nature of, 39
origin of higher, 71f., 100f., 120
pampered, 98, 99
perfect, 132
public, 39
states of, 95
stultified, 98, 99
unconscious, 105
Belief
explanation of, 3, 4
indubitable, xxii, 4

Bentham, J., xiii
Bergson, H., 7, 8, 9, 20, 21, 101
Berkeley, G., 83, 122
Bias, 42, 68, 194, 261
Bible, 121
Biology, xiii, 72, 121, 123,
  metaphysics of, 81ff.
Birth, 134, 141, 153, 242, 265
Blake, W., x, xi
Blinking, 154, 157
Body, 82, 96, 97, 99, 102, 103, 104,
  106f., 109, 115, 215, 225
  and mind, xiii, xvi, 200ff., 215, 217,
    218ff., 223, 224, 225, 230, 232, 234,
    236, 237, 238, 241, 244, 265
  and self, 139, 223, 225, 239, 241ff.,
    253, 256, 257
  and soul, 27, 128ff.
  and will, 223, 230
  animal, 100
  bias of, 68, 217
  boundary of, 115
  cells of, 141
  changes in, 134ff., 197, 253
  child's, 158
  concern of, 71, 159, 222, 256, 257,
    259, 261, 262
  demands of, 194, 196
  economy of, 225
  embryonic, 153
  feeling in, 109ff., 115
  function of, 71f., 76, 123, 129, 159
  good of, 129, 165, 226, 266
  human, 26, 27, 122, 123, 128, 132,
    133, 137, 139, 158
  infant's, 153f., 265
  living, 26, 27, 100, 103f., 122, 136, 139,
    146, 150, 153, 164, 242, 243, 259
  mastery of, 116, 194f., 199, 237, 242
  necessity for, 128, 129, 133, 239, 253,
    267
  needs of, 194. *See also* Food
  objective of. *See concern* of
  of inanimates, 73, 130
  parts of, 141, 145, 242
  preparation of, 224
  rejuvenation of, 150
  resistance of, 33, 70, 71, 73ff., 100,
    102, 105, 116, 140, 143, 144, 159,
    194, 217, 227, 267
  satisfaction of, 94
  sensitized, 103f., 146, 164
  state of, 242, 243

Body—*Continued*
  tendencies of. *See* Tendencies,
    bodily
  wisdom of, 85ff., 92, 94
Bondage. *See* Barriers
Boundaries, 7, 39, 40, 42, 43, 44, 45,
  46, 48, 49, 56, 57, 115, 142, 146,
  174, 195
Brain, 91, 109, 110, 111, 112, 114, 123,
  137, 153, 241
Bravery, 195, 196

Calls, 178, 179, 180
Calvin, J., 132
Cancer, 76, 92
Capacity, 125, 231
Career, 34, 41, 56, 142
Casanova, G., 248
Categoreals, 183,
Categories
  basic, 56,
  daily, x,
  universal, xvii
Categorization of future, 168, 195
Causation, v, xvi, xviii, xix, 14ff., 19,
  34, 123, 164, 183, 202ff.
  and freedom 4, 6, 19, 203
  belief in, 4
  course of, 5, 6, 7, 9, 10, 12, 13, 18,
    19, 21, 32, 34, 204, 213
  deterministic theory of, 20f.
  efficient, 19,
  final, 19, 54, 55, 97
  lines of, 6, 12, 32,
  rationale of, 9ff.
  terminus of, 12,
  unit of, 33
Cause, 19, 57, 121
  and effect, 3ff., 18, 19, 20ff., 202ff.
  Aristotelian, 32
  components of, 57
  efficient, 19
  final, 19, 54, 55, 97, 203
  impotence of, 5, 9, 20
Caution, excessive, 175
Cells, 141ff., 150
  bodily, 141
  change in, 134, 150, 266
  complex, 143,
  constitution of, 150
  dependent, 145
  human, 141f.
  nature of, 142

Cells—*Continued*
 origin of, 141, 145
 reproductive, 141, 142, 145
 specialized, 145, 146, 148, 149
Certainty, xxi, 29
Chance, 22, 23, 123, 162, 177, 202
Change, 6, 21, 24, 65, 70, 96, 100, 111, 115, 116, 120, 130, 131, 135, 150, 264
 and constancy, 135, 136, 138, 253, 254
 evolutionary, 101
 in future, 36, 54, 55, 254, 262
 in man, 134ff., 254
 in self, 255
 in society, 255
 reason for, 119
Chants, language of, 189
Character, 61, 66, 264
Chemistry, xiii, 72
Childhood, 134, 135, 136, 251
Children, ix, 127
 sexuality in, 249ff.
Choice, 65, 231
Christian Scientists, 128
Christianity, xiii, 131
Circumstance, 155, 157, 265f.
Citizens, 37, 60
Civilization, ix, 164
Clarification, 173, 181
Clear, the, 115
Clouds, as signs, 167, 170, 171, 172, 174, 175, 187, 188
Coexistence, 4
Coherence theory, 183
Cold, common, 148
Collections, 82
Color, 42, 125
Coming to be. *See* Becoming
Command, 192, 241, 248
Commandments, the, 17, 22
Communication, ix, xxi, 176, 177, 178, 188, 190f.
Components, 4, 32, 34ff., 142, 162
Compounds, organic, 72
Compulsion, 21, 25, 33, 58, 60, 61, 65ff., 68, 74, 76, 195, 202, 203
Conceit, natural, 107
Concept, 215, 217
Conception, 141, 228
Concern, 53ff., 58, 61, 84, 99, 100, 120, 231
 allocation of, 71

Concern—*Continued*
 animal, 139
 change in, 70, 73ff., 100, 101, 102, 105, 106, 120, 140, 143, 144
 convergent, 258, 263f.
 demands of, 69, 71, 76, 116
 expression of, 62ff., 73, 76, 100, 103f., 107, 112, 139, 140, 143, 144, 159, 162, 200, 246f.
 individuality of, 71, 203
 intelligent, 206
 human, xvi, 84, 101, 120, 138, 139, 140, 144, 239, 249, 251ff.
 object of, 53, 54, 58, 59, 61, 64, 67, 68, 70, 71, 73, 74, 89, 95, 140, 141, 177, 205ff., 210, 215, 253, 258ff.
 of body, 71, 159, 222, 256, 257, 259
 of living beings, 74, 90,
 of mind, 219
 of self, 164, 225, 238, 239, 244ff., 252f., 260
 of subhuman, 264
 of will, 222
 purposive, 205
 satisfaction of, 71, 75, 116, 117, 157, 244, 252
 sensitive, 103ff., 108, 109, 116, 267
 shared, 205, 207, 209, 211
 vital, 205, 206, 211
Conclusion, 9, 11, 214, 216, 227
 contingent, 212, 213
Concrete, 6, 11, 13, 14, 15, 17, 18, 29, 30, 36, 38, 39, 47, 167, 199, 258
Condillac, de, E. B., 124
Conditioning, 158, 203, 225
Confirmation, 16, 25
Conflict, 58, 61, 63, 64, 95, 226, 237, 239, 261
 of desires, 227, 248
Conscientiousness, 264
Consciousness, v, xix, 92, 100, 102, 104, 111ff., 115, 119, 143, 164
 nature of, 105, 116, 117
 objects of, 109, 117, 119. *See also* Pain, Pleasure
 of guilt, 135
 origin of, 102, 116, 203
 self-, 124
Consistency, 183
Constant, human, 134ff., 151, 157, 253ff., 262, 266
Constituents. *See* Components

Constraint, 19, 34, 36, 37, 46, 68, 196, 197, 217, 236, 264
Contagion, 176, 208
Contemplation, 15, 249
Contemporaries, 55, 56, 81f., 84
Continuum, xvii, 43, 84, 89, 136
Contradiction, xviii, 56
Control, 64, 73, 109, 144, 153, 154, 156, 157, 159, 160, 164, 165, 169, 194, 195, 196, 197, 203, 224, 242, 244, 266
Convention, ix, 185ff., 192
Conversation, 32, 35, 252
Copula, 50, 189
Cosmology, 210
Courage, 66, 82, 160
Course, 5, 7, 8, 28, 33, 34, 161
  canalized, 6
  constitution of, 32, 36,
  constraint of, 35, 36, 37
  determinateness of, 10, 212
  future of, 36
  of causation, 5, 6, 7, 9, 10, 12, 13, 18, 19, 21, 32, 34, 204, 213
  of inference, 11, 212, 213
  uniqueness of, 6, 9, 13
  unit of, 33
Cowardice, 156
Creation, 28, 46, 121f., 124, 131, 132
Creativity, x, 34, 35, 52, 64
Cries, 178, 179, 180
Crime, 65, 135
Criminal, 197, 198
Criticism, 86, 119
  self-, 243
Curiosity, 92, 227, 250, 251, 252
Curvature of space, 43
Custom, 160

Danger, 91, 92, 101, 103, 117, 168, 169, 173, 174, 176, 180, 181, 187, 237
Darwin, C., xii, 82, 124ff.
Date, 20, 167,
Death, 71, 72, 75, 92, 96, 112, 116, 117, 119, 129, 131, 134, 136, 145, 146, 165, 196, 241, 264
Decisions, 86, 95, 96, 105, 241
Deduction, 7, 9, 10, 22, 29, 31
Defects, 90, 132
Defiance, social, 196, 197
Definiteness, 19, 130, 173
Deliberate, 25, 127, 157. *See also* Action, voluntary

Democracy, 61,
Democritus, 200
Denial, xix, xx, 4, 24, 25, 26. *See also* Affirmation
Denotation, 47, 48, 50, 51, 52, 56, 182
Descartes, R., xii, xiv, 27, 82, 109, 110, 111, 112, 114, 128, 200, 215
Description, 86, 182
Desires, xvi, 23, 29, 61, 92, 117, 154, 156, 222, 227, 228, 244, 248
Despair, 96, 265
Destiny, 157, 241
Determinateness, 6, 11, 12, 13, 15, 16, 18, 19, 32, 33, 67, 169, 199, 203, 224
  of effect, 10, 24, 29, 203
  of good, 67, 258, 259
  of possibility, 15, 16, 199,
  of self, 257, 258
Determination, 24, 36, 37, 39, 55, 68, 70, 138, 183, 184, 199, 236, 254
  self-, 22, 23, 33
Determinism, 20, 27, 28, 29, 32, 37, 65, 83, 175, 202, 213, 232
  paradox of, 24f.
Development, 97, 141, 145, 152, 163, 200, 248
Dewey, J., 16, 218
Dialectic of history, 36, 201
Dialecticians, 191
Dialogue, 189, 192
Dictatorship, 160
Digestion, 74, 155, 159
Dingle, H., 83
Diplomats, 248
Discernment, 97, 117, 118, 119, 205, 207, 211
Disciples, 59, 60
Discipline, xi, 237, 238
  self-, 243
Discourse, x, 25, 166, 181, 183, 188, 189, 190, 251
Discrimination, 171, 172
Discursive, 53
Disease, 86, 123
Disintegration, 44
Disputation, 7, 8, 178
Distance, xvii
  infinite, 46, 47, 185
  spatial, 39, 43, 46, 254
  temporal, 4, 6, 7, 8, 9, 19
Distinctions, 39, 53, 100, 130, 171, 174, 231

Disturbances, 105, 111ff., 123, 141, 156, 180
Division, 146, 147
Doctor
    medical, 187, 245
    of philosophy, 187
Dogma, 196
Dominance, 94, 95, 97, 219
Don Juan, 248
Doubt, self-imposed, xxi, xxii
Dualism, xvi
Duns Scotus, 186
Drive, 89, 91, 248f.
Drunkard, 160, 233
Durée, 6
Duty, v, xiii, 200, 240, 261, 267. *See also* Obligation

Earlier and later, 33
Eating, habit of, 158, 159, 160, 225
Echolalia, 179
Economics, xii, xiii, 192
Ecstasy, 116, 117
Education, xiii, 126, 128, 153, 186
Effect, 3ff., 21, 33
    analytic component of, 4, 5
    and cause, 3ff., 18, 19, 20ff., 202ff.
    avoidability of, 10
    coming to be of, 10, 18. *See also* Causation, Course
    deduction of, 9, 10, 29, 31
    determinateness of, 10, 24, 29, 203
    kinds of, 6
    knowledge of, 10, 12, 13, 20, 31, 32, 33, 34, 67, 203
    necessity of, 10, 11, 18, 24, 33, 202
    possible, 5, 10, 11, 13, 20
    subordinate, 5
Effort, 199, 201
    of will, 232f.
Egg, 142, 143
Einstein, A., 82
Electrons, 44
Embryo, 131, 134, 135, 137, 140f., 143, 144, 145ff., 152ff., 157, 266
Emotions, 30, 150, 205, 207, 221f., 225, 226, 227, 241, 244
Empedocles, 121, 242
Empirical, 184
Empiricists, 7, 40
Endings, xvii, 6, 19, 32, 235
Ends, xiii, 23, 36, 97, 98, 99, 199, 231, 246. *See also* Concern

Ends—*Continued*
    object of; Good; Objective
Energy, 27, 31, 64, 65, 99, 152, 159, mental, 230, 233
    potential, 47
Entelechy, 83
Environment, 39, 44, 56, 94, 95, 96, 103, 114ff., 120, 153, 156, 157, 158, 162, 217, 265, 266
Epicurus, 60
Equilibrium, 108, 117, 157, 236
Error, xii, xxi, 59, 86, 87, 175, 235, 239,
    explanation of, 30, 31, 169, 170
    in response, 113,
    of addition and subtraction, xv, xvi, xvii
Essence, 130, 135, 156, 166, 249
Esthete, 117
Esthetics, xii
Eternal, 131, 200
Ethics, v, xiv, xviii, xxii, 4, 14, 65, 77, 144, 156, 240, 249, 252, 257, 264, 267,
    Aristotelian, xiii
    cosmic, xv
    laws of, 17
Euclid, 59
Evaluation, 25, 26, 86, 87, 89, 90, 91, 96, 257, 258, 265
Event, 6, 10, 16, 31, 167. *See also* Course
Evidence, 106, 126, 202, 203, 204, 219
Evolution, 72, 83, 87, 100f., 120, 123, 140, 148,
    freedom and, 102, 201
Excellence, intrinsic, 90
Exchange of calls, 178
Excitation, 159, 205, 247
Exclamations, 180ff.
Existence, 41, 46, 58, 130, 167, 242
    difficulties of, 93
    effective, 101,
    mediated, 49
    possibility of, 254f.
Expectation, 4, 31, 55, 74, 119, 166, 168ff., 170, 174, 175, 176, 178, 180, 181, 190, 193, 205, 206, 208, 209
Experience, 10, 40, 42, 92, 93, 94, 112, 114, 115, 125, 197, 201, 203, 206, 211, 219, 227
Experiment, 82, 83, 84

Explanation, xviii, xxii, 6, 38, 58, 65,
    77, 119, 202
Explosion, 5, 6, 44
Exposure, 64
Expression, 39, 58, 59, 61, 62ff., 67, 68,
    74, 99, 101, 115, 129, 136, 175, 191,
    199, 246
    dangerous, 247
    limited, 246, 252
    of absolute, 48
    of animals, 124
    of concern, 62ff., 73, 76, 100, 103f.,
        107, 112, 139, 140, 143, 144, 159,
        162, 200, 246f.
    of freedom, 199
    of inanimates, 64, 74
    of men, 64, 164, 249
    of self, 138, 139, 215, 216, 220, 241ff.,
        244ff.
    of sensitivity, 103f., 139, 140
    of tendencies, 149, 150, 154, 156, 157,
        159, 163, 262
    patterns of, 266
    repression of, 246
    resistance to, 71
    sexual, 246ff.
Extensiveness, 43, 49
Extrapolation, method of, 47, 49, 52
Extroverts, 62,
Eye, origin of, 101

Fact, xiii, 4, 16, 26, 29, 51, 65
Failure, 58, 60, 62, 63, 70, 76, 89, 168,
    169, 255
Falsehood, 26, 50, 237
    and truth, 24, 25
    test of, 49
    See also Error
Family, 37, 123
Fanatic, 219
Fatigue, 149
Fear, 155, 157, 169, 176, 194, 205
Feeling, xvi, 100, 106, 109, 113, 115,
    117, 148, 176, 208
    immediate, 111
    location of, 109ff.
    psyche as, 119
Fictions, 183, 184
Fidget, 248
Field, 198, 199
Fighting, instinct for, 155, 156, 158
Finitude, xxii, 54, 87, 122, 210
Finger-mouth problem, 222

Flexibility, ix, 156, 238
Fluidity, 45
Folly, 92, 93ff.
Food, 97, 128, 158, 159, 224, 225, 227f.,
    235, 243
Force, 31, 37, 52, 82
    cosmic, 20f., 24, 25, 32
    creative, 35,
    of desire, 227,
    of will, 229, 235
Form, xii, 130ff., 186, 243, 258, 259,
    261, 263
Fossils, 73
Frank, E., vi
Freedom, v, xiii, xviii, 4ff., 12, 18f.,
    20f., 26, 29, 31, 34, 35, 38, 69, 74,
    75, 76, 141, 147, 191, 222
    and activity, 26, 31, 33, 62, 67ff., 69,
        101, 198, 199, 200, 236
    and causation, 4, 6, 19, 203
    and consciousness, 102
    and evolution, 102, 201
    and mind, 201, 203ff., 215, 217, 222
    and necessity, 18ff.
    animal, xviii
    embryonic, 141,
    explanatory nature of, xviii, xxii
    human, v, xiii, xiv, xv, xvi, 4, 139,
        192, 198ff., 217, 267
    legal, 66
    limits of, 31
    nature of, 199
    of self, 240
    of will, 22, 23, 236
    three-fold, 198ff.
    universality of, xiv, xv, xix
    See also Spontaneity
Freud, S., 244ff.
Frustration, 70, 73, 75, 246ff.
Future, 15, 17, 19, 35, 36, 56, 98, 99,
    118, 125, 202, 203, 236, 259, 262
    and determinism, 29, 30, 83
    as object of sign, 167ff., 202f.
    being of, 13,
    categorization of, 168, 195
    change of, 36, 54, 55, 254, 262
    common, 37, 38, 53, 56, 170, 171,
        208, 258
    concrete, 12, 13, 30
    cosmic, 37, 38, 53, 258, 263
    constitution of, 36, 37, 168, 196
    knowledge of, 12, 13, 17, 30, 32, 55,
        67, 204, 205

Future—*Continued*
  of perceived, 119
  reaching to, 53, 56, 244
  predictability of, 11, 15
  undetermined, 7, 8, 11, 67, 168, 170,
    175, 196, 203, 217,
  See also Good, Possibility, Predic-
    tion

Galileo, G., xii, xiv, 82
Gaps, xvii. *See also* Distance
Generals, 6, 11, 13, 15, 18, 29, 36, 130,
  167, 199. *See also* Universals
Generalization, xx, 16, 88, 210
Geology, xiii, 73, 82, 83, 121, 122, 124
Geometry, *n*-dimensional, 219
Gestalt, 83
Gesture, 182, 188
Giant, 110, 150
Gland, 137, 219
  pineal, 109,
  transplantation of, 150
Glutton, 160
God, 8, 13, 17, 22, 40, 46, 72, 121, 132,
  148, 210, 247
  Aristotelian, 244
  limitations of, 13, 14, 132
  name of, 187
  pantheistic, 107
Good, v, xiii, 35, 53, 56, 57, 58ff., 65,
  76, 85, 86, 88, 129, 217, 258
  absolute, 53, 238, 256, 258, 260f., 267
  abstract, 258, 260
  and self, 254f., 258f., 261
  and will, 223, 238, 263
  arbitrary, 88
  as object of concern, 53, 54, 58, 59,
    61, 64, 67, 68, 206, 210, 253, 258ff.
    See also Concern
  as possible, 53, 68, 199, 207, 256, 258,
    259, 261
  as real, 199
  common, 53, 54, 94, 144, 256f., 263,
    264
  concordant, 59f., 261
  concrete, 258
  cosmic, 53, 54, 253, 256, 257, 259
  demands of, 239
  elected, 57
  for animals, 87ff., 97
  great, 59f., 63, 64, 66, 258
  knowledge of, 55, 70, 86, 87, 97, 260
  minor, 59, 60, 62f., 66

Good—*Continued*
  of body, 129, 165, 226, 266
  of living, 74, 88
  of mind, 226
  of others, 206, 207, 254ff., 261f.
  prescribed, 95, 138, 259, 260ff.
  private, 61, 67, 88
  qualified, 54, 260
  realization of, 57, 58f., 62, 65f., 69,
    70, 75, 76, 88, 89, 90, 95, 119, 129,
    138, 145, 164, 199, 207, 254ff.,
    261f., 267
  social, 61, 97, 144
  thought of, 129
  total, 53, 54, 265
  ultimate, 238f., 256, 258. *See also*
    Good, absolute
  universal, 239, 256
  See also Future, Objective, Possi-
    bility
Grace, 93, 98f, 140
Grammar, 188, 189, 190, 192
Grammarian, 17, 191
Gravitation, 39, 44, 82, 198
Greek thought, xiii
Gregory XIII, Pope, 186
Ground, ultimate, 211. *See also* Good;
  Objective, ultimate
Group mind, 35
Growth, 61, 64, 97, 98, 106, 123, 134,
  141, 143, 145, 146, 151, 153, 248, 262
Guilt, v, 135, 240, 253, 254, 257
Gymnastics, 128

Habit, 13, 33, 93, 94, 98, 99, 104, 114,
  140, 144, 152, 153, 155, 156, 157,
  160, 163, 189, 191, 193, 196, 204,
  218, 225, 226
  and instinct, 155, 156
  and scientists, 29
  cause for, 3
  embryonic, 154, 156, 157
  formation of, 113, 153, 156, 157
  mental, 158f., 192, 204, 216, 217, 218,
    225, 226
  of artists, 118
  of matter, 218
  organization of, 157ff., 161
  stabilization of, 156
Hands, 123, 147, 148
Happiness, 124, 249
Harmony, xvii, 54, 59f., 63, 164, 195,
  222, 227, 238, 239, 242, 258ff.

Health, 86, 92, 94, 98, 137, 150, 151, 249, 256
Heart, 146, 147, 151, 152, 153, 162
Hebrews, 17, 131
Hegel, G., 24, 27, 35, 40, 41, 47, 48, 49, 52, 53, 82, 122, 201
Hegelians, 8, 40, 201,
Heisenberg, W., 22, 23
Heresy, 60, 196
Heroes, 34, 156
History, 4, 24, 29, 34, 36, 73, 125
  and art, 184
  and signs, 166
  dialectic of, 36, 201
  natural, 121, 122, 124
Hobbes, T., xiii, 230, 231, 232
Hope, xvi, 54, 55
Humanists, 186
Hume, D., 3, 7, 8, 21, 40, 41, 44, 45, 83, 202ff.
Humility, ix, xiii, 19, 52, 53
Huxley, T., 218
Hypothesis, 22, 23, 82

Idea, ix, 211, 217, 232, 236, 241,
  obscuring, ix, 224
  origin of, 225
  true, 230, 231
Ideal, 58, 59, 62ff., 86, 129, 217, 239, 241
Idealism, 48, 122, 183, 201, 202
Idealists, absolute. *See* Hegel
  practical, 60
Identity, self-, 134ff., 241, 243, 251, 253, 254, 255, 262, 266, 267
Idiot, 127, 132, 138, 204, 262
Ignorance, 195
Illusion, 8, 56, 106, 118
Imagination, 124, 215
Immaturity, 99
Immediate, 48
Impartiality, 86, 88
Impotence, 96, 107, 188, 202, 203, 218, 251
Impulse, 109, 110, 159, 160, 245ff., 252
Inanimate, 43, 71, 81, 116, 130, 263
  acts of, 67, 69
  body of, 73f., 130
  expression of, 64, 74
  form of, 130
  freedom in, xviii
  knowledge of, 84
  nature of, 64
  spontaneity of, 69, 70, 76

Inclination, 149, 150, 157, 222, 234, 237
Indefiniteness, 130. *See also* Definiteness
Independence, 46, 57, 141, 142
Indeterminate, 6, 7, 11, 15, 18, 19, 55, 167, 175, 184, 199. *See also* Determinateness
Indeterminacy, theory of, 22, 23
Indeterminism, human, 27. *See also* Determinism
Indication. *See* Denotation
Indifference, 85, 86, 254
Individualism, 34, 35, 88, 89
Individuals, 35ff., 57, 76, 81, 88, 93, 94, 96, 99, 130, 142, 201, 204, 206, 207, 215
  and absolute, 35, 37, 40, 45, 201
  and activity, 38, 99, 163
  aspects of, 39ff.
  as substantial, 38
  concern of, 71, 203
  localized, 43
  origin of human, 140ff.
  privacy of, 45
  resistance of, 45ff., 57
  unity of, 163, 244
Indivisible, 39
Infants, 138, 157, 204, 205, 262
  and ethics, 77
  body of, 153f., 265
  fear of, 176
  helplessness of, 140, 155, 161
  intelligence of, 208, 209
  mind of, 206, 209
Inference, xxi, 11, 208, 209, 211ff., 226
"Information," xii
Inheritance, 143
Inhibition, 112, 161, 162
Innate, 154, 155
Innocence, x, xxii, 132, 240, 253, 254, 257
Inquiry, 86, 125
Insensitivity, 126
Inside, 14, 49ff., 62, 67, 84, 122
  from the 39, 40, 41, 53, 55, 56, 73, 257
  inviolability of, 46, 49, 52
  knowledge of, 49, 50f., 84
  on the, 39, 40, 41, 55, 56, 58, 73, 253, 254, 256
  self-transformation of, 61
Insight, 191

Insistence, 42ff., 49ff., 56, 57, 233, 253
Instinct, 83, 155ff., 231, 232
Institution, 35, 36, 160
Instrument, 35, 71, 82, 147, 218, 219
Intellect, 69, 137, 159
Intellectuals, 159, 216, 217
Intelligence, 66, 119, 124, 177, 205f., 210, 211, 261
Intensity, 49
Intention, 66, 68, 100, 137, 157, 158, 174, 193, 197, 198, 199, 241
Interactionism, 218f., 234
Interest, 43, 88, 117, 118, 164, 171, 173, 197, 222, 243, 247, 249, 251
Intrusion, 42f., 45, 46, 52, 53, 254
Intuition, 53
Inwardness, 14. *See also* Inside
Iron, alteration of, 73f.
Irrationality, 126
Irregularity, 18, 24
Irritation, 105, 111, 114, 115, 117, 154
Is, 183, 184
It, 47, 48, 49, 51, 52, 185

James, W., 221, 232
Jaw, human, 123
Joy, 114, 117, 265
Judgment, 14, 15, 16, 25, 26, 27, 28, 47, 49, 50, 52, 53, 86, 88, 196, 232, 235, 240, 243, 247
Jumping, habit of, 155, 156
Jung, C., 251
Justice, 132

Kant, I., xiii, 27, 110, 122, 134, 135, 215
Kindness, habit of, 157
Knee-jerk, 156
Knowledge, ix, x, xix, 13, 14, 15, 17, 21, 28, 47, 50, 53, 55, 84, 125, 206, 208, 216, 229, 243
  abstractness of, 50
  and being, 51, 185
  and determinism, 25, 26
  and emotions, 30
  before birth, 242
  God's, 13
  intuitive, 14
  mediated, 48, 49
  nature of, 119, 218
  of action, 67
  of antecedents, 9
  of becoming, 6
  of change, 135

Knowledge—*Continued*
  of concrete, 13, 14, 15, 50ff.
  of effect, 10, 12, 13, 20, 31, 32, 33, 34, 67, 203
  of ends, 97, 98
  of error, 30, 31
  of future, 12, 13, 17, 30, 32, 55, 67, 204, 205
  of good, 55, 70, 86, 87, 97, 260
  of inside, 49, 50, 51, 52, 53, 84
  of irritation, 113
  of outside, 46
  of persons, 14, 179, 184
  of possibles, 15, 17, 203, 208
  of reality, 13f., 40, 47, 50f., 125, 234
  of self, 138, 240
  rational, 130
  scientific, 22, 23,
  self-, 84, 138, 206, 259
  through body, 130
  universal, xxii

Laboratory and life, 76
La Mettrie, de, J., 124
Lange, C., 221
Language, x, 166, 178, 195, 204
  analysis of, 182
  and philosophy, 192
  animal, 178, 179
  artificial, 182
  as absolute, 48
  dead, 182
  nature of, 179, 180, 182, 189, 190, 192
  referent of, 190, 191, 192
  shared, 190, 191
  unit of, 181
  use of, 192
Laplace, de, P., 21, 22, 23, 24, 27
Law, xvii, 17, 20, 81
  exemplification of, 17
  generality of, xv, 11, 36
  moral, 17
  of courses, 36
  of logic, 11
  of matter, 218
  of men, xv, 27
  of motion, 21
  physical, 17
  three-fold status of, 17
Leaders, 60, 63, 266
Learning, 94, 113, 117, 125, 156, 157, 160, 161, 163, 174, 178, 186, 215, 237.

Lee, D. D., 173n.
Leibniz, von, G., xii, 40, 41, 49, 51, 122, 244
Liberty, 67
Libido, 245, 249
Life, v, xvi, 9, 19, 27, 43, 64, 74, 81, 82, 85f., 92, 99, 103, 104, 116, 119, 120, 130, 136, 141, 143, 145, 150, 153, 215
  daily, 118, 219
  in body, 136, 146, 150, 153, 164, 243. *See also* Body, living
  nature of, 74, 75, 76, 196
  origin of, xvi, xvii, xxii, 71ff., 76, 141, 147
  rhythm, 74, 150
  social, 206, 207
  span, 151, 152
Limits, outside, 7, 39, 40, 42, 43, 44, 45, 46, 48, 49, 56, 57, 115, 142, 146, 174, 195
Line and point, 6
Link, missing, 101
Listener, 180, 181, 189, 190
Listening, habit of, 155
Living. *See* Animals, Life, Subhuman
Location of feeling, 109ff.
Locke, J., xii, 137
Loeb, J., 142
Logic, xii, xiii, 9, 10, 59, 218
  laws of, 11
  of absolute, 201
  of fiction, 183
Logicians, 19, 59, 174, 213, 214
Loneliness, 61, 62
Love, 66, 124, 155, 158, 226, 248
  of child, 158, 249ff.

Machines, 85, 87, 109
Man,
  abilities of, xv, 126, 157
  action of, 23, 27, 67, 128, 136, 163, 200, 263
  and animal, xiii, xv, 120, 121ff., 127, 128, 133, 134, 139, 140, 144, 148, 166, 264
  and apes, xvii, 100, 123
  and determinism, xiii, 26, 27
  any, 184
  Aristotelian, xiv, xv
  as constant, 134ff., 151, 157, 253, 262, 266

Man—*Continued*
  as ethical, v, xiii, xviii, xxii, 14, 144, 156, 252
  as free, v, xiii, xiv, xv, xvi, 4, 139, 192, 198ff., 217, 267
  as self, 239, 241ff.
  compactness of, 148, 149
  concern of, xvi, 84, 101, 120, 138f., 144, 239, 249, 251ff.
  equality of, 264, 266
  expression of, 64, 164, 249
  improvement of, 148, 157, 200
  knowledge about, 14, 179, 184
  life of, 192
  meaning of, 265, 266
  nature of, xiii, 119, 120, 127, 129ff., 132, 133, 134, 137, 156, 165, 184, 191, 215, 223, 241, 251, 252, 264
  natural, v, vi, xiv, xvi, xviii, 4, 27, 87, 88, 132, 195, 252, 267
  obligations of, xiii, xiv, xv, xviii, 156, 261, 263, 264
  origin of, xiv, xviii, xxii, 71, 89, 101, 120, 121ff., 131, 133, 139ff., 144, 148, 202
  perfectibility of, 263
  promise of, xvii, 156, 158, 266
  right of, xviii, 240, 263, 264, 267
  task of, xvi, 77, 144, 156, 200, 254, 264, 267
  unity of, 26, 27, 133, 138, 163
  value of, 65, 120, 129, 260, 264f., 267
Manifestation, 62
Manners, 186, 190
Many, the, 40, 41
Marx, K., 24, 201
Mastery, 54, 104, 107, 116, 117, 120, 144, 157, 198, 199, 200
Materialism, 218
  dialectical, 201, 202
Mathematics
  and logic, xiii
  and science, 210
  metaphysics of, 82
  nature of, 210, 213
Mating, 97, 98, 154
Matter, 218, 241
  and form, xii, 130f., 186
Maturity, xi, 99, 114, 123, 126, 140, 204, 237, 262
Mead, G. H., 181
Meaning, 118, 119, 125, 180, 182, 185, 186, 193, 206, 209, 211, 236

Meaning—*Continued*
  multiple, 207, 208, 211
  of man, 265, 266
Means, 199
Mechanism, xv, 65, 85, 87, 154, 202,
  203
Mediation, 48
Medievals, 86
Memory, xxi, 124, 135, 137, 138, 150,
  253
Men, 8, 21
  and wars, 35
  as walkers, 164
  bad, 65
  comparability of, 251
  complete, 238
  dilemma of, 65
  discouraged, 59
  ethical, 77, 238
  high-minded, 61
  of action, 63
  origin of, 140f.
  political, 60
  practical, xxi, 19, 64, 117, 238, 239
  primitive, 204
  reflective, 59, 60
Metaphor, 183, 207, 210
Metaphysicals, 182ff.
Metaphysics, xii, 82f., 122, 184, 245
Method, xii, 84, 126, 160, 210
  of extrapolation, 47, 49, 52
  philosophic, xx
Middle Ages, 86
Mind, v, xvi, 30, 69, 82, 111, 130, 138,
  139, 144, 149, 253, 265, 266
  absolute, 48, 122
  and body, xii, xvi, 200ff., 215, 217,
  218ff., 223, 224, 225, 230, 232, 234,
  236, 237, 238, 241, 244, 265
  and freedom, 201, 203ff., 215, 217, 222
  and intelligence, 206f., 210, 211
  and language, 193
  and man, 215
  and self, 215, 216, 220, 223, 239,
  241ff.
  and will, 223
  Aristotelian, 130
  as barrier, 215ff.
  development of, 204, 209, 210, 211
  direction of, 217, 220
  divine, xxii
  finite, 122, 214
  goal of, 218

Mind—*Continued*
  group, 35
  habits of, 204, 216, 217, 218, 225, 226
  impulsive, 159
  infallible, 201
  instrumental theory of, 218, 219
  knowing, 50, 51, 201, 216, 239
  levels of, 205, 208, 211
  need for, 140, 215, 239, 261
  of artist, 210
  origin of, 200f., 203ff., 218
  philosophic, 210
  potentiality of, 51
  resistance of, 227
  scientific, 209, 210
  submitted, 50, 51
  work of, 211, 213, 214, 218, 219, 262,
  267
Miracle, 3, 72, 202
Misogynist, 158
Mob, 35, 43
Modern times, xii, xv
Modesty, xxii
Momentum, 22
Monads, 40, 41, 244
Monkeys, 124
Monsters, 86
Montaigne, de, M., 124
Moods, 105f., 150, 219
Moralism, 87, 89
Morality, laws of, 17
Moral-sense, 124
Motion, laws of, xvii, 21
Movement, 19, 21, 24, 92, 99, 100, 113,
  114, 130, 162, 218
Muscles, use of, 161, 233, 250
Musculature, human, 123
Mutation, 101, 102
Mysticism, 191, 215
Mythology, 204

Names, 182, 185
Nation, 34ff.
Naturalism, 217, 219
Nature, v, xv, xvii, xix, 4, 21, 26, 44,
  86, 87, 122, 195, 198, 217, 218, 237
Necessity, 8, 18, 20, 24, 29, 202, 203,
  213
  and freedom, 18ff.
Needs, 65, 90, 92, 94, 98, 156, 163, 194,
  224, 243
Neighbors, 33, 37, 96, 119, 176, 191,
  194, 195, 197, 199, 217, 236, 264

Neo-Platonism, 218
Nerves, 110, 114, 123, 153
Newton, I., 82
Nirvana, xxii
Nonexistents, 235
Norm, 151
Northrop, F. S. C., vi
Nothing, 10, 46
Noun, 182
Novelty, 10, 12, 18, 68, 69, 94, 99, 149,
   153, 215, 226, 238
Number, 82

Objectives, 35, 56, 66, 68, 76, 177, 198,
   199, 227, 231, 260ff.
  change in, 70, 73, 74, 101, 199
  common, 176, 225, 239
  immediate, 238
  insistence on, 233
  mental, 234, 236
  of body, 71, 159, 222, 256, 257, 259,
    261, 262
  of self, 244ff., 254ff., 265
  ultimate, 199, 200, 210, 217, 238, 239
  willed, 233, 234, 236, 237, 239
  See also Concern, object of; Ends;
    Good
Objects, 35, 36, 40, 41, 73, 115, 117,
   118, 158, 229f., 232
  of concern. *See* Concern, object of
  of emotions, 226
  of knowledge, 51, 234f.
  of signs, 167, 168, 170, 175, 180, 183
  willed, 233, 234, 236, 237
Obligation, xix, 125, 156, 238, 240,
   252, 264. *See also* Duty, Ought
Observation, 23, 84, 177, 203, 245
Obstacles, xviii, 67, 69, 71, 119, 120,
   200, 251. *See also* Barriers
Occasionalists, 58
Occurrence, 173, 177
  vocal, 178
Offspring, 67, 76
Omnipotence, 13, 46, 54, 107
Omniscience, xxii, 13, 14
One and many, 40, 41, 108
Operation, field of, 199
Opportunity, 93f., 197, 238
Opposition, 26, 33, 54, 68, 69, 108, 198,
   199, 236, 254
Order, 98
Organic, the. *See* Animals, Life, Or-
  ganism, Subhuman

Organism, 82, 83, 91, 101, 111, 145,
   146, 150, 155
  unity of, 91, 146, 242
Organs
  action of, 147, 152, 266
  auxiliary, 147, 152
  embryonic, 152, 153
  functions of, 149, 150, 151
  habituated, 153
  human, 123, 130
  modification of, 150, 152
  origin of, 101, 146
  relation of, 146, 150, 151
  sense, 117, 118, 123, 125
  separation of, 141f.
  specialization of, 148, 151
  use of, 148, 149, 177
  vital, 147, 151, 152, 153
  vocal, 177
Organization, 36, 160, 242
  of habits, 157ff., 161
Origin. *See* Consciousness, Life, Man,
  Mind, Organs
Ought
  idea of, 85, 86
  intrinsic and extrinsic, 89ff.
  to be, 60, 62, 64, 66, 67, 85, 144, 151,
    217, 254, 259, 260, 264
  to do, 64, 66, 67, 85, 87, 88, 89, 91,
    93, 94, 157, 229, 235, 238, 262, 267
Outcries. *See* Cries
Outside, 48, 62, 66, 84
  from the, 39, 40, 41, 42ff., 47, 55
  knowledge of, 46
  on the, 39, 40, 41, 47, 56, 58, 65, 73,
    253, 256
Overconditioned, 99
Overdetermination, 30, 31, 39
Oxydation, 73, 74

Pain, xix, 100, 104, 105ff., 111ff., 115,
   116, 117, 118, 119, 123, 143, 168,
   180, 215
  feeling of, 109, 111, 113, 115, 116
  location of, 109ff., 113, 114
  public, 107
  pure, 108
Panpsychism, 71
Pantheism, 107
Parallelism, 220, 230
Particulars, 6, 11, 16, 18, 21, 24, 28, 35,
   104

Parts and whole, 91, 102, 145, 150, 163, 242
Passing away, 46. *See also* Death
Passion, 107, 159, 231
Passivity, 21, 24, 42, 49, 50, 96, 130, 136, 195, 196, 201
Past, 6, 10, 17, 31, 167
  causes as, 5, 202ff.
  determinism and, 29, 133
  errors of, 59
  limitation by, 11, 33, 68, 191, 194, 195, 196, 199, 216, 217, 236, 267
Pasteur, L., 72
Peace, 59f., 196, 248
Peirce, C. S., 212
Perches, mental, 213
Perceived, 211, 214, 227, 235
  as sign, 118, 119, 205, 207, 208, 209, 211
  unity of, 210
Perception, 44, 100, 117f., 123, 143, 144, 169, 205, 206, 208, 222, 235, 261
Perfection, 54, 58, 66
  self-, 263
Persistence, 255
Perspective, 39, 164, 199, 205
Perversion, 132, 246ff.
Philistines, 191
Philosophers, 22, 23, 31, 173, 192
Philosophy, x, xviii, 109, 125, 132, 192, 210, 211, 252
  and art, 184, 185
  and language, 192
  and science, 82, 83, 184, 185
  and signs, 166, 192
  and theology, 210
  animal, 126
  contemporary, 81f., 84
  controversies in, 30
  conventional, xi
  error in, xi, 30, 31
  method of, xx
  task of, xv, xviii, 82, 210
  terms of, 83, 192
Physics, xiii, 17, 22, 23, 72, 114
  metaphysical, 82
  See also Science
Physiology, 109, 110, 113, 134
Pincus, G., 142
Plans, city, 158
Plants, 71, 100, 102, 106, 114, 121, 130, 142

Plato, 60, 82, 128, 133, 185, 200, 242
Play, 249, 250, 251, 252
Pleasure, 100, 104, 105ff., 111f., 115f., 119, 123, 125, 143, 215, 237, 249, 250
  acute, 116
  feeling of, 109, 111, 115, 116
  location of, 109ff.
  pure, 108
  private, 107
Plotinus, 200
Poets, 173, 191, 225
Point and line, 6
Politics, xii, xiii
Position, 20, 21, 23, 42
Positivism, 48, 82
Possibilities, 5, 6, 8, 10, 12, 15ff., 29, 30, 34, 38, 53, 54, 61, 168, 184, 205, 208f., 211, 258
  alteration of, 36, 38, 54
  and actuality, 15, 17, 18, 32, 199, 203, 235
  as objects of signs, 168, 170ff., 188, 208f.
  common, 171, 172, 256
  constituents of, 34
  determinate, 15, 53, 55, 168
  double, 207
  distinction between, 172
  localization of, 117
  of existence, 254
  of self, 254ff.
  realization of, 17, 34, 36, 38, 118, 168, 199, 254ff., 260, 261
  totality of, 53
  See also Future, Good, Objectives
Postulate systems, 213
Potentiality, xii, 46, 47, 51, 121, 184, 231, 265
Power, x, 6, 13, 19, 20, 27, 35, 36, 46, 77, 99, 120, 127f., 177, 219, 229ff., 251
Practice, 6, 154, 160, 172, 175, 195, 202, 218, 219, 220
Pragmatism, 48, 222
Prescience, 171, 174
Predetermination, 20, 25
Predicates, 50, 51, 182, 183, 185, 189, 253
Predictions, 6, 11f., 15f., 20, 21, 29, 31, 33, 67, 69, 99, 153, 191, 196, 202, 204
Preference, 87, 231
Premises, 9f., 212f.
Preparation, 96, 103, 224

Prescriptions, 54, 58, 65f., 74f., 95f., 159, 259, 261

Present, 5, 6, 12, 16, 17, 29, 30, 55, 56, 59, 67, 99, 167, 168, 185, 203, 244

Preservation
of society, 160
self-, 88, 155, 156

Primitives, 204

Principles, 209f., 262

Privacy, 27, 40f., 45, 49, 51, 52, 56, 57, 59, 253. *See also* Inside

Process. *See* Course

Procreation, 131

Production, 5, 6, 9, 18, 20, 131, 202, 203

Progress, 59, 101

Prohibitions, 247, 248

Projection, 109

Promise, x, 54, 55, 59, 84, 118, 129, 130, 184, 215
of man, xvii, 158, 166, 266

Pronouns, 182

Propositions, 214

Prose, 190

Prospects, 36, 168, 233, 236. *See also* Possibility, Promise

Protection, self-, 156

Provocations, 111, 113, 154, 195, 221, 224, 227, 228, 232, 233, 235, 237, 245

Psyche, 82, 119, 130, 143, 144, 145, 147, 150, 151
and self, 138, 139, 144, 256, 261

Psychoanalysis, 249

Psychology, 81, 155, 252
animal, 85, 86, 87, 88
metaphysics of, 82

Psychoneurosis, 248

Ptolemaic astronomy, 90

Public. *See* Limits, Pleasure, Space, Traits, Words

Purpose, 98, 177, 215

Purposiveness, 93, 97f., 100, 102, 143, 205

Pythagoras, 242

Quality, 3, 42, 45, 115

Questions, 189, 250
philosophic, 122

Rational, 10, 19, 127, 137

Rationalists, 7

Reaction, 91, 154, 159

Reality, xiii, 35, 39, 40, 50, 57, 167, 184, 192, 236

Realization, 17, 34, 36, 38, 58, 61, 62f., 69, 70, 157, 168, 184, 199, 244, 254
of good, 57, 58f., 62, 65f., 70, 75, 88, 89, 90, 95, 119, 129, 138, 145, 164, 199, 207, 254ff., 261f., 267
of possibilities, 17, 34, 36, 38, 118, 168, 199, 254ff., 260, 261

Reason, 10, 83, 127, 128, 130, 131, 137, 138, 214, 216, 217, 239

Reasoning, 11, 124, 127, 131, 213, 214

Reconstitution, 36, 216

Reference, 167, 168, 176, 180, 183, 207, 228f., 235

Referents of signs, 183ff.

Reflection, 59, 191

Reflex, 91, 155, 157, 231, 232

Reform, 196, 265, 266

Re-formation, 199

Rejection, 95

Rejuvenation, 150

Relation, 40, 46, 47, 50, 202, 203, 209, 212

Religion, 125ff., 204, 252
and signs, 166
function of, 117, 210

Rembrandt, 65

Repression, 159, 194, 195, 225, 234, 246ff.

Reproduction, 125, 131

Resistance, 39, 40, 42f., 44, 45ff., 54, 55, 56, 69, 70, 99, 108, 197, 200, 207, 259
infinite, 47, 51, 52
of body, 33, 70, 71, 73ff., 100, 102, 105, 116, 140, 143, 144, 159, 194, 217, 227, 267
potential, 46, 47

Response, 68, 70, 76, 94, 97, 98, 111f., 116, 117, 143, 149, 154, 158, 159, 162, 180f., 225, 227, 230, 247

Responsibility, vi, xv, 25f., 135, 138, 240, 253, 254, 261, 263, 264, 267

Responsiveness, 93, 94, 97, 99, 100

Retreat, 61, 62, 71, 74, 119, 129, 191, 215f.

Revolution, 248

Revolutionary, 197, 198

Right and wrong, xix, 25, 87, 124, 125

Rights, xiv, xviii, 66, 88, 263
human, xviii, 240, 263, 264, 267

Rights—*Continued*
  natural, 264
Rigidity, 45
Ritual, 117,
Roesler, M., vi
Romantics, 7, 19, 30, 40
Ruler, 261
Rust, 73, 74

Sacrifice, self-, xiv, 89
Salutation, 173ff., 180, 189
Sanity, xx, 108, 160, 226
Santayana, G., 218
Satanic, 107
Satisfaction, spiritual, 250
Schopenhauer, A., 40, 41, 55
Science, xi, xii, 6, 7, 17, 18, 21, 22, 30,
    72, 125, 198, 249
  and art, 184, 185
  and Bible, 121
  and determinism, 22, 23, 29
  and mathematics, 210
  and philosophy, 82, 83, 184, 185
  and signs, 166
  as absolute, 48
  limits of, 122
  principles of, 209, 210
  progress in, 82
  scope of, xv
  terms of, 83, 184
Scientists, 29
  animal, 126
  Christian, 128
  mind of, 209
  philosophy of, 83, 241
Selection, 91, 93f
Self, v, 26, 141, 145, 150, 151, 161, 239
  activity of, 243, 253, 254, 260
  and body, 139, 223, 225, 239, 241ff.,
    253, 256, 257
  and desire, 146, 227, 244, 245
  and good, 254f., 258f., 261
  and mind, 215, 216, 220, 223, 239,
    241ff.
  and psyche, 138, 139, 144, 256, 261
  and will, 229, 236, 239, 241ff., 244
  as body, 241ff., 252ff.
  as substance, 253
  concern of, 164, 225, 238, 239, 244ff.,
    252f., 260
  constancy of, 139, 151, 220, 243,
    252, 253, 254ff.
  demands of, 159

Self—*Continued*
  embodied, 139, 243ff., 257ff.
  enjoyment of, 216
  features of, 252ff.
  freedom of, 240
  knowledge of, 138, 220, 240
  magnitude of, 241
  objective of, 244ff., 254ff., 265
  of others, 226
  possibility of, 254ff.
  pre-existence of, 242
  renewal of, 255, 262
  separability of, 128, 131, 256
  task of, 244, 255f., 260
  uniqueness of, 253, 256f.
Self-criticism, 243
Self-identity, 134ff., 241, 243, 251, 252,
    253, 255, 262, 266, 267
Selfishness, 262
Self-perfection, 263
Self-preservation, 155, 156
Semantics, 53
Sensation, xii, 112, 114, 117, 232
Sense
  common, 83
  of beauty, 124, 125
  of pain and pleasure, 112
  of right and wrong, 124, 125
  organ, 117, 118, 123, 125
Sensibility, 103f., 117, 144
Sensitivity, 93, 95, 97, 102f., 111, 116,
    117, 118, 125, 136, 143, 144, 147,
    177, 205, 207, 208, 211, 261
  ethical, 261
  function of, 103
  growth in, 262
  of inanimate, 263
  of plants, 100
  reach of, 95, 96, 100, 103, 105, 108,
    114, 139, 140
  to value, 253, 261, 262
Sentence, 181ff., 190
Separation of cells, 141f.
Servants, 63, 66
Service, 63, 90, 249
Sexuality, 125, 245ff.
Shape, 42, 45, 134
Shock, 141, 155, 156
Signals, 188
Significance, 208, 219
Signification, 167ff., 178, 179, 182, 185,
    188, 190
Signs, 166ff., 191

Signs—*Continued*
conventional, 186ff.
definition of, 166, 167
distinction between, 170ff.
equivalent, 170, 172, 173
nonvocal, 188
objects of, 167, 168, 170, 175, 180, 183
perceived as, 118, 119, 205, 207, 208, 209, 211
reference of, 167, 187
technique of, 165
use of, 166, 167, 168, 177, 187, 188, 191, 193
Skill, 93, 134
Skills, 128
Slavery, xiii
Sleep, 106, 115, 135, 136, 166, 215, 252
Smith, A., xii
Smoke, as sign, 166, 170, 171
Sociality, 95, 97, 175, 180, 190, 195, 206, 207, 249, 251f.
Society, 63, 159, 160, 185, 195f., 206, 267
Socrates, 9, 65
Soddy, F., 83
Solidarity, 176
Solipsists, 83
Solitude, 195, 216
Sophist, 185, 191
Soul, 26, 27, 67, 122, 130f., 243. *See also* Self
Sound, 45, 177
as sign, 177, 178, 179, 181
Space, 43ff., 56, 82, 130, 186, 241
Speaker, 180, 181, 189f.
Specialists, 172, 213
Species, 92, 97
fixed, 72, 83, 122, 123
members of, 88, 93, 94, 96, 99, 175
Specification, 29, 30, 36, 38, 167
Speculation, xxi, 83, 85, 125, 126, 127, 191, 204, 245
Speech, x, xii, 125, 126, 149, 166, 178, 191, 193
of birds, 178
Sperm, 142, 143
Spinoza, B., xiii, 7, 8, 9, 20, 21, 110, 217, 230, 231, 232
Spirit, 128, 238, 241
absolute, 241
cosmic, 24, 35
See also Self, Soul

Spiritualists, 128, 241
Spontaneity, 69ff., 76, 103, 116, 164, 165, 198, 199, 200, 222
function of, 69, 71, 225
Standard
of behavior, 85ff.
of evaluation, 258
State, 35, 248
formation of, 24
purpose of, xiii
States,
bodily, 242
emotional, 221
Statesmen, 63, 248
Status quo, 196
Stimuli, 39, 76, 94, 98, 109, 112, 113, 143, 153, 154, 157, 158, 159, 247, 250
Striving, 55, 200, 232
Structure, 130, 138, 155, 157, 158, 159, 182, 243, 258
Struggle, 93, 198f.
Stupor, 104
Subdivision, 145, 146
Subhuman, xiv, 84, 85ff., 100, 123, 131, 144, 264
action of, 67, 97, 98, 254
concern of, 264
expression of, 64,
freedom in, xvi
grades of, 100
intelligent, 206
perfectibility of, 263
use of signs, 166, 173, 175, 179
Subject matter, 15, 16, 50, 51, 183, 184
Subjects, 40, 41, 50, 51, 183, 189
Submission, 49, 52, 54, 57, 95, 97, 192, 195ff., 217
Substance, 38ff., 44, 50, 52, 53, 131, 135, 183, 185, 200, 216, 235, 253, 256
Subtraction, error of unwarranted, xv, xvi, xvii
Sucking instinct, 154
Suggestiveness, 173
Suicide, 252
Suppression, 155, 159, 162
Surgery, 157, 197
Susceptibility, 156
Swearing, 179
Syllogism 9
Symbols, xiii, 125, 188
Sympathy, 14, 66, 107, 216

Symptoms, 151, 187
Synonyms, 172
Syntax, 53
Systems, xi, 37, 213

Taboos, 186, 247
Taste, 42, 148
Teachability, 93
Techniques, 82, 139, 144, 156, 157,
   160ff., 166, 191f., 200, 217f., 239,
   266
Technology, 185, 192
Teeth, 124
Teleology, 19, 54, 55, 97, 203
Temperance, 61
Temptation, 62
Tendencies, 231
   ascendant, 156, 161, 162, 194, 224,
      225, 228, 229, 232, 233, 237
   bodily, 93, 97, 116, 147, 149, 154,
      156f., 161, 178, 224ff., 231, 237
   embryonic, 154
   expression of, 159, 162, 246
   repression of, 246
   to affirm or deny, 231
Tension, 221, 237, 244
   felt, 95
   fluctuation of, 105, 108, 113, 114, 116
   origin of, 105, 143, 248
Terms, ix, x, 182ff., 214
   new, x, 173
   philosophic and scientific, 83
Thales, 82
Theology, x, 126
Theory, 24, 25, 26, 83, 222, 239
Thing in itself, 50, 52
Things. *See* Inanimate, Objects
Thinkers, free, 117
This, 47
Thought, 24, 154, 193, 253, 265
   abstract, 164
   activity of, xii, 164, 215, 221f.
   and freedom, 217
   and nature, 122
   beginning of, xx
   Christian, xiii
   creative, x, xii
   conventional, ix, 192, 196
   depressing, 219
   disciplined, x, 83, 164
   disconnected, 209
   Greek, xiii
   habit of, 158f., 192, 204, 216, 217,
      218, 225f.

Thought—*Continued*
   idle, 224
   mathematical, 213
   possibility of, 241
   simple-minded, 159
   speculative, 83
   willed, 229
Time, xxii, 4, 17, 28, 82, 123, 130, 203,
      244, 254, 255
   atomic, 31, 33
   distance in, 4, 6, 7, 8, 9, 19
   external, 28, 32
   passage of, 12, 28, 167
   process in, 7, 11
Timidity, 92, 194
Tolerance, 60
Tolstoy, L., 156
Tools, 124
Totality, 53, 60
Tradition, intellectual, x, xx
Traffic control, 158
Tragedy, 64, 106, 117, 265
Training, 98, 140, 195
Traits
   human, 123, 124
   public, 42, 43, 45, 46, 47, 51, 65
Transformations, 15, 17, 34, 36, 37, 38,
      61, 147, 209, 230
Transmission of impulse, 109ff., 114
Transplantation, 82, 150
Truth, x, xii, 10, 50, 51, 82, 83, 184,
      214, 217, 219
   and falsehood, 24, 25
   assertion of, 25, 230f.
   coherence theory of, 183
   concrete, xix
   contingent, 11
   empirical, 224
   eternal, 201
   love of, 61
   necessary, xviii
   of fictions, 183
   of logic, xviii
   philosophical, xviii, xxii
   second-hand, 219
   test of, 49
   tragic, 106
   universal, 210, 211

Understanding, ix, 62, 130, 190, 216
Unintelligible, 130, 216
Union, 57, 133
   of sperm and egg, 142

Uniqueness, xix, 6, 13, 141, 253, 256f., 264, 265
Unit
  indivisible. *See* Atoms
  of language, 181
Unity
  cellular, 141
  good as, 258, 259
  man's, 26, 27, 133, 138, 163
  of inquiries, 210, 211
  of perceived, 235
  organic, 146, 147, 150, 242
  spatial, 44
Universals, 47, 258. *See also* Generals
Universe, 19, 85, 95, 195
  creation of, 121
  deterministic, 21, 24, 28
  future of, 37
  of becoming, 37
  of necessity, 19
  physical, 22
  singleness of, 40, 41, 72
  static, xxi
  See also World

Vagueness, 21, 30
Values, xiv, xvi, xix, 23, 60, 64, 65, 90, 97, 107, 108, 120, 216, 234, 253
  acquired, 264
  anthropomorphic theories of, 88ff.
  increase in, 90, 260, 263
  new, 265
  of man, 65, 120, 129, 260, 264f., 267
  prospective, 235
  reduction of, xix
  sensitivity to, 253, 261, 262
  unique, 264
Variations, 101, 177
Vegetarian, 159
Velocity, 21, 23
Verbs, 183
Virtue, xiii, 60, 120, 157, 197, 253
Vision, 15, 39, 148, 176
Vitality, 27, 136, 147, 191
Vivisection, 127
Vocabulary, 187, 193, 245
Volition, 230, 235, 236. *See also* Will

Wakefulness, 104
Walking, 123, 160ff., 220, 235
War, 34, 35, 249
Weight, 241
Whitehead, A. N., 40
Wholes, 35, 209
Whorf, B., 172*n.*
Will, v, 69, 83, 126, 138, 139, 140, 241, 253
  action of, 114, 200, 223, 228, 230ff., 235
  and desire, 228
  and good, 223, 238, 263
  and self, 229, 236, 239, 241ff., 244
  concern of, 222
  effort of, 233
  faculty of, 231
  free, 22, 23, 236
  grades of, 223
  inconstancy of, 138
  limitations of, 231
  nature of, 228ff.
  need for, 230, 236, 237, 239, 261, 267
  power of, 229, 230ff., 241
Wing, origin of, 101
Wisdom, 35, 60
  natural, 87f., 91f., 99, 155, 206
Wish, 241
Words, 161, 179, 188, 189
  and language, 189, 190
  creation of, 184ff.
  elementary, 180
  exclamatory nature of, 181, 182
  function of, 188
  interchange of, 190
  kinds of, 181ff.
  silent, 189
Work. *See* Action, Effort
World, xiii, xviii, xxi, 19, 21, 24, 25, 31, 32, 37, 92, 119, 192, 194, 199, 217, 236, 264, 265, 267
  external, xiii, xix, 104, 105, 183, 192, 215, 216
  of artist and scientist, 43
  of idealist, 61
  retreat from, 61, 199, 200
  See also Universe